The Administration of the British Army

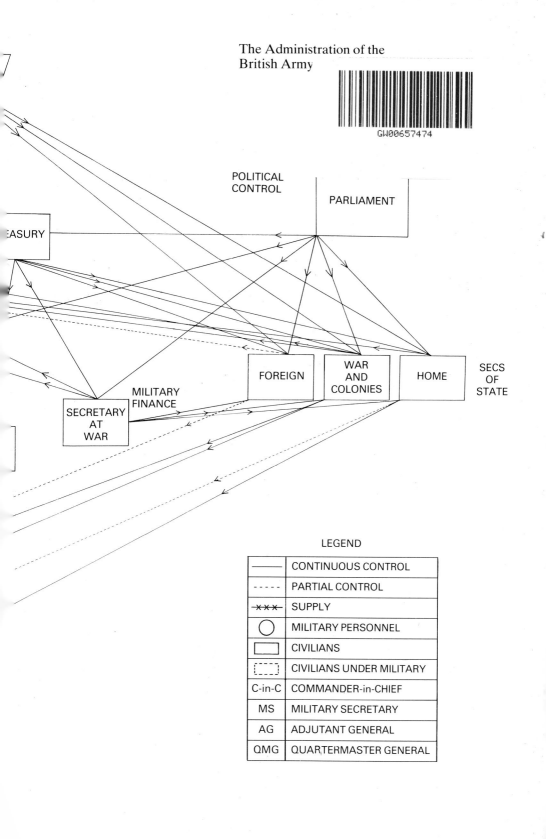

POLITICAL
CONTROL

PARLIAMENT

EASURY

FOREIGN

WAR
AND
COLONIES

HOME

SECS
OF
STATE

MILITARY
FINANCE

SECRETARY
AT
WAR

LEGEND

——	CONTINUOUS CONTROL
- - - - -	PARTIAL CONTROL
×××—	SUPPLY
◯	MILITARY PERSONNEL
☐	CIVILIANS
⌐ ¬	CIVILIANS UNDER MILITARY
C-in-C	COMMANDER-in-CHIEF
MS	MILITARY SECRETARY
AG	ADJUTANT GENERAL
QMG	QUARTERMASTER GENERAL

Ex Libris

IAN HARVIE

War and Administration

WAR

AND

ADMINISTRATION

The Significance of the Crimean War
for the British Army

JOHN SWEETMAN

1984
SCOTTISH ACADEMIC PRESS
EDINBURGH

Published by
Scottish Academic Press Limited,
33 Montgomery Street, Edinburgh EH7 5JX

© 1984 J. Sweetman

First published 1984

ISBN 0 7073 0332 X

Cataloguing in Publication Data

Sweetman, John
  War and administration: the significance of
  the Crimean War for the British Army.
  1. Great Britain, *Army* — History — 19th century
  2. Great Britain — History — Crimean War, 1854–1856
  I. Title
  355′.00941   UA649

Printed by Clark Constable (1982) Ltd., Edinburgh

ACKNOWLEDGEMENTS

I am grateful to the following for permission to quote from manuscript collections as indicated: Marquess of Aberdeen (Aberdeen Papers); Sir John Cotterell (Airey Papers); Trustees of the National Library of Scotland (Brown Papers); Earl of Dalhousie (Dalhousie Muniments); Gloucestershire Record Office (Estcourt Papers); University of Newcastle (Grey Papers); Sir William Gladstone (Gladstone Papers); Earl of Pembroke (Herbert Papers); Gloucestershire Record Office (Kingscote Papers); University of Nottingham Library Manuscripts Department (Newcastle Papers); Baron Raglan (Raglan Military and Private Papers). Extracts from the Palmerston Papers and Palmerston Letterbooks are published by permission of the Trustees of the Broadlands Archives; extracts from Crown copyright material by permission of the Controller of Her Majesty's Stationery Office.

My sincere thanks for their help at various times are also due to current and former members of the academic staff at the Royal Military Academy Sandhurst, notably: E. A. Brett-James, Dr. E. R. Holmes, J. D. P. Keegan and the late Lt. Col. (Retd) J. P. Lawford. The bulk of the work for this book, however, was undertaken when a postgraduate student in the Department of War Studies at Kings College, London, and for their invaluable advice and encouragement I would particularly like to thank Professor Michael Howard, Brian Bond and Dr. M. L. Dockrill. I must not forget either Mrs. G. Mulford, who struggled so valiantly with my handwriting to produce the final typescript or Mrs. M. Lever for ably assisting with subsequent corrections.

(Camberley, 1983)   John Sweetman

Contents

Acknowledgements   vii

INTRODUCTION:
     The Nature of Administration   I

CHAPTER:

I: The Administrative System   8

II: Wellingtonian Twilight, 1830–1852   15

III: Before the Storm, 1852–1854   29

IV: Transport and Supply
        The Commissariat and Ordnance Departments   41

V: Military Command
        The Commander-in-Chief   77

VI: Ministerial Responsibility
        Secretary at War and Secretary for War   97

CONCLUSION:
     The Significance of Change   128

Notes   134
Selected Bibliography
     Manuscript Sources   164
     Autobiographies, Edited Papers and Miscellaneous
     Unpublished Material   165
     Official Publications   166
     Secondary Publications   168
     Other Miscellaneous Pamphlets   170
List of Major Office Holders, 1830–1856   172

ILLUSTRATIONS

front endpaper
The Administration of the British Army in 1852

Figure 1   *facing page* 58
The Advance to Sevastopol, 1854

Figure 2   *facing page* 59
The Siege of Sevastopol, 1854–1856

back endpaper
The Administration of the British Army, 1856

Introduction

The Nature of Administration

Military administration is more decisive in war than diplomacy in the Cabinet or courage in the field. (*The Times*, 27 February 1854).

British military action against Russia between 1854 and 1856 excited keen interest from its outset. National shock caused by the inability of forces, traditionally successful on colonial battlefields, to subdue the Tsar's barbaric hordes secured the attention of early writers.[1] Later, starved of major nineteenth century European triumphs after Waterloo, other authors also settled greedily on the struggle. Perhaps significantly the various encounters, known collectively to contemporaries as "The War against Russia" or "The War in the East", have in retrospect been narrowed to "The Crimean War". At least on that forlorn Tartar peninsula victories might be identified: operations in the Baltic, White Sea, Pacific, Caucasus and on the shores of the Ukraine offered few opportunities for eulogy. In the Crimea British troops were inferior in numbers to the French and even, at times, the Turks. During the decisive final phases of the battle for Sevastopol, they secured little positive advantage for the Allies: unlike the Malakoff across the Channel, memory of the Redan has not been perpetuated in buildings and avenues.

Perhaps as something of a psychological reflex action, British historians have concentrated on the earlier, more glorious feats of arms — Alma, Balaclava, Inkerman — and on supply difficulties in the first winter, which emaciated men and animals alike. Yet the real British success of 1855 was reorganisation of 'army administration'. This process entailed cause and effect: revelations of deficiencies at the front, made known by W. H. Russell through *The Times* and a host of private correspondents in letters to their familes, created such a furore of public indignation that a disoriented collection of authorities was forced into a reasoned, organic whole. The War exposed unrealised shortcomings, and great benefit accrued to the Army. Somehow, the emphasis has thus been shifted from military activity against the enemy to purification of the administrative system. Losses on the Sevastopol Heights, although regrettable, were worthwhile. So military heroes have been over-shadowed by Russell and Florence Nightingale, and uninitiated laymen can read several British accounts of the War without realising that the French, Turks and Sardinians ever went to the Crimea.

Those linking the battlefield experiences directly with administrative change have been numerous: within personal memory of the events, Thomas Thackeray and Sir Garnet Wolseley, for instance; in the twentieth century, among others, the editors of Lord Panmure's papers, Major-General A. Forbes, Brigadier A. Symons, Olive Anderson and W. S. Hamer, whose individual conclusions Major-General W. H. Anderson adequately summarised in a lecture to the Staff College, Camberley: "The outcry against the mismanagement of the Crimean War led to changes in the system of army administration, which had lasted since 1689".[2] But the timetable of reform does not bear out this contention and, to some extent, these and other commentators may have been misled by evidence from certain contemporary sources. The press, particularly *The Times*, sought to underline its responsibility for remedial action by emphasising exposition of chaos in the theatre of operations, colourful hyberbole from Florence Nightingale has not assisted clear appreciation of the issue and politicians, faced by severe losses before Sevastopol, claimed to have solved appalling difficulties produced by the incompetence of their predecessors. Death of almost half the Mounted Staff Corps' horses during the first fortnight of December 1854, and sweeping accusations, such as the letter produced by Colonel Knox stating "we bury a thousand a week", could not be ignored.[3] So Lord Clarendon attributed mid 1854 administrative changes to "public opinion", Lord Palmerston promised swift action from his new government and Lord Panmure, preparing the way for his own scheme concerning the Ordnance, declared that hitherto the administrative system had been defective. It was in their political interest to publicise unprecedented initiative. In reality, the primary effects of information from the front were overthrow of Lord Aberdeen's coalition and establishment of a succession of inquiries into the conduct of the War. Forty years later, Russell reflected: "The Commissions of Inquiry and Committees of Investigations, which were appointed in consequence of the popular outcry, at the time led to no important (administrative) changes".[4]

Understanding of the subject of 'administration', in the military context, has been complicated by different interpretations placed upon the term. Seven years before the Crimean War, the Deputy Inspector-General of Hospitals used it to describe a whole range of activities concerned with soldiering. Shortly afterwards Thomas Thackeray, in his book about French military administration, applied it to the provision of each soldier's needs from enlistment until death or retirement, and E. B. de Fonblanque wrote: "Military administration is the machinery through the agency of which armies are raised, organised, maintained and governed".[5] Such all-embracing explanations are actually vague. Nor is the narrow concentration on supply of equipment and provisions more helpful.[6] For meeting an army's physical needs is only the end-product of its administrative system, the essence of which concerns policy not boots. Lord John Russell, in a Parliamentary exchange with Benjamin Disraeli in 1848, came close to a satisfactory definition: "The chief portion of the time and attention of Ministers must be given to those questions of administration, which devolve upon them in the exercise of the discretionary power vested in the Crown". How valid the concept of the monarch's 'discretionary power' remained in the mid nineteenth century must be a matter of judgement, but the association of 'administration' with 'power' is crucial to an understanding of its nature. Administration is the means by which power is exercised: it is no accident, therefore, that governments, and more precisely cabinets, are freqently referred to as Administrations. So military administration involves the exercise of political power with reference to the Army: shortcomings in supplies at the front may bring calumny on responsible heads, but they are unlikely to affect the distribution of power between politicians or civilian and military authorities at a high level. Army administration cannot be divorced from the central business of government.[7]

Changes in its emphasis or its nature may occur after fundamental political upheaval in the state: many of the Comte de Guibert's reform proposals, published anonymously in 1772, were not introduced until after the French Revolution.[8] Adjustments in the distribution of power and the process of government inevitably result in reorganisation of military administration. But, as war constitutes the proving ground for all armies, failure in the field may independently affect army administration. Prussian defeat at Jena is possibly the most striking example of such interaction. During five traumatic days the weaknesses of an army, trading on past glories and suffering in the hands of five "virtually equal and autonomous" administrative authorities, were revealed: Scharnhorst needed the shattering impact of these events to surmount opposition to administrative reform. A half-century earlier Field-Marshal Daun had used less striking reverses to purge the Austrian system.[9]

In autocracies administrative change may be imposed, as seventeenth and eighteenth century Prussian rulers demonstrated. Reforms in Russian military administration during the early nineteenth century, carried through by Count Chernyshev, relied heavily upon Nicholas I's support, and the Decembrists discovered to their cost that the Tsar jealously guarded his rights in this respect.[10] Shielded from the effects of an absolute monarchy, with neither military disaster nor political upheaval to change the locus of power, Britain nevertheless showed that administrative change could take place. Development of improved techniques of accounting, recording business and organising manpower, as the demands of production, distribution and trade increased, created an impetus for efficiency at a functional level which reflected throughout

the administrative system. *Laissez-faire* stemmed as much from inability
to cope with problems as disinterest: until its precise nature had been
identified, medical practitioners could not fairly be censured for failure
to cure cholera. Before the work of William Farr in 1849, a theory
predominated in Britain that it spread through the atmosphere, and not
for a further six years was a firm link established between the disease and
water. Even then an influential body of opinion still held that it thrived
mainly on a combination of filth and human contact. British medicine
did not stand alone in ignorance: in Spain doctors poured pints of olive
oil down the victim's gullet, in China after being thrashed with rods he
had his stomach heavily jumped on. The problem was not confined to
one illness. The standard treatment for typhus at the time of the
Crimean War was to fill the patient with wine and hopefully build up his
strength against the virus. A marked tendency also existed to employ
panaceas like bleeding for everything from fever to swellings. The
reaction of Captain Hawley to sickness among friends before Sevastopol
was not therefore extraordinary: "I swallow the contents of a mustard
pot and five quarts of water: effect, instantaneous and effective".[11]

Like the first industrialists, early Victorian administrators suffered
from crudity of the means at their disposal. Slow inter-departmental and
overseas mail services, absence of telephone and electric telegraph,
caused lengthy delays.[12] Improvement in techniques alone, however,
did not produce administrative reform: social and political changes in
the country greatly affected redistribution of power. The minutiae of an
administrative process at functional level represents but the polish on a
rough-hewn base: administration is concerned with political responsibility, not the outpourings of menial clerks. Reorganisation in national
and local government through legislation, such as the Great Reform and
Municipal Corporations acts, signifying effective shifts in influence
within the state, have even more relevance to the whole sphere of
administration than improved techniques. So the emergence in the early
nineteenth century of industrial businessmen, who challenged aristocratic monopoly of political responsibility, and subsequent alterations in
the pattern of society were not irrelevant. Richard Cobden concluded:
"At certain periods in the history of a nation, it becomes necessary to
review its principles of domestic policy, for the purpose of adapting the
government to the changing and improving conditions of its people".
Government responsibility cannot be separated from administration.[13]

Administrative reformers thus strove for something beyond improved
order in official transactions — rationalisation of a system, which
allegedly depended on anachronistic views of the nature of British
society. Hence national institutions, including the Army, were subjected
to close scrutiny in the light of philosophical concepts and a search for
efficiency. Disjointed efforts were made to evolve a theoretical basis for
the exercise of power, in place of blind adherence to tradition. Radicals

argued that descendants of the feudal lords retained unrealistic control in positions of influence, including the armed forces. Cobden maintained: "The aristocracy of this country have the army, the navy, the colonies, and a large amount of expenditure at their disposal". John Bright, referring to Parliament, wrote: "In fact our representative system is for the most part a sham and the forms of representation are used to consolidate the supremacy of the titled and proprietary class". On the eve of the Crimean War *The Times*, attacking its reliance upon aristocratic patronage, declared that the Civil Service was characterised by "incapacity, indifference and idleness", representing "a relic of the world which preceded the Reform Bill".[14] In military terms, purchase of position was connected with patronage, and criticism of this system should not be seen in isolation from the assault on civilian patronage. To do so would be to misjudge both the nineteenth century Army as an institution of the state and the effect upon it of political, economic and social movement within the country as a whole. The Army did not, and could not, exist independent of other institutions in Britain nor outside political control. Like them it was sensitive to administrative change even beyond its immediate concern.[15]

Although they must broadly conform to accepted values, as disciplined bodies armies never faithfully reflect civilian society; and factors peculiar to them often exert influence upon their administrative development. Deep-rooted suspicion of the Army, evident in Britain since the Stuarts and possibly reinforced by the advance of French conscripts into central and southern Europe after the Revolution, heightened as establishment of the Royal Military College suggested increased professionalism. For, in any state, the military normally has at its disposal the overwhelming majority of force. Direction of this lies at the centre of civil-military relations. As military expertise increases, fears may arise that those able to dispense force might also aspire to control it. In this sense, the work of men like General Le Marchant, coupled with specialisation required by the technical developments of the Industrial Revolution and the impact of the French Revolution on the very nature of warfare, focused attention upon control of military force, which had not been so clear since the seventeenth century. There is some truth in Denis Le Marchant's claim, that previous plans for increasing military professionalism in national training institutions foundered through political dread that officers might become divorced from the community at large — with the consequent danger of a new Cromwellian era.[16] Ironically, more dedicated and efficient officers became a potential threat to society.

Criticism, especially from the radical left, served to make the Army more introspective and defensive. As opposition in the Civil Service to competitive examinations and in the universities to abolition of religious tests showed, conservatism tended to characterise long-standing institutions. But the Army used its need for stability — as a platform for discipline — to pursue the cause of paternalism. The Duke of Wellington frequently defended retention of aristocratic officers, though his justification wavered between the worth of private means as a bulwark against mercenary interests and the desire for social superiors worthy of the rank and file's respect. Sir William Napier introduced political overtones into his defence. He claimed that non-aristocratic officers would republicanise the Army "and then we must republicanise the Government, for the Army is the principal support of the aristocratic form of our Government". Writing during the War, although his remarks were published after its conclusion, Sir John Burgoyne, like Wellington, held that abolition of purchase would weaken the Army's efficiency, as officers and men might then be drawn from the same social class. This whole line of argument became less credible as aristocratic influence declined politically, socially and economically throughout the United Kingdom. Expressed by high-ranking officers, too, it represented an unrealistic attempt to dam the floodgates of civilian interference in the Army. Thus, equally defensively, Sir George Brown declared the British superior to any continental force, insisting that "the mass of the army" was opposed to change. These various, complicating factors did not prevent army administrative reform: they determined that its pace would be slow.[17]

Moreover, it was comparatively simple for Lord Ellenborough to declare that the military ought to be "entirely subordinate" to civil authority, but the administration of the Army depended upon a fine balance between constitutional conventions, national ethos and the attitude of the Army concerning the exercise of power in military matters. More precisely, it concerned which government minister should discharge responsibility towards the Army and what were the political parameters within which military officers should operate. By the mid nineteenth century the structure of army administration was clearly outdated, but politicians and officers could not agree on the form of its reconstruction. While there was peace apart from remote colonial enterprises, no urgency pressed to narrow differences or, for the most part, even to think constructively about them.[18]

Superficially, crystallisation of attention on the Army, and the desire and capability to reform army administration, occurred once the Crimean disasters prompted a more sympathetic atmosphere at Westminster. In practice, administrative reorganisation originated in the Parliamentary session which terminated in August 1854, before any troops landed in the Crimea. Decisions to divide government responsibility for 'War' and 'the Colonies', so creating a fourth Secretary of State, and to transfer the Commissariat from the Treasury to the War Department, were taken in May. Possibly but for a stubborn defence by its holder Sidney Herbert, the office of Secretary at War would have been abolished shortly afterwards: certainly, the arguments in favour of abolition then and later had little association with military events in the War. Similarly, ending the independent Ordnance Corps and Ordnance Department relied upon well-worn arguments and may have been postponed in mid 1854 only because two important administrative changes were already under way. As it was, the Secretary of State for War apparently could not take control of the Commissariat for six months, because he lacked suitable office accommodation. The war effort did not loom large among reasons for these changes. Eventually the fate of the Ordnance was determined in February 1855 — with more than a suspicion that Lord Palmerston supported the project in order to base his new government firmly on reform. Already Lord John Russell had tacitly admitted using the cause of administrative reform in a bid to eject Lord Aberdeen from the premiership.[19]

The Crimean War was not the catalyst which woke Britain from military torpor induced by an erstwhile famous victory and an obstinate, aged hero. It did not cause political trauma at home; nor did its setbacks for Britain, if less harrowing than those at Jena, engender fundamental reform — although the relation of administration to the exercise of power was underlined. Adjustments in military administration evolved from changing philosophy in the state, signalled by legislation twenty years earlier. Such was the nature of nineteenth century British politics that, until a national emergency occurred, military conservatism, political indifference and budgetary reticence denied necessary improvement. Sympathy for army administrative reform, which could ostensibly be linked with the national war effort, determined the timing of changes. The reasons for them were buried in history, not sired by transient problems about the supply of bedsteads and entrenching tools at a functional level.[20]

Military administration in time of war is of prime importance: an army's strength and efficiency ultimately depend upon it. To regard it merely as a supply exercise is to trivialise its significance. Without rational and reasoned administration, expressed in a well organised structure of command and control, diplomatic skill and battlefield courage count for little. The British, however, did not need the lessons of the Sevastopol Heights to appreciate this.

I

The Administrative System

It is not individuals, but the system that I condemn. (Lord Grey, 1854).[1]

In 1851 a Parliamentary Select Committee chaired by Lord Seymour agreed that "effective and economical conduct of military business is divided among too many offices totally separate and independent of each other"; and a fortnight after the Crimean War began one newspaper correspondent described army administration as "a heterogeneous mass". Condemnation has scarcely moderated with the advantage of hindsight. In 1869 C. M. Clode thought the administrative machine "hybrid ... discharging functions, vast, miscellaneous and undefined"; and eighteen years after him Lord Wolseley looked back in disapproval on "this curious Chinese-puzzle-like system".[2] A succession of twentieth century writers have reached similar unflattering conclusions. The claim made as Britain entered her last major war before the Crimean, that military administration was based upon the principle of "multiple fission", neatly summarises these opinions.[3]

An impression of confusion has been heightened by apparent inability of critics to agree about the precise number of departments responsible for army administration in 1854: estimates varied during the War between five and eight,[4] afterwards from seven to fourteen.[5] Unfortunately, the task of determining which were the relevant authorities has been complicated by traditional reluctance to commit details of responsibility to paper. As Lord Melbourne explained: "The work of conducting the executive government has rested so much on practice, on usage, on understanding, that ... description of it ... is to be sought in debates, in protests, in letters, in memoirs, and wherever it can be picked up".[6] Nevertheless, if the different estimates are examined, several authorities from the longer lists (such as the Commissioners of Chelsea Hospital, Paymaster-General and Audit Office) may be effectively excluded as subordinate bodies or ones concerned with minor areas of administration. Less disagreement, therefore, actually exists about the departments conducting the major business of army administration than a cursory glance at material might indicate.

Furthermore, suggestions of an irrational, haphazard growth of authorities within the system are unjust. Public administration, of which the military sector formed an integral part, had been developed with areas of overlapping responsibility for sound constitutional reasons. Charles James Fox remarked in 1793: "The theory of the constitution consists in checks, in opposites, one part bearing up and controlling another", a view to which Lord Palmerston and T. B. Macaulay, both with experience at the War Office, subscribed some fifty years later.[7] Possibly, too, emotional demands for individual liberty helped to weaken central administration and keep local government strong, so reinforcing the broader constitutional argument.[8]

Lord Grey drew attention to another crucial factor concerning the development of military administration: fear that a powerful Army might overawe the Government.[9] Origin of this dread may be traced to 1641, when troops raised by Charles I for Ireland seemed destined rather for action against Parliamentary opposition in England. Oliver Cromwell's use of major-generals to force an unpalatable way of life on the country, and James II's menacing deployment of troops outside London during his disagreements with Parliament, increased civilian unease.

The Revolution Settlement, by placing the Army firmly under Parliamentary control in matters of finance and law, did something to allay this fear without fully curbing it.[10] A hundred years after the accession of William and Mary, Edmund Burke declared that "an armed disciplined body is in its essence dangerous to Liberty", and there were numerous references to the subject in the first half of the nineteenth century. Early in 1815 a Member of Parliament complained that "he had been nearly rode over by a squadron of Horse, who had formed themselves in front of the door of the House . . . in a situation to overawe their (House of Commons) deliberations". The Speaker had to assure the Commons that the cavalry were present only to deal with anti-Corn Law demonstrations. The following year during a debate on the Army Estimates, Lord John Russell, alleging "daily increase" in the influence of the Crown, declared: "How much that influence would be augmented by a great standing army, required no illustration". He argued that if the monarch were permitted "to keep up an immense regular force . . . the people must bid farewell to that freedom which they had so long and so consciously preserved".[11]

Use of troops to suppress disorders in the immediate post-war era kept this argument alive, as an anonymous pamphleteer noted in 1825. Nineteen years later Sharman Crawford claimed: "That the large amount of standing army . . . (is) contrary to the principle of constitutional liberty, and dangerous to the rights of the people", shortly afterwards in the House of Lords the Duke of Wellington admitted: "This country does not like an army under any circumstances"; and in 1850 Sir Francis Head ironically illustrated persistence of the claim that a standing army was unconstitutional. Midway through the Crimean War Lord Panmure, Secretary of State for War, acknowledged that "deep jealousy of a standing army" was ingrained in Parliamentary thought.[12] Grave suspicion of unchecked military force was thus a long-standing factor in shaping the Army's administrative system and determined its mixture of civilian and military elements, nurtured since 1688. Then, a broad distinction was drawn between command of the Army, exercised by military officers, and its administration in the hands of civilian ministers responsible to Parliament. The system of checks practised in the administrative system as a whole was applied clearly to the Army.[13] As an additional safeguard to civil liberty, the concept of reserve forces acting as a counterweight to regulars was encouraged, with the Militia recognised as "the constitutional force".[14] Discussion of certain matters in the years immediately prior to the Crimean War emphasised that fear of an unrestricted army remained an important issue. Tentative proposals for the replacement of civilian officials of the Board of Ordnance by military officers foundered on the question of consitutional principle, a Bill was introduced to restrict movement of soldiers within two miles of polling stations during an election and Sidney Herbert opposed introduction of 'short service' on the grounds that too many men trained in military service might consitute a danger to the state.[15] So the Duke of Wellington could accept that separation of command of the army and provision of its pay, equipment and quarters was a fundamental, consititutional principle and the Duke of Newcastle reiterate that civilian administration of the Army was of "material importance".[16]

Corruption and peculation also contributed to the need for independent checks. In the late eighteenth century traces of investment in regiments remained and a procedure was instituted to prevent excessive personal gain from this and other practices. At this time, too, the Navy sought to put its house in order.[17] Seventy years later connivance between regimental colonels and contractors to profit from the supply of inferior clothing to troops caused a political storm. Such shortcomings were not purely a military problem. In November 1841 an Exchequer clerk was found guilty of forging Treasury bills and shortly afterwards two Members of Parliament were discovered perpetrating frauds.[18] It did not seem unreasonable, therefore, that within the Ordnance Department the Clerk should draw up contracts, the Surveyor-General check them and the Principal Storekeeper record delivery. Nor was it surprising that a Royal Commission under Lord Howick proposed offices with separate responsibility for supply and finance to guard against corruption. Almost twenty years afterwards Sir Charles Trevelyan, Assistant Secretary to the Treasury, argued against changing financial aspects of military administration, because they had successfully prevented fraud.[19]

Not only is it clear that the Army's administrative system developed for recognisable reasons, but in addition broad areas of responsibility

were apparent within it, and a definable structure did exist.[20] At its head
the Crown exercised purely *nominal control*, as Prince Albert recognised,
but under Queen Victoria this function was never neglected. The Queen
prodded ministers constantly and was not slow to offer them advice.[21]
This active interest gave added cohesion to the different administrative
authorities, although the Crown's influence owed more to sentiment
than to real power. Queen Victoria might claim that ministers acted
under her authority rather than that of the Cabinet, but all official
documents were counter-signed by a Secretary of State.[22]

The report of Lord Howick's Royal Commission emphasised that
executive control lay with the three Secretaries of State, of whom two had
only tenuous links with the regular army. The Secretary of State for
Foreign Affairs was concerned with the efficiency of troops, which would
not normally be used abroad outside the colonies without his approval.
Control of British ambassadors, who frequently relayed information of
military importance to him and arranged supplies from local sources in
time of crisis, gave him more frequent contact with the Army. But, in
truth, his connection with it was not strong.[23] Through Lieutenants of
Counties, the Secretary of State for the Home Department controlled all
reserve forces. Among his ministerial responsibilities were "the repelling
and prevention of any invasion and the suppression of any rebellion or
insurrection within the United Kingdom", and so he also supervised the
disposition of regular forces in Great Britain. Legally no troops could be
employed in disturbed areas without a magistrate's permission: then the
Home Secretary must be informed. He in turn notified Parliament or, if
it were not sitting, caused a Proclamation to be issued through the Privy
Council. The Home Secretary authorised issue of all military arms in the
United Kingdom and was consulted by the Commander-in-Chief (C-
in-C) before the appointment of commanders to home districts. He
supervised camps of instruction and, during the period when no C-in-C
existed, approved publication of General Orders.[24]

The Home Secretary's responsibilities, however, were confined to the
United Kingdom and, although stronger than that of the Foreign
Secretary, his connection with the regular army was relatively weak. As
Lord Howick's Royal Commission acknowledged, the third Secretary of
State, responsible for "War and the Colonies", had "authority in all
matters relating generally to the army". He was the most important
minister concerned with army administration. Specifically, he controlled all forces overseas (except those under the East India Company)
and supervised in various ways the C-in-C, Secretary at War and
Master-General of the Ordnance as well as other civil and military
authorities connected with military administration. That dispute
existed about the exact nature of his responsibility may partly be
explained by the Duke of Newcastle's claim that the limits of his office
were defined "by agreement or understanding with the head of the

government" and might therefore vary according to the personalities involved. The fact of that responsibility, however, was accepted.[25]

Military finance was in the hands of two authorities, the Secretary at War and the Treasury. The former was a government minister, who dealt with matters such as military grants, pensions and allowances and introduced the Army Estimates in Parliament: the latter exercised general supervision over army finance as over all public expenditure. The Treasury ruled on the interpretation of regulations and applications for extra finance; and the files of departments connected with army administration record that its supervision was not remote, nor its intervention casual.[26] *Supply* responsibility, principally for land transport, military equipment, food and forage, rested with the Commissariat (directed by the Treasury) and Ordnance Department (under the Board of Ordnance). *Military discipline* was the province of the C-in-C for the infantry and cavalry and Master-General of the Ordnance for the artillery and engineers.[27]

In fact, as none of these authorities could act constitutionally without its sanction, *effective control* of the entire administrative system was vested in Parliament. Four years before the Crimean War, Sir Charles Wood referred to "the constant supervision which is exercised by the House of Commons over matters of a more minute detail than they ever before interfered with", notwithstanding the recent increase in public business.[28] In essence, under Parliament, five agencies dealt continuously with matters of major administrative importance connected with the regular army: two government ministers (Secretary of State for War and the Colonies and Secretary at War), two military officers (C-in-C and Master-General of the Ordnance) and one civilian department (the Commissariat, under the Treasury), although another civilian department (the Ordnance) was responsible through the Board of Ordnance to the Master-General. Observers at the time, therefore, understood army administration more clearly than later writers: Sir John Pakington named the five in July 1854. Demonstrably, too, allegations of a thoroughly disorganised administrative system have been astray: discipline, finance and supply were each under two authorities because of the accepted need for checks. Later descriptions of administrative chaos — increasingly colourful with the passing years — owe more to evidence of local deficiencies in the Crimea than a balanced evaluation of the whole system.[29] Moreover, two figures, who portrayed administrative disorganisation at the time, exaggerated for their own purposes. Lord Grey, a persistent critic, constantly drew attention to alleged evils; in mid 1855 William Monsell described earlier shortcomings to justify expenditure on reorganisation in his department since 1854. Neither Grey nor Monsell can be regarded as reliable sources on this subject.[30]

By the middle of the century the strength of arguments in favour of the current structure of army administration had diminished. Firm

Parliamentary control of finance and decline in the independent power of the monarch had virtually eliminated fear of the Army in a political role. As Sir John Burgoyne noted in 1834: "The House of Commons hold the purse strings, and become a perfect check ... the under-secretary, who would have the immediate superintendence of the civil branches, would be another, and the variety of political feelings in the Army itself — all render such a fear chimerical".[31]

Following the growth of British colonial responsibilities after 1815, the volume of the Army's administrative business mushroomed. With existing checks, long delays became inevitable. An enormous amount of correspondence passed between departments, often housed in the same building; issue of equipment occurred only after completion of lengthy procedures; and it took eleven years to repair barracks in Trinidad through inter-departmental wrangles.[32] Hence, efficiency and economy, which pointed towards fewer responsible authorities, became twin targets for reform opinion. Lord Seymour's Select Committe concluded: "The more responsibility is concentrated, the greater ... will be the chance of efficiency and economy in the service". The Navy had already made some advance in this respect. In 1782 thirteen separate departments in different parts of the country controlled naval affairs, but, through reform measures by the Earl of St. Vincent and abolition of the Navy Board in 1832, administrative responsibility within the Service had been consolidated and clarified. Significantly, the theme of much mid-century literature on army administration concerned efficiency.[33]

The Army's difficulties were not peculiar, for parallel problems appeared in other areas of public administration. Centralisation of responsibility became something of a remedy for all evils. The Metropolitan Commission of Sewers replaced six separate authorities, the Poor Law Commission and the Board of Health came into existence, and Civil Service reorganisation was mooted partly for the same reason.[34] In practice, however, expertise is a prerequisite for successful reform, and moves towards centralisation were also caught in the tangled web of resistance to government control, intransigence of local officials and insistence on the rights of individuals, as the Poor Law Commission discovered to its cost. Inter-departmental strife proved another potent factor: forty years elapsed before the 1832 naval reforms, especially recognition of the position of the First Sea Lord as principal adviser to the First Lord of the Admiralty, were fully accepted in the Service.[35]

Palmerston wrote in 1836: "The present subdivision of the ad-ministration of the affairs of the Army into several departments is inconvenient". But ministerial memoranda, like reports from com-mittees, are not self-executive. Apathy and preoccupation with more pressing political matters combined to frustrate reform, until develop-ment of a national crisis. Then, in the more favourable climate of 1854, administrative reorganisation could be introduced under the umbrella of military urgency. When reform did come, it involved simplification of a structure which, despite contrary opinions, was less than chaotic.[36]

II

Wellingtonian Twilight, 1830–1852

Thus saith the Duke – thus hath the Duke inferred. (*Satirical pamphlet*, 1850).[1]

The years between the Duke of Wellington's resignation as Prime Minister and his death[2] witnessed a wide range of administrative reform measures involving Parliament, local government, industries and urban concentrations.[3] Insignificant parallel advances occurred in the Army; and, for this, through his obstinate resistance to progress, Wellington has been blamed. In fact, a number of complex factors, far beyond the influence of one man, conspired to frustrate aspiring reformers during "the long dead period of the long peace", when allegedly "basking in the glow of its victories in Spain and at Waterloo the British Army dozed and enjoyed its laurels".[4]

The very scope and importance of changes in the civilian sector reduced prospects of major military reform, as writers, philanthropists, reform associations and philosophers directed public interest towards social problems and encouraged a rash of surveys, select committees and royal commissions. Parliamentarians concerned themselves with mines and factories, gaols and education; Dr. Kay and Dr. Arnott discovered stagnant water, fetid drains and paltry ventilation in the Metropolis, Dr. Smith 27,000 paupers in Bethnal Green and Whitechapel; and in 1842 Edwin Chadwick produced a disturbing report on the health of the labouring classes.[5]

The two decades after 1830 consequently witnessed a deluge of official action: bills or select committee reports concerning prisons totalled fifty-eight, health fifty-one, education forty-four and factories thirty-two: exclusive of the Militia, the figure for army administration was twenty-three.[6] Philanthropic ardour cannot entirely explain this abundance of activity. Select committees had reported deficiencies in operation of the poor laws before, but recommendations of the 1832 Royal Commission were preceded by unpleasant riots. Similarly, a Royal Commission on the State of Children in Factories was appointed in 1832 only after strikes and industrial unrest. Nobody signed petitions or burned hayricks in the cause of army administrative reform. Once the turmoil of the 1840s had subsided, the country indulged in an orgy of pacifism over the Great Exhibition, and interest in military matters, not closely connected with national defence, sank to a low ebb.[7]

Unease, too, about growth of professionalism among officers discouraged reform which might appear to strengthen the Army.[8] This was not connected with fear of direct intervention in politics. The constitutional position of the C-in-C in relation to the Crown and Parliament became a matter of political discussion; so royal endeavours to maintain some independent control over the Army through him assumed more significance. Abroad, prompted by the example of Prussian military reformers, other European armies were looking to make their officers more professional; and, in Britain, an expansion of civilian professions was taking place.[9] In the early part of the nineteenth century, the Royal Military Academy, Woolwich, improved its standards, the C-in-C introduced examinations for first commissions and promotion to captain and the Ordnance Corps established its own school at Carshalton House for aspiring cadets.[10] Precisely what constituted 'professionalism' was not clear then and has been a subject of debate ever since, but it clearly involved greater expertise. More efficient officers might become a constitutional embarrassment.[11] The Duke of Wellington, Sir George Cathcart and, shortly after landing in the Crimea, Lord Raglan all saw themselves primarily as personal servants of the Crown.[12] This devotion, based on belief not lip-service, was innocuous when no distinction occurred between Parliament, government and Crown; but Wellington and Raglan individually made statements, which created some confusion of thought about the role of the Army in a constitutional crisis. The extent of professionalism, therefore, became important. To introduce administrative reform might reduce certain restraints on the military officer and was a subject best left alone.[13]

Various other elements of anti-military thought also discouraged administrative reform as well. Conditions of service — poor food, rampant disease, harsh discipline — attracted only low quality recruits and made the Army despised. W. E. Gladstone, Richard Cobden and John Bright all deplored the immoral nature of armies, which brutalised and degraded their soldiery.[14] Calls to improve this unsatisfactory situation were made on moral and humanitarian grounds, without concentrating narrowly on the conditions of service and without pressing for administrative reorganisation.[15] Furthermore, support for pacifism, reinforced by merchants in search of markets, the short-lived peace society and general euphoria surrounding the Great Exhibition also distracted attention from military matters which undoubtedly did not assist the cause of administrative reform either.[16]

Possibly the most important ingredient of anti-militarism was resentment at the use of troops to cope with civil disorder.[17] Deployed to control polling at elections, suppress opposition to the revised Poor Law and deal with Chartism, the Army appeared an opponent of civil liberty.[18] Reduction of the Army, rather than administrative reform, therefore became a pressing demand. Sharman Crawford argued that the size of regular forces at home represented the Government's aim "to coerce the people of Great Britain" and William Williams protested at some 20,000 police "being equipped in all respects regularly like soldiers" for the same reason. So there were complaints of military interference with an election in Ireland and objection to the organisation of out-pensioners for duty in riot situations.[19] Enjoying support in Parliament, anti-militarism could not be ignored, and its advocates eyed proposed administrative change with considerable scepticism.[20]

Demands for military economy, usually resurgent in Britain as danger recedes, proved an important bar to reform. With the coming of peace, forces were quickly reduced and military arrangements defended on the grounds of less cost. Normally regiments stayed overseas for ten years, though in India the period was fifteen because of the heavy expense involved in movement: Wellington protested strongly at a government plan to keep men abroad even longer to save money.[21] The first interim report of the Seymour Committee in 1849 needed to explain that increases in Ordnance expenditure had resulted from vastly expanded responsibilities, including those acquired from other departments.[22] So in its final report the Committee rejected abolition of army agents mainly because increased expenditure of £8,937 would result. Not surprisingly it applauded a total saving of £884,000 for non-effectives since 1828; and another select committee opposed expansion of government small arms factories due to necessary initial outlay. The administrative reformer, whose measures involved expense in the short term, had little hope of success.[23]

The bulk of support for reform came from radicals, some of whom also expressed anti-military views. This paradox pinpointed radical lack of success in this and other spheres, for as a group they lacked cohesion: Joseph Hume remained tinged with the toryism he had abandoned, A. H. Layard fanatically anti-Russian; John Roebuck was frequently bellicose, while Richard Cobden preached disarmament.[24] A few, like David Urquhart and Thomas Anstey who branded Palmerston as a Russian client, appeared ridiculous; others like Sharman Crawford habitually queried military estimates, but enjoyed sparse influence. Many of the radicals spread their interests too wide and, through obsessive carping in and out of Parliament, alienated potential friends.[25] Layard admitted that his political activity cost him support; and Benjamin Disraeli remarked that, in the 1840s, Cobden's appeals had become "both to the nation and parliament a wearisome irritation". In these years, as military reformers, the radicals achieved nothing directly.[26]

Yet, partly through their persistence, military administration was not altogether ignored. In the period between the formation of Sir Robert

Peel's second ministry (September 1841) and Wellington's death (September 1852), the House of Lords debated relevant subjects on only seventeen occasions and divided twice. But there was more interest in the Commons. Although divisions were infrequent, Army and Ordnance estimates were often discussed at length: a long debate occurred on the Ordnance Estimates in April 1850 and seventeen Members spoke on the Army Estimates in March 1852. Lord John Russell claimed, with justification, that debates were sometimes curtailed only because the Estimates had been "proposed ... at one o'clock in the morning, and they had been allowed to pass without discussion".[27] Including resumed debates and those connected with supplementary requests, the Army Estimates were discussed on seventeen occasions with fifteen divisions: two divisions failed to attract 100 M.P.s, but those on 31 March 1848 (two), 19 March 1849 and 11 March 1850 involved 332, 291, 222 and 273 respectively. Attempts to achieve economy were the main reason for interest. The Ordnance Estimates were debated on fifteen occasions, although only on 12 July 1849, and then three times, did the House divide with 111, 133 and 136 M.P.s present.

From time to time other issues connected with army administration occupied the House: eight debates concerned military punishments (three divisions of 246, 127 and 106 M.P.s), nine military pensions, rewards and medals (one division), nine Chelsea out-pensioners (six divisions, of which two exceeded 100 M.P.s) and eight concerned army enlistment and the Army Service Bill (two divisions of eighty-nine and 133). Administration of the Board of Ordnance concerned the Commons on two occasions, so did the position of the C-in-C (Wellington) in the Cabinet, and military finance was raised six times during debates on the whole range of national expenditure. Allowances, for instance connected with clothing, were dealt with on four occasions and duelling five: national defences were specifically considered only twice and single debates occurred on a variety of issues, such as soldiers' knapsacks, allocation of Crown troops in India, regiments in Ireland, alleged death of a soldier through over-drilling, barrack canteens, and examinations at Sandhurst. There were, therefore, a considerable number of matters on the fringe of military administration discussed without an issue of major importance being raised, competence of the Board of Ordnance and the constitutional position of the C-in-C being the most significant. During these eleven years, spanning sixty-three volumes of Hansard (lix–cxxii), in all the Commons dealt with army administration on ninety-five occasions (fifty-two directly concerned with finance) and divided twenty-nine times.

Absence of important reform measures from the floor of both Houses, indeed from wider civilian and military discussion, has been attributed to one indomitable figure: the Duke of Wellington. Two years before

Wellington's death, Fox Maule considered that until the Duke and Lord Anglesey died no administrative reform would be achieved; and the same year a critical pamphlet declared that, while Wellington remained C-in-C, the Horse Guards would sanction no change. Lord John Russell wrote to Prince Albert: "It may be useful if Your Royal Highness will see him (Wellington) from time to time in relation to the Army", as he felt that the Prince's influence might "overcome the indisposition to change which he naturally entertains". After Wellington's death newspaper comments were less restrained. *The United Service Gazette*, quoting a letter of October 1812 from the Duke of Wellington to Lieutenant-Colonel Gore, "'if once we begin to alter, we shall have nothing fixed, as there are no bounds to fancy'", concluded that "the passion for 'as you were' oppressed the Duke to the last"; the *Manchester Guardian* decided: "While the Duke of Wellington lived no-one ventured to question either the civil or military administration in opposition to his great authority". At the outbreak of the Crimean War, *The United Service Gazette* and *Illustrated London News* returned to the theme.[28] A succession of later authors, not all unsympathetic towards Wellington, have also adopted this standpoint. "He let things go from bad to worse and in several directions checked what should have been normal progress by the obstructive display . . . of a bigoted conservatism", Captain Owen Wheeler has written: spanning over a century G. R. Gleig, Major Arthur Griffiths, General E. B. Hamley, J. B. Conacher and W. S. Hamer have reached like conclusions.[29]

Wellington's opposition to a host of proposals cannot be denied: introduction of the Minié rifled musket, improved staff training, army schoolmasters, abolition of purchase, pensions to N.C.O.s under certain circumstances.[30] Frequently he referred to his military past: the retreat from Kabul in December 1842 "was not as clean, as we term it, as my Retreat in the Peninsula", retention of the smooth-bore musket was justified by Marshal Marmont's praise of its effectiveness during the Napoleonic Wars, and his last significant speech in the House of Lords referred to the performance of the Hanoverian Militia at Waterloo. *The United Service Gazette* not inappropriately referred to his Torres Vedras mentality.[31] He was conservative, even ostrich-like, and he bitterly attacked efforts to obtain important administrative reform. But his opposition was not in itself decisive, although between 1815 and his death he held an influential political or military position almost continuously: Master-General of the Ordnance for eight years, then C-in-C on three separate occasions (the last during the final ten years of his life), he went on diplomatic missions to Vienna and Verona, was Prime Minister twice (1828–30 and for nine brief days in May 1832) and for three weeks in 1834 dealt with the business of every government department. In both of Sir Robert Peel's ministries he held Cabinet rank.[32]

Despite such an impressive array of appointments, after his retirement as Prime Minister his health was never good and temporary resurgence of energy during the Chartist crisis could not conceal this. He suffered from deafness and rheumatism, in 1838 Charles Greville recorded: "He is no longer so straight and upright, and old age is taking possession of his features in a way that it is distressing to see", and in the following two years he suffered four strokes.[33] At the time of the Bedchamber Crisis he pleaded to be excused office because "he was so deaf and so old and unfit for any discussion"; for similar reasons, he declined specific responsibility in Peel's Second Ministry two years later, preferring to become "Cabinet Minister Without Office". In view of contemporary concern about his repeated illness, there must be more than a suspicion that this unspecified Cabinet office and his return to the Horse Guards a year later were seen more as nominal rewards for a national hero than positions involving real authority. In practice much of the C-in-C's military work during his last years was left to personal staff under the guidance of Lord Fitzroy Somerset.[34] There is something pathetic, also, about an aged warrior being swindled through a series of begging letters from pseudo-impoverished veterans and indulging in seventeen years of piffling correspondence with a female religious fanatic. Moreover, evidence exists that Wellington's advice was not always accepted: in February 1852 Lord Derby ignored his objections to plans for the Militia. The few attempts to achieve important administrative reform during these years failed for a wider variety of reasons than the opposition of an elderly C-in-C.[35]

Abolition of the office of C-in-C, leaving administrative control at the Horse Guards in the hands of Adjutant-General and Quartermaster-General, was briefly raised in 1833. But, founded more on feelings of political antipathy than arguments for efficiency, the proposal lacked tangible support and required no pressure to ensure its failure. In the same year a Royal Commission under the Duke of Richmond was appointed to examine the whole structure of army administration, and it made two basic recommendations.[36] Command of the Ordnance forces should be transferred to the C-in-C, who would therefore head all regular troops. Secondly, "the finances of all the land forces, together with every matter not now cognizable by the Commander of the Forces, should be under the direction of a Board, to be called the Army Board", with a Cabinet Minister as First Commissioner exercising the same authority as the Secretary of State over the Admiralty Board. This Board would assume the duties of the War Office, Pay Office, Ordnance Office, Commissariat and Comptrollers of Army Accounts and, with the abolition of civilian and military posts connected with those authorities, the Commission argued that £21,080 per year would be saved. In effect all military forces would be commanded by one officer and the Army's administration would come under one Cabinet Minister. These proposals were neither "half-hearted" nor "mild", as Brigadier Symons claimed a century later.[37]

Richmond's proposals were never adopted. In fact no report was presented, and the draft recommendations were not widely known until published as an appendix to the findings of Lord Howick's Royal Commission in 1837. Before that body Richmond needed to summarise his scheme of reform, which Wellington especially condemned in connection with the Ordnance. The Duke's disapproval was probably not decisive. For Richmond admitted that his draft had neither been seen nor accepted by all the other commissioners. He explained that, on resigning from the Government and his place on the Commission in May 1834, he had passed the relevant papers to Lord Russell for completion of the task, and this had not been carried out. Lord Howick suggested that the Duke's resignation determined failure of this reform attempt, but neither in nor out of office did Richmond express enthusiasm for the project. Perhaps fundamentally he recognised that adequate support for his measures could not be mustered at this time: two changes of government in one year and preoccupation with events in Ireland might well explain this. Furthermore, proposed abolition of so many influential civilian and military posts guaranteed fervent opposition. In particular, Sir James Kempt would have almost certainly resisted disappearance of his office; so, even if agreement had at length been reached between the commissioners, the final report could have assumed a different shape to that of the draft version.

One interesting aspect of the Commission's work involved views expressed by Sir John Burgoyne, who opposed formation of the Army Board as liable "to be more expensive, dilatory and inefficient" than existing arrangements and particularly objected to the Ordnance changes. But he suggested an alternative plan, which apparently went further than Richmond's proposals: "I would propose uniting in one person the offices of Secretary at War, C-in-C, Master-General under the title of 'Secretary of State for the War Department', or as he would be more appropriately styled on the Continent 'Minister of War' ". This minister should if possible be a distinguished soldier — Wellington, Richmond, Sir George Murray or Sir Henry Hardinge — though, in default, an influential civilian would be acceptable. Burgoyne believed that this idea would awaken "many prejudices, but I am myself satisfied that they are but prejudices". The precise nature of his scheme, however, was unclear. Possibly he envisaged an overlord, with subordinate officers divested of their concern with policy making: known by another name, a commander-in-chief would still command the Army. There was no need for Wellington to attack such a vague project. Even if it were logically and persuasively presented, reduction in influence or abolition of the country's two most senior military appointments would provoke bitter controversy. Direct subordination of the Army to a civilian minister invited violent reaction from the Crown, military figures and political opinion. Richmond's was at root a personal, unapproved outline of proposals, Burgoyne's scheme never a viable undertaking.[38]

The major attempt at army administrative reform during these years centred on the report of Lord Howick's Royal Commission in 1837 which held that Richmond had provided "no adequate remedy to that which we consider the chief defect of the present system, namely the want of one authority having an efficient control over the whole military expenditure of the country and responsibility for both its amount and for the manner in which the sums voted by Parliament are applied". It therefore proposed that "the greater part of the authority with reference to the Army, which at present belongs to the Secretary of State, should for the future be invested in the Secretary at War", who, as a member of the Cabinet, would assume all "the formal duties" of a Secretary of State "such as preparing and counter-signing of all Military Commissions and the issuing of orders for the delivery of arms to the troops" without actually holding that rank. His powers would be wide: "He should be the Minister by whom the advice of the Cabinet as to the amount of the military establishments should be laid before the King; and he should be the person to communicate on all points with the C-in-C on behalf of the Administration and be immediately responsible to Parliament for all the measures of the Government with reference to the Army". Specifically, he would assume control of the Commissariat (from the Treasury) and the civil business of the Ordnance: the three civilian members of the Board of Ordnance would henceforth be answerable to him, not the Master-General. All military supplies and finance would be under his control and he would exercise "general superintendence" over the C-in-C and Master-General in place of the Secretary of State for War and the Colonies. Unlike the Richmond Report no change in the military duties or responsibilities of these two officers was proposed.[39]

Lord Howick's report was not implemented, although the Prime Minister, Lord Melbourne, informed Queen Victoria in December 1837 that he could not ignore the advice of five Cabinet Ministers who had signed it and that he had also taken professional advice from the C-in-C (Lord Hill) and the Master-General of the Ordnance (Sir Hussey Vivian). Enclosed in this letter to the Queen was a draft Order in Council to introduce the proposed reforms.[40]

Seventeen years later Lord John Russell claimed that it was decided "not to enforce the new arrangement against the authority of the Duke of Wellington, who on this point entertained decided objections". Wellington certainly did react strongly. A month after production of the report he wrote a long memorandum to Lord Fitzroy Somerset, raising three basic points. Constitutional practice had hitherto separated responsibility for command and supply and, now taking His Majesty's pleasure, the Secretary at War would control the C-in-C and the Master-General of the Ordnance to the detriment of both officers. Most crucially, however, the authority of the Crown would be affected: "This measure will transfer the effective command of the Army from the King to the House of Commons — of which body the Secretary at War will be the most powerful Member". Wellington repeated these arguments to Lord Melbourne, further insisting that the measures would make the Secretary at War superior "instead of being as heretofore the subordinate in office to the C-in-C", and emphasising added objection to the proposed changes in the Ordnance and Commissariat. Elsewhere he described the Secretary at War as the "new Leviathan".[41]

Objections were also raised by other influential figures, not all of whom were swayed by Wellington's views. Before completion of the report, Edward Ellice expressed preference for Richmond's solution and William IV opposed the recommendations; Lord Glenelg wrote that "the whole scheme itself is I must think open to a good deal of objection", Lord Hill reacted critically to diminution of the C-in-C's status and the King of the Belgians feared an adverse effect on the monarchy. Even the Deputy Secretary at War warned about defects in the proposals: "A board is a tedious and bad way of transacting business", this Board would be unworkable without the C-in-C and, in any case, the Army would not accept subordination of its professional head to the Secretary at War. Howick's own deputy therefore cast doubt on the scheme at an early stage.[42]

The Ordnance, almost inevitably, proved hostile. The Surveyor-General, Sir Rufane Donkin, believed that if the civil business of the Ordnance were to be lost "neither Parliament nor the Country would consent" to the Master-General and his Staff merely exercising military command of the Ordnance Corps and, "shorn of power and patronage", the Master-General himself might not wish to continue. He doubted, too, whether "as a mere military man", the Inspector-General of Fortifications would be able to supervise military works as anticipated. In fact, Sir Hussey Vivian, the Master-General, did constitute a stubborn opponent, despite a conciliatory letter from Howick with his copy of the Report: "We have not meant to cast the slightest blame upon anyone belonging to that department (Ordnance), but merely to show that its present constitution is defective". Although Sir Hussey agreed that the proposals were not vindictive towards his Department, he maintained that they were impracticable. He was not in principle opposed to a civilian head of military departments, but this new Secretary at War patently would not be able to cope with his extended duties: Sir Hussey preferred Richmond's plan. Once the business of Queen Victoria's accession and the consequent Parliamentary election had been settled, Howick prepared to draft a Minute hoping to allay the Master-General's fears about loss of patronage. And he tried once more to gain Sir Hussey's support. Declaring that "utter confusion" would arise if the report were accepted as it stood, Sir Hussey argued that Howick would find opposition in Parliament from both those who thought that he had gone too far and those who believed that he had not gone far enough. Bluntly he pointed out that no support would come from responsible Ordnance officers: "Your Proposed Minute of the Queen in Council would in Execution be found neither satisfactory to us as Chiefs of our respective Departments nor advantageous to the Publick (sic)". In vain Howick referred to Sir Hussey's letter of March and later conversations which had led him to count on Ordnance support. He now realised that Sir Hussey's opposition was implacable and agreed that the matter should be left to the Cabinet for decision.[43]

While the final draft of the Report was in preparation, individual Commissioners appeared to doubt its wisdom. In October 1836 Howick thought Russell preferred Richmond's scheme, at the end of that month Lord Strafford revealed that the opinion of Wellington "and several very distinguished officers" had caused him to reconsider his support for "some such consolidation": particularly he feared that with all his other duties, in wartime the Secretary at War would not be able to handle the Commissariat efficiently. By the end of the year Sir J. Cam Hobhouse was also wavering. At this time, however, Palmerston seemed firm: he favoured the plan "to build up the Office of Secretary at War again, and to restore to it some of its ancient Functions and Importance", adding that the minister's permanent place in the Cabinet would mean a further check on the C-in-C. Early in the new year he wrote: "I entirely concur in this Report".[44]

Not until late in 1837 did the matter again receive serious consideration and, by then, Palmerston evidently had second thoughts: "I still think that with some modifications and additions it would be the best that could be adopted". He believed that army administration should be divided into two departments: executive and military, civil and financial, with the latter supreme. The Secretary at War would still be "the person responsible to Parliament for the whole Military expenditure and through whom the orders of the Government would be conveyed to the Military authorities". But, in addition, Palmerston now felt that the post of Master-General of the Ordnance should be abolished and the Ordnance Corps brought under the C-in-C. Diametrically opposed to his views, these ideas obviously owed nothing to Wellington. Palmerston also wrote that if objections were raised to a consolidation of military finance under one head, the Ordnance Estimates might still be presented to Parliament by the Clerk of the Ordnance and the Commissariat transferred to the Ordnance Department, as Sir Hussey Vivian had suggested. Palmerston therefore apparently favoured strengthening the civilian Board of Ordnance. He further confused the issue by suggesting that Lord John Russell's idea of a Board of the three Secretaries of State, Secretary at War, C-in-C and Master-General might be possible, although contradicting himself with a marginal comment: "I am not sure that it would not be liable to greater objection". Whatever Palmerston did support, he had evidently moved away from the Commission's original recommendations.[45]

Four days later Russell used Sir Hussey Vivian's objections to claim that Howick's proposed Minute must fail and underlined his alternative of "the Big Board". Shortly afterwards he wrote: "I do not think the transfer of the Pay and Allowances of the Ordnance Department to the Secretary at War is worth the pen and ink which you and Sir Hussey have expended upon it". And he showed disagreement with Palmerston by favouring ultimate, not immediate, transfer of the Ordnance Corps to the Horse Guards. Before the close of the year, therefore, Lord Melbourne made the Queen aware of these difficulties, warning that "Your Majesty must contemplate the possibility, not to say the probability, of his not being able to succeed" in composing them. In January of the new year Howick's hopes effectively vanished. Russell agreed that the present system constituted "a strange division of powers" and was "anomalous", but that the time was "inconvenient" for reorganisation. Recognising the seriousness of this contention, Howick reminded Melbourne that the Report had been on the Table nearly twelve months and that this "difficult" subject would not become less so with time. Russell then put forward three possible courses of action: merge the Secretary of State's military responsibilities with those of the Secretary at War, create a new Secretary of State to absorb the Secretary at War's duties (which he now preferred) or form a Board such as the Board of Admiralty. Howick still pressed for expansion of the Secretary at War's powers, however, because effective consolidation was his aim and the Ordnance business must be included in any satisfactory scheme. Russell had thus shifted his ground during this month and seemed most unlikely to agree with Howick on any measure. The project was finally abandoned in the summer of 1839. Russell's assertion that Wellington's opposition proved decisive was no more convincing then than in 1854: "If they (the Cabinet) had acceded, the Duke of Wellington followed by the whole Army would have opposed it and surely defeated it". But immediately he followed this with indications that the plan was in itself unworkable: "Ellice's scheme, which I thought the best, of having a 4th (sic) Secretary of State you would not hear of — so the subject has been dropped from necessity".[46]

A number of other urgent problems undoubtedly contributed to this decision by distracting political interest and prompting the Commissioners to think again. Lord Melbourne's Government was not in a strong position and, while the final draft of the Report was under consideration, Howick and Hobhouse both viewed its future with apprehension. This situation did not improve during the ensuing year.

Commenting on the result of the summer election in 1837, Russell wrote: "It is not to be denied that this near balance of parties makes the task of conducting the government difficult for any ministry". The Government experienced considerable domestic trouble over such measures as Church Rates and Irish Municipal Corporations, and serious insurrection in Canada demanded special note: the Canadian problem remained unsolved when possible intervention in the Low Countries against France was considered, and disaffection about the new Poor Law and support for the Peoples' Charter also mounted. Lord Howick, at the War Office, was closely connected with army administration, but his colleagues had different problems to occupy them. As Lord Melbourne informed the Queen, compared to "Canadian affairs . . . the question of the administration of the army . . . is of less immediate importance ". Furthermore, such a controversial measure might lead to political suicide for a precarious government.[47]

Howick's own political inexperience, stubbornness and volatile temperament were disadvantages in these circumstances, and he became increasingly isolated within the Cabinet. When sending a draft of the Report for Russell's approval, he adopted a self-effacing attitude: "The whole subject is so perfectly foreign to any to which I have ever been accustomed to attend or take any interest in, that I am very incompetent to deal with it properly". Four days later he described his proposals as "less objectionable" than those of Richmond, "but I think this plan though not really good in itself would be a material improvement upon the existing system". Such temporary diffidence neither inspired confidence nor commanded respect. A year later Melbourne revealed that Howick disagreed strongly with his Cabinet colleagues over action in Canada, and Howick conceded that he was "always in a minority in the Cabinet". He continued to make trouble over Canada and early in 1839 Melbourne reported a "very stormy and unpleasant" Cabinet meeting about army administration: "Lord Howick made a most violent speech strongly condemning the whole of the present system and arraigning the conduct of the Treasury and other Departments". Howick threatened to "express his entire disapprobation of the present system" in Parliament and Melbourne, with a hint of exasperation, informed the Queen that the Cabinet bore Lord Howick "with great patience". He foresaw difficulty, possibly disaster, for the Government if Howick continued in this vein. In May, during the Bedchamber Crisis, Howick was with difficulty persuaded to support fellow Cabinet members and, eventually, the possibility of easing him out of office arose. Perhaps aware of this, in August 1839 he resigned. No vestige of hope now remained for introduction of the Commission's recommendations.[48]

Failure to introduce the proposals cannot, therefore, be ascribed simply to Wellington's disapproval. Their crucial weakness lay in the position of the Secretary at War: although with vastly expanded authority, he would not be a Secretary of State. In this fundamental respect the scheme was ill-conceived. Furthermore, by 1839 Wellington's health was not good and a determined government could have introduced administrative reform if he had been the sole, even the main, barrier to it. A number of different political and military figures clearly had qualms about many of the proposals and, even before its production, Commissioners themselves were expressing their own doubts. A likely explanation for events surrounding the Commission and its report is that experienced politicians, confident that his recommendations would never reach the statute book, were prepared temporarily to give Howick his head in the hope that he would support them on other current matters. For them Wellington provided a useful cover. Howick's dealings with Sir Hussey Vivian and Lord John Russell displayed a certain naïvety; and, as the incumbent, he would himself enjoy the improved prestige and power of the Secretary at War. Sidney Herbert's comment on him is therefore of interest: "very honest ... but rather impracticable". His colleagues were prepared for him to produce a report, but not enhance his personal authority.[49]

In the ensuing years there were occasional hints that independence of the Ordnance Department and Ordnance Corps was about to end and regrets expressed that these changes were yet delayed. In January 1850 Fox Maule, the Secretary at War, circulated a Confidential Memorandum proposing consolidation of responsibility for army administration: "Let the patronage of the army be left to the C-in-C and its strategy to its officers, but let all other matters rest with a responsible Minister of the Crown". The memorandum contained no specific plan of reform, however, and may have been designed primarily, by demonstrating interest outside the narrow confines of his office, to support Fox Maule's claim for entry into the Cabinet from which he was excluded until 1851.[50]

These were not major efforts at reform. The most positive attempt came from Wellington, which, had it succeeded, would have had far-reaching political and constitutional significance. He proposed that on his death Prince Albert should become C-in-C and the posts of Adjutant-General and Quartermaster-General he amalgamated into that of one Chief of Staff. Prince Albert agreed that if he did become C-in-C this amalgamation would become "indispensable", but would create "confusion" if he did not and possibly even lead "to the abolition of the office of C-in-C". In fact, the Prince recognised overall difficulties more clearly than Wellington — perhaps an indication of the Duke's waning powers — and declined the offer on the grounds of constitutional impossibility: as C-in-C he would be associated with one institution of the state and in this capacity receive the Queen's commands through a Secretary of State. Impartial advice in his other role as the Queen's consort would be difficult, if not impossible. Wellington's scheme was unrealistic.[51]

Lord Seymour's Select Committee on Army and Ordnance Expenditure considered the findings of both Richmond and Howick, together with contemporary oral and written evidence, producing two interim reports and a final report between 1849 and 1851. In the interests of "greater simplicity", it expressed "general acquiescence in the principles of the Report of 1837". Urging the Government "to adopt measures to consolidate, economise and simplify the Civil Administration of the Army in all its branches", it offered no "detailed course of action", however, leaving those with "official positions and authority . . . (to) remedy the present imperfect system". Wellington had no material influence on these conclusions, which offered considerable licence for procrastination.[52]

The two decades after formation of Lord Grey's Whig government in 1830 showed that need for army administrative reform was recognised. Measures later introduced — creation of a separate Secretary of State for War, ending of Treasury control over the Commissariat, abolition of the appointment of Master-General of the Ordnance, transfer of the Ordnance Corps to the command of the C-in-C and elimination of the post of Secretary at War — were all discussed at some length. Their introduction would have rationalised the system, but only a persistent few evinced interest in them. For this a combination of financial, military, social and moral reasons was responsible, in which opposition from the Duke of Wellington was by no means the most important: economy proved a much more potent force. Periodic French war scares caused feverish activity around south coast fortifications, but administration rated low priority. Until a crisis evolved, the national purse strings were tightened against military expenditure. This attitude, demonstrated neither for the first nor the last time in British history, owed scarcely anything to Wellington. As Lord John Russell commented during controversy over the Howick report in 1838, the time for administrative reform was "inconvenient".

III

Before the Storm, 1852–1854

England slumbered on, until the Crimean War awoke her. (*Anonymous pamphlet*, 1870).[1]

In retrospect, it is clear that Wellington alone did not prevent administrative change before 1852. At the time, however, his death was expected to herald reform, and the choice of his successor at the Horse Guards could not be divorced from anticipation of it. So their advanced age ruled out the Marquis of Anglesey and Lord Seaton as serious contenders. Of Anglesey, who was eighty-four, *The United Service Gazette* queried "Is he not too old?"; and, although eight years younger, Seaton had recently suffered a long illness, after-effects of which forced him to stay with his family near Bagshot rather than in camp during the Chobham manoeuvres in 1853.[2] The Queen's cousin, the Duke of Cambridge, was thought too young and inexperienced for overall command, and Sir John Burgoyne, despite his great experience, as an Ordnance officer could not be considered.[3] On constitutional grounds Prince Albert had already rejected Wellington's plea to succeed him, hence only two candidates remained: Lord Fitzroy Somerset and Lord Hardinge.[4]

Within a fortnight Hardinge had become C-in-C and a disappointed Somerset been offered the Master-Generalship of the Ordnance and a peerage, as Lord Raglan. Charles Greville wrote in his diary: "I have no doubt that the Court insisted on having Hardinge, who is a great favourite there". No firm evidence has survived to sustain this allegation. Hardinge was undoubtedly on friendly terms with the Queen, as his correspondence from India showed, but Somerset was not unpopular: when he hesitated to accept a peerage because of the cost involved, the Queen offered to pay the fees.[5] Nor was age decisive: both were Peninsular veterans and, at sixty-seven, Hardinge actually three years older than Somerset. Hardinge had considerably more military and political experience than his rival, though this was of marginal importance. The C-in-C's post virtually restricted its occupant to office work in London with little prospect of command in the field and with no political initiative.[6]

Hardinge's wider experience in military and political appointments may have made him more attractive to the Crown, which feared diminution of the C-in-C's status: Prince Albert felt "that many attacks on the Army which have been sleeping on account of the Duke will now be forthcoming". Nevertheless, however strong its view, the Court could not constitutionally act independently of, nor in opposition to, the Government. Hardinge went to the Horse Guards because he had shown energy in bringing about military change, albeit of a narrow Service nature, and he represented a break with the past. His appointment was linked with hopes of reform.[7] When Secretary at War, he had introduced measures to improve the Army's morale and efficiency. More recently, during seven brief months as Master-General, he had displayed considerable activity in touring coastal defences and increasing the number of field guns available for national defence and overseas operations. He therefore appeared actively aware of the need for change.[8] In contrast, Somerset had been Wellington's 'alter ego' and, in the atmosphere of hero worship surrounding the Duke's death, it might to some "seem but meet that the present system of command should be prolonged in his person". On the other hand, "the Horse Guards has for too long a time been dominated by a variety of influences, none of which should have been allowed any weight in the adjustment of military appointments"; and Lord Fitzroy Somerset had been there for a lengthy period. So *The United Service Gazette* summarised hopes for improvement, which were decisively connected with Hardinge's appointment as C-in-C: "In many important respects the change at the Horse Guards will, we suspect, be found advantageous to the Service".[9]

Prince Albert's fear that the Army would suffer extraordinary public and political pressure was not realised. Pacifist figures like Cobden still uttered anti-military sentiments and use of troops to suppress disorder continued to prompt unpopular reaction. But these activities constituted an irritant rather than a menace to the military.[10] More important was preoccupation with social reform. Shortly after his coalition government took office, Lord Aberdeen announced its intention of introducing measures connected with education, legal reform and Parliament, and early in 1853 a leader in *The Times* argued that education, income tax and the government of India were the most important issues of the moment. The latter, in fact, occupied a considerable amount of Parliamentary time: Sir Charles Wood's new bill to replace the current India Act received the royal assent on 20 August 1853 only after two months of bitter controversy. Already, too, Lord John Russell and Lord Granville had drawn attention to the need for educational reform, although emphasising the difficulties surrounding introduction of any worthwhile measure. Russell did sponsor a bill to allow corporate towns to levy an education rate under certain conditions, but after three months it was quietly shelved in the light of strong religious opposition.[11]

A number of minor acts, from employment of children in factories, licensing of common lodging houses and vaccination to smoke nuisances in London, consumed Parliamentary time and political attention: 136 public acts were passed during the 1853 session, of which about one-third concerned the budget, income tax and other fiscal matters. Even as tension mounted over events in the eastern Mediterranean and British military intervention grew ominously near, the Queen's Speech in January 1854 laid down an ambitious social reform programme, and *The Times* urged that the international crisis should not interfere with important domestic legislation. Until early in 1854, in fact, habitual disinterest in military affairs persisted. A division on the Army Estimates in February 1853 attracted 119 Commons' members; but, apart from debates on the Mutiny Act and purely colonial matters, during the eighteen months between Wellington's death and the Crimean War the House of Commons was occupied with military affairs on only nineteen occasions. Including two important debates initiated by Lord Seymour and Joseph Hume, a mere five of these were directly connected with army administration; and in this period only four select committees considered associated subjects.[12] To some extent this apathy was an indication of the lack of political influence of Sidney Herbert, whose replacement of William Beresford at the War Office soon after Hardinge's arrival at the Horse Guards had been greeted en-thusiastically by reform opinion. Herbert's reputation was largely based on seventeen months of previous activity at this office, which had in reality narrowly involved military discipline and soldiers' comfort. He had never supported a major administrative reform measure, nor had he the political weight to combat other strong personalities.[13]

Reminiscent of the previous decade, the only military issue to attract significant attention, at a time of political upheaval across the Channel, was national defence.[14] Shortly before Wellington's death, as Master-General of the Ordnance, Lord Hardinge initiated an inquiry into the effectiveness of existing coastal batteries against ships steaming at eight to ten knots and their vulnerability to bombardment. While the new Militia Bill was under consideration, the Queen expressed concern about the deficient state of coastal defences and in the autumn of 1852 the Board of Ordnance looked closely at the fortifications of Alderney and Guernsey. At the end of that year Sir John Burgoyne emphasised the military vulnerability of the new dockyard at Portland, and pointed out that an invader landing west of Portsmouth could progress rapidly up the Meon valley to Windsor and London in the absence of viable barriers in his path. General anxiety about defences from Granton in Scotland to Plymouth in Devon continued into the new year, and particular fears were expressed in January 1853.[15] Detailing a contemporary pamphlet, *The United Service Gazette* alleged that the naval dockyard at Portsmouth "would fall in a very few days" and, furthermore, that "nothing can prevent the landing of an enemy upon the Kentish coast". Two days after, Palmerston wrote to Aberdeen about deficiencies in harbour and port defences, and Sir John Burgoyne also produced an exhaustive analysis of individual areas. At the end of the month Palmerston admitted that two years would be needed to improve dockyards' defences satisfactorily, and Sidney Herbert too voiced his misgivings on the subject. Joseph Hume, objecting to increased Ordnance Estimates, protested that people were "quite mad on the subject of defence", but failed to quieten the nervous.[16] In the spring Lord Seaton added his fears, throughout June the Ordnance concerned itself with extraordinary defence repairs; in the autumn Sir James Graham, First Lord of the Admiralty, undertook an extensive tour of dockyard fortifications and land was purchased on Whaley Island and at Sconce Point, Isle of Wight, to improve the defences of Portsmouth. This myopic concentration on coastal fortifications determined that, as war with Russia became likely, *The United Service Gazette* called for an extension of east-coast defences to guard against surprise attacks over the North Sea. A fortnight after war had been declared, and on the day that Lord Raglan was officially appointed to command the expeditionary force destined ultimately for Sevastopol, Sir John Burgoyne complained that "a single man of war or even an armed Privateer" could severely damage most commercial harbours in Britain "within the period of an hour or two".[17]

Concern about coastal fortifications was not at first entirely irrational, given suspicion about French military intentions. At the end of October 1852 Lord Grey noted that Lord Clarendon was perturbed about expanding French military power, and he himself recorded: "The common tale of the French army and of his (the Emperor's) entourage is about the 'descente sur l'Angleterre' and the occupation of London". During this winter Ordnance records show that scrupulous attention paid to defence work stemmed from fear of French attack: build-up of the Militia was also founded on this and press articles emphasised its probability. Grey professed himself "a great deal alarmed about France ... the new Emperor is clearly not to be trusted".[18] Lord Malmesbury protested that these fears were entirely unfounded. Nevertheless the Commons increased expenditure on coastal fortifications to counteract improved French naval armament. Cobden held that reports of possible French invasion were a "wicked delusion", only to be decried as an unrealistic, "cotton-spinning mountebank", on the same day that Palmerston emphasised French hostility privately to Sidney Herbert. A week later *The United Service Gazette* announced that a "discarded mistress" had reached England with Napoleon III's actual invasion plans, and two days later Cobden referred to an alarmist letter in *The Times* claiming "positive information" of an increase in French forces preparatory to invasion: Disraeli's scorn at the flimsy basis for such rumours had scant effect.[19] Disquiet, therefore, continued and in June 1853 an editorial in *The United Service Magazine* quoted confident statements by two French admirals concerning an invasion of England. One month before the official declaration of war against Russia, and when British and French joint naval action had already taken place, Queen Victoria demanded: "Who can say it is impossible that our own shores may be threatened by Powers now in alliance with us?"[20]

This absorption with defence matters in an indirect fashion brought about establishment of barracks at Aldershot and the Army's long association with that area. After a personal inspection in August 1853, Lord Hardinge proposed purchase of ground on Aldershot Heath for a permanent training ground, arguing that in the long run this would prove more economical than annual hiring costs plus inevitable compensation for damage. His main arguments were strictly military, however: access by railway would be easy, good water available and "every continental army (even those of second and third-rate powers)" had a permanent practice camp, where regular and reserve troops could train together. Palmerston supported the plan for reasons of defensive utility: "I believe that the possession of a large encampment like this, in the situation in which this ground is placed, would tend more to the Defence of London and at a less cost than any such fortified works". It would certainly pre-empt an advance up the Meon Valley, which so worried Burgoyne.[21]

Military initiation of moves to obtain land at Aldershot, like evident concern over defective forts, created the impression of an alert Army, eager to obtain maximum professional efficiency: civilians need not therefore worry. Complacency in this respect was encouraged by evidence that the Ordnance was similarly mindful of maintaining its own efficiency. Its methods of operation had been modified in accordance with recommendations from two Parliamentary Select Committees. And a Treasury Committee of Inquiry in December 1853 stated: "We are gratified by finding that the officers of the Board of Ordnance have been for a long series of years engaged in the work of self-reform", adding with approval that an internal Ordnance Committee of Inquiry had recently re-examined the structure of the Department. Early in 1854 examinations for Ordnance clerks were made compulsory and the duties of the Principal Storekeeper reviewed, when he became "Comptroller of Stores and Principal Storekeeper". As the international situation deteriorated, plans were put in hand to raise 1,145 additional Ordnance troops. The Clerk of the Ordnance thus declared that the organisation and efficiency of his department were good.[22] This general picture of well-being and professional watchfulness was enhanced by Sidney Herbert's recitation to the Commons of recent advances in Service education, health and prisons, and his assertion that "he did not believe that at any period had the soldier been more comfortable than at the present moment". Establishment of a permanent musketry range at Hythe to improve marksmanship added to the overall impression of military efficiency.[23]

The greatest single opiate for the complacent involved army manoeuvres, comprising some 10,000 troops under Lord Seaton, on Chobham Common in June and July 1853. The exercise was apparently a great success. *The United Service Magazine* published an "official summary of the Camp at Chobham", which expressed "one cordial feeling of praise ... (at) the state of discipline and internal economy of the regiments", Sir George Brown, the Adjutant-General, congratulated the troops on their performance and Lord Hardinge held that he "never saw a finer body of men".[24] In this welter of self-satisfaction, indications of military shortcomings somehow escaped official eyes. Moreover the Commissariat, which was so lavishly praised, did not operate under battle conditions and freely made use of contractors from the surrounding area and even London. As the Crimean troops were later to discover, success in Surrey did not guarantee effectiveness in the field. The Chobham camp provided an encouraging panorama of combat-readiness for the complacent. Through the expense that it incurred, it also guaranteed limited finance for other military purposes.[25]

Ironically, the one important development in administration, which took place during these months, came about almost by accident and as a result of concentration on coastal fortifications. Although evidence for their origin and continuation is sparse, regular meetings involving civilian and military figures to plan national defence were evidently arranged. Lord Hardinge revealed later that in 1852 and 1853 the Master-General of the Ordnance, Secretary of State for War and the Colonies, First Lord of the Admiralty, C-in-C, Secretary at War and Chancellor of the Exchequer met under the Home Secretary to discuss preparation of the annual Estimates with reference to defence matters. These meetings were primarily concerned with finance and were unoriginal, as Hardinge pointed out: "There was no novelty in such a step, for it was one adopted in the time of Lord Liverpool".[26]

An entirely separate and more significant body developed early in 1853, concerned itself with defence policy, and was novel. Impetus for it may have come from Queen Victoria in October 1852, when she requested the Prime Minister to collect opinions from the C-in-C, Master-General, First Lord of the Admiralty and Home Secretary about the country's defences. But Lord Palmerston, the Home Secretary, seems to have been responsible for its organisation. On 10 January 1853, he recorded having written to the C-in-C "a few days ago" suggesting "periodical meetings". Hardinge replied on 9 January more specifically suggesting meetings "at least once a month ... (which) especially if we get Graham (the First Lord of the Admiralty) to join us may afford the means of systematizing our Defence arrangements by Land and by Sea". He believed that this procedure would keep responsible officers "informed" and "confident", and Palmerston agreed that "it would enable me to report from time to time to you (Aberdeen) and the Cabinet". Aberdeen fully approved Hardinge's modified proposals, although Palmerston could not carry out his scheme for an initial meeting on 10 January as Sir James Graham had not then been consulted. Apparently the First Lord consented to take part and "three or four" meetings did occur. Lord Hardinge's vagueness about the number of meetings suggests that proceedings were neither formalised nor, perhaps, successful. There is no indication why they were discontinued but, if held monthly and allowing for some delay until Graham's participation was assured, they may have lasted until April or May. By then the Cabinet (and Palmerston in particular) was preoccupied with the worsening Eastern Crisis and threat of imminent Russian invasion of Moldavia and Wallachia. By mid 1853, therefore, military action abroad in association with France was becoming more likely than a French invasion of Britain; and coastal defence seemed correspondingly less important. There is some evidence, however, that a Defence Committee did meet again later. In November 1856 Lord Panmure referred to the reconstitution of "a Committee upon coast defences (sic)" and, almost four years after, a "Defence Committee Minute on the Royal Commission's report on National Defence" was produced. Both the regularity of meeting and the composition of these later bodies are uncertain, for the name may have been applied to a Committee of purely Cabinet members. Nevertheless, the principle of regular policy-making consultations between responsible ministers and military officers had been established in 1853.[27]

Meanwhile the perennial, peacetime drive to curb expenditure continued to influence many proposals for military change, whatever their character. Joseph Hume called for a thorough overhaul of army administration, claiming that "by judicious alterations an enormous saving of expense might be effected"; and an attempt was made to withhold grants of public money from RMA Woolwich to make it self-supporting like RMC Sandhurst. On the grounds of expense the Treasury refused to sanction a War Office request for increased staff to cope with a larger army establishment and additional work after passage of the Militia Act. Following demand for their improvement, Hume and Sir George Pechell complained about heavy expenditure to improve the calibre and number of artillery pieces, and a Treasury Committee, specifically appointed to examine the possibility of inter-departmental amalgamation in the interests of economy, recommended consolidation of the Commissariat and Naval Victualling departments.[28]

Not surprisingly one measure of administrative consolidation, which

was achieved, owed its origin largely to a search for economy —
establishment of the combined Army and Ordnance Medical Department. Co-incidentally, negotiations towards this end revealed the
narrow, obstructive departmentalism which bedevilled working of the
entire machine. And the unsatisfactory end-product emphasised need
for careful planning and preparation of military and political opinion
before successful administrative reorganisation could be attained.

Reporting in July 1851, the Seymour Committee drew attention to
the wasteful system of maintaining two separate medical staffs and
different hospitals for the Army and Ordnance. Although it urged that
"no time should be lost in effecting ... one control and one system of
management", no significant action was taken until Lord Hardinge
became C-in-C.[29] In November 1852 he agreed that Ordnance troops in
Malta might be treated by Army doctors, where no Ordnance doctors
were available: a previous attempt to allow Ordnance troops to be
treated in line hospitals and to abolish all Ordnance hospitals except
Woolwich was resisted by the Marquis of Anglesey. When Master-
General of the Ordnance, Hardinge had agreed to the convention of a
Commission of Inquiry by the War Office, which reported that
Ordnance troops were already being treated in a number of line
hospitals and recommended that, in order to reduce expense, this
practice should be extended. On learning that the Secretary at War was
preparing a Royal Warrant to put these economies into effect, Lord
Raglan, by then Master-General, declared himself unaware that
Hardinge had "officially consented" to amalgamation of the Ordnance
Medical Department with that of the Army: he proposed to "look
carefully" at the Warrant to ensure that Ordnance medical officers were
not "even indirectly ... (brought) under the sway of the War Office".[30]

Apart from underlining the parochial attitude of departmental heads,
Raglan's protest did not affect the issue. For, eight days before his
letter to Hardinge, Treasury instructions to the Secretary at War for
preparation of the Royal Warrant emphasised that the authority of the
Master-General should not be impaired and that regimental hospitals
must be maintained. Early in 1853 Hardinge produced a memorandum
which, following the Treasury instructions, showed only partial
amalgamation of the two medical organisations. He proposed overall
administrative consolidation, provided that Ordnance regimental
hospitals continued and a separate Ordnance medical officer was
appointed wherever three or more companies of Ordnance troops were
stationed. Hardinge agreed to one Director-General, but that only
amalgamation of administrative functions, not military absorption,
should be entailed. With regard to Ordnance troops, the new Director-
General should consult the Master-General in military, and the Board of
Ordnance in financial, matters. The Royal Warrant of 14 February
1853, which officially laid down this reform, closely followed Hardinge's

proposals; so the Army medical staff was reponsible to the C-in-C and Secretary at War, the Ordnance to the Master-General and the Board of Ordnance. Administratively, however, they both came under one Director-General, the current Director of the Army Medical Department. Such an incomplete arrangement, apart from the prejudice of the separate authorities involved, resulted from a lack of clear purpose — except a general desire to save money.[31]

Calls for administrative reform not obviously based upon economy fell on deaf ears. During the debate on the Ordnance Estimates in February 1853 Joseph Hume, referring to the recommendations of the Howick Royal Commission, observed that it was "very objectionable" to keep the Army and Ordnance troops under separate commanders. In reply Sidney Herbert, the Secretary at War, pointed out that since 1837 every member of Lord Howick's Commission had held office and "modified" his views, though he personally believed that "the whole subject (ought) to be reconsidered". But nothing was done.[32]

Further probings were delayed for almost a year and, by then, the Russian naval attack on Sinope had occurred, British warships were in the Black Sea and national interest had focused on the possibility of war.[33] On 31 January 1854, Lord Grey again urged administrative reform in the Lords and, shortly afterwards, The Times called for "a real Minister of War" — one minister responsible for the Army. In the third week of February Lord Seymour requested that the Militia and Commissariat Estimates be presented to the Commons before those of the Army, "so that the House may be enabled to consider at the same time the whole military expenditure of the country". He continued: "The second question is, whether it is the intention of the Government to introduce any measure with the view to bringing the several departments connected with the administration of the Army under the superintendence of one responsible department?"[34]

Lord John Russell answered Seymour's first question by pleading that the military situation demanded immediate consideration of the Army Estimates, which could not wait for preparation of those for the Militia and the Commissariat. He then unequivocally stated: "There is no present intention on the part of the Government to introduce any measure with the view of bringing the several departments connected with the administration of the Army under the superintendence and control of one responsible department". The matter was not pressed.[35]

On 2 March 1854, Joseph Hume initiated the most important consideration of army administration immediately prior to the War, proposing in Parliament "to consolidate the different branches of Military Service and expenditure ... (under) one efficient and responsible department ... to strengthen, if possible, the hands of the Government in the administration of the Army". Arguing that "for years past" the Army, Ordnance and Commissariat had lost £200–300,000 annually,

he emphasised that he brought this matter forward in "no hostile spirit
. . . only with the view of showing the anomalies of the present system
and the importance of remedying those anomalies". He particularly felt
the "impossibility of allowing these matters to remain in their present
condition . . . (because) if any gentleman connected with a large
establishment acted on the principle on which the business relating to
the Army was conducted, he would very soon bring himself to ruin". At
the very least, the system was inefficient.

Once more Hume signified that he "entirely concurred" with the
Howick recommendations, which included putting army administration under "a Minister of War or Secretary at War". Those who had
read the Report, he claimed, would "have a fair notion of the anomalies
and inconsistencies of the present system". In particular, Hume wanted
"the whole expenditure" under one responsible minister ($£8$ million
was asked for by different ministers), the Ordnance Corps brought
under the C-in-C and establishment of one supply system for all forces.
Seymour supported him, pointing to the cumbersome nature of the
existing system, in which one man was responsible for all business
connected with the Army and colonies. Edward Ellice declared: "It
was impossible, in a rational country, long to continue a confused and
perplexed administration, like that the merits of which they were
discussing . . . the Ordnance, the Commissariat, the paymasters, the
doctors and everything else" should come under one authority.

Sidney Herbert replied for the Government with a strange mixture of
arguments. During "the last few years . . . great changes have from time
to time originated at the War Office and these changes have ultimately
been invariably successful": unconvincingly he mentioned introduction
of ten years' limited service and pre-commissioning examinations. He
then held that no change was necessary because "complete harmony
(existed) between civil and military departments" and further pleaded
that Hume's proposals were impracticable, because the Secretary at
War would be too overburdened. None of these arguments was
developed satisfactorily though, possibly aware of the paucity of his
material, Herbert assured the Commons: "Theoretically, no doubt, it
(the present system) has many faults, but practically it works very well".

There he might have concluded with consistency, if not depth.
However, he apparently accepted the validity of the very motion which
he opposed. Believing that "the main reason why the administration of
the army is more economical than that of the Navy is . . . that the
Secretary at War watches over every step of the C-in-C", he felt that this
control should be extended to the Master-General of the Ordnance.
He revealed that "privately" he thought the Ordnance troops should
come under the C-in-C, leaving the Master-General in charge only of
matériel. Cryptically he added: "This is an opinion not shared in by
others" and confessed, moreover, that he could not understand why the

Commissariat acted as Treasury banker abroad. Thus Herbert seemed in sympathy with the call for administrative consolidation. He ended his speech with another confusing passage. Looking "with great alarm" upon Hume's motion, which would put "the whole machinery out of gear", he declared that it would take "years of trouble" to get men used to the present system to work in a different way. Apparently, after all, he opposed all change; because these final words implied denial of change at any time.

Lord John Russell, another Cabinet Minister, proved hardly more convincing. He blamed the Duke of Wellington for non-introduction of Howick's proposals, rather vaguely agreed with Hume that "better arrangements are required" and purported to see in Sidney Herbert's speech that "no want of attention will be shown to this subject (of reform)". Positively he proposed that a military officer should become Under Secretary of State for War and the Colonies, suggesting that this would occur "in a very short time". Then he destroyed the illusion of further reform intent by announcing that he intended to oppose the proposals, because British troops were already on their way to the east. Patriotically, Hume withdrew his motion for the same reason.[36]

Hume could hardly have anticipated a successful review of administration, as British troops were already sailing for the Mediterranean and the country teetered on the brink of war. In any case his main aim was economy. But the debate prompted by his motion served to bring administrative problems to the fore, as impending national crisis discouraged opposition to military change. There was hope, too, that the equivocal remarks of Herbert and Russell indicated a Cabinet not stubbornly united against reform.

Belief that Wellington's death would open the floodgates to administrative reform, founded on misunderstanding of the complexity of reasons preventing successful change, put undue pressure on those expected to achieve it, particularly Herbert and Hardinge. Herbert was not physically strong. He mainly influenced individuals through personality and private argument; for as his opposition to Hume's motion in March 1854 revealed, he was not always convincing in debate. Possibly Herbert did not appreciate wider aspects of the problem: in 1853, he concerned himself with musket production at Enfield, the camp at Chobham and coastal defences. Reservations, expressed in *The United Service Gazette* after he took office, about his "knowledge of Military matters" proved not unjust.[37]

At the Horse Guards Hardinge was confronted with an ultra-conservative Adjutant-General, Sir George Brown. Objecting to Hardinge's intention of rearranging duties within Headquarters, Brown drafted his resignation in January 1853, withdrawing it after intervention by Richard Airey and Raglan. In December, however, he did resign and his twenty-one page apologia, produced three months later, not only confirmed adverse opinions expressed about his resistance to change, but suggested that he had prevented implementation of reform at the Horse Guards for some time. It is an indication of Hardinge's personal weakness that, as C-in-C, he did not remove Brown from office. Fifteen months after Hardinge succeeded Wellington, *The United Service Gazette* regretted that he had not "precipitated (expected) measures of reform": perhaps, exhausted by the exertions of a strenuous military and political life, Hardinge simply could not cope with the opposition before him. But to expect that the C-in-C, whose initiative was limited by constitutional practice, and the Secretary at War, a comparatively junior minister, could effect reform unaided was to display utmost naïvety about the political framework within which the British Army operated.[38]

Furthermore, the naval lobby remained a powerful influence in a country where considerable, active opinion declared in favour of a defensive posture. A correspondent to *The United Service Gazette* protested that James Fergusson's arguments for improved dockyard defences were irrelevant: the Navy could best defend British ports by blockading enemy harbours. Almost simultaneously, an article in *The United Service Magazine* declared: "The enemy must be kept from our shores by the Navy, which is our real defensive power"; and Sir George Pechell, dismissing many coastal forts as "objects of ridicule", claimed: "If they wanted to have the country really defended, as it ought to be, it must be by the instrumentality of an efficient navy, not bricks and mortar". Expressions of such confidence in British maritime strength encouraged lassitude towards other forms of military preparedness.[39]

Wellington's death, in itself, could not change entrenched attitudes. There were still those, who recognised the need for administrative reform, but few to agree with them. Like Howick in 1837 it was their misfortune to deal with a weak government, which even had it wished to do so, could not risk a controversial measure in the interests of political survival. Faced by other political diversions, the eternal drive for economy and national preoccupation with defence, sufficient support could not be mustered to outweigh prejudice and apathy. In the absence of a sympathetic climate of opinion, administrative reform remained a tantalising dream. The pear was not yet ripe.

IV

Transport and Supply
The Commissariat and Ordnance Departments

Although military administration involves decision making and civil-military relations at the highest level, provision of supplies to an army remains a truly vital part of its function: in the mid nineteenth century, this principally entailed food, fodder, ammunition and the means to distribute them. The British system neither concentrated transport and supply in one organisation nor exclusively in military hands, but in two entirely separate departments: the Commissariat and Ordnance. The former was wholly civilian and controlled by the Treasury; the latter, although largely manned by civilian personnel, came under the military officer who also commanded Ordnance troops.

Abroad the departments frequently maintained parallel staff, who carried out similar duties, and attempts to rationalise this situation met with obstruction in the interests of departmental status. The web of army supply services alone demonstrates the danger of a complicated administrative system: borne down by a mass of finicking regulations and wearied by the delays of tortuous procedures, Commissariat and Ordnance clerks strove to carry out their duties. The extent to which they failed was revealed on the Heights of Sevastopol. By then, however, changes had already been determined. As with other elements of the administrative machine, the Alma, Inkerman and privations of the winter served mainly to illustrate faults, which could not be rectified until more favourable opinion prevailed nearer Westminster than Sevastopol. Before the troops had even settled in Bulgaria, this became apparent.

The Commissariat

An army is quite as helpless without a properly trained commissariat as without ammunition. (Sir Charles Trevelyan, 1850).[1]

In the field, land transport and non-military supplies, such as food and forage, were provided by a civilian organisation (the Commissariat) under the direct control of another civilian agency (the Treasury). This arrangement had evolved from the medieval practice of hiring waggons and contracting for food: in a time of seasonal campaigning and when large-scale desertion might occur if troops were free to forage, there was much to recommend it. Its survival into the nineteenth century may be explained partly by the failure of efforts, like the Royal Corps of Waggoners, to establish a regular military transport service.[2] There was the belief, too, that if the Army must rely on civilians for its means of movement and sustenance, it would be less likely to indulge in unpalatable political adventures. The civilian Commissariat, therefore, acted as a constitutional safeguard. Furthermore, it could be argued that soldiers were paid to fight and problems of recruitment were too acute to permit the luxury of non-combat regulars. The difficulty of establishing military supply depots before permanent barracks were built also weighed in favour of the *status quo*.[3]

Need to rely for supplies upon civilians, who never willingly exposed themselves to enemy fire, and the frustration of military officers, who had no power to coerce commissaries whom they believed to be endangering their troops through dilatory behaviour, caused constant friction. The Duke of Wellington was well aware of this problem, which led one officer in the Crimea to despise "that most infernal Commissariat" and mischief makers in the Mess to perpetuate a legend that the last commissary-general in England had been shot by Sir Thomas Picton for incompetence. Before the Sevastopol Select Committee, Sir Charles Trevelyan admitted that the Commissariat was an "unpopular arm of the service and has been so time out of mind", and Lord Seaton found it necessary to caution his son, Major Francis Colborne, to treat Commissariat officers with consideration: "You will find them most useful, if they are treated with respect and consulted as to the affairs under their charge". Whether Colborne, who served on the staff of the Third Division in Lord Raglan's expeditionary force, heeded his father's advice is uncertain, but other officers clearly did quarrel with their commissaries. G. R. Emerson reported "continual bickerings" in Bulgaria between commissaries and commanding officers, and Major-General Estcourt's conclusion that civilian control of the Commissariat Department constituted "a great evil" represented a numerically-strong section of military opinion.[4]

The Commissariat, which "had its origin in the commissaries who were appointed from time to time to conduct on behalf of the Treasury the extraordinary expenditure caused by the Army taking the field", developed during the eighteenth century as a distinct corps with its own uniform and discipline. Controlled by the Treasury, it was neither subject to military discipline nor in any way under the C-in-C.[5] As an organised non-combat body closely connected with military forces, almost inevitably the Commissariat acquired responsibility far beyond its original scope: in West Africa its officers acted as chaplains, in Canada they collected canal tolls and in the West Indies paid stipendary magistrates. Other areas of control also accrued to it. In 1822 the separate Irish Commissariat, under the Lord Lieutenant since its inception twenty-four years previously, was transferred to the Treasury and consolidated with that of Great Britain. So by the mid nineteenth century the responsibilities of the Commissariat Department were indeed immense. Early in the Crimean campaign Sir Charles Trevelyan justifiably pointed out that it had become "much more complex" since 1809, when the Treasury had temporarily relinquished immediate control to a Commissary-in-Chief. It was arguable that in 1850 the commissary-general in the field was the most important figure in any military operation, simply because of the reliance that an army must place on him.[6]

Once the Treasury had resumed direction of the Commissariat in 1816, its Assistant Secretary (after 1840, Trevelyan) acted as its head, corresponded with commissary-generals on all matters and prepared the Annual Estimates. The corps that he controlled, although civilian, maintained a quasi-military organisation with a strict table of ranks and comprehensive regulations covering entry and promotion.[7] After 1834 the Commissariat surrendered normal, peacetime duties within the United Kingdom, while retaining widespread responsibilities in the colonies and with expeditionary forces in time of war.[8] In addition to the provision of military land transport and supplies, the Commissariat acted as Treasury banker abroad.[9] In theory the Department "blended with the Army, Ordnance and Navy and many other branches of the public service" and the commissary-general or senior commissary was responsible for his conduct to the military officer in charge of a particular station. But, as he corresponded directly with the Assistant Secretary to the Treasury and was bound by departmental regulations to report to London immediately if requested to act in a manner with which he disagreed, the executive power of the military over the Commissariat was very limited. An obstinate commissary could declare that supplies were not available.[10] Each commissary-general was thus in charge of the Military Chest, negotiated all bills, made advances to regimental paymasters for the troops' pay and to the Ordnance and Navy, and he was responsible for the local payment of military pensioners overseas. However, he had authority to advance money for immediate requirements or repairs, only subject to formal approval by the Treasury exercising its constitutional supervision of public finance, for the Department could not initiate expenditure.

Specifically, the Commissariat provided food, non-military stores, forage, fuel and light in all foreign stations. Often it needed to secure requirements from the United Kingdom, though usually supplies and transport were obtained through contracts with local civilian operators. The success of this practice depended very much upon availability of produce, cooperation from other government departments and the honesty of contractors, as the Army discovered painfully in the Crimea.[11] For once a military expedition was mounted, possibly on the fiction that another "colony" or "station" had been created, the Commissariat performed precisely the same functions with that force. Hence the Army's money, supplies and land transport were handled by a civilian body, which was not in practice subordinate to it and over the appointment of whose personnel its commander had no authority. The commissary-general was a Treasury official attached to an expeditionary force, not a military officer under the General's command. Captain Wrottesley erred in maintaining that "the Commissariat officers are under the command of the Commander of the Forces abroad strictly" and Sir George de Lacy Evans that Lord Raglan had the power to dismiss Commissary-General Filder in the Crimea.[12]

This civilian organisation, therefore, had a wide diversity of responsibility. On service it produced "articles of diet to which they (the troops) have been accustomed in this country", provided for the Army in the United Kingdom during time of war and ministered to the needs of countless stations from the Cape of Good Hope to Van Dieman's Land.[13] But the Commissariat had no regular recruitment policy, nor did it undergo field training in peacetime. Whenever an expedition was launched, recruits were hastily found and retired officers recalled to serve. This haphazard method of gaining personnel in time of crisis, and the disadvantages of relying upon civilians not under the Army's direct command for vital needs, were unsatisfactory. In a wider sense, too, it was clearly inconvenient for the Treasury (which exercised an overall constitutional check on national finance) physically to control one subordinate department.[14]

The folly of relying on rapid recruitment when serious trouble arose was harshly illuminated as the regiments set sail from England: on 1 February 1854 the entire list of active Commissariat officers spread throughout the world numbered 178. Sixteen days later James Filder, aged sixty-four, was recalled from retirement to act as Commissary-General in charge of a planned forty commissariat officers for an expedition of 10,000 men.[15] It was predictable that, when Sir Charles Trevelyan commended Filder and other commissaries to Lord Raglan, he listed their colonial experience at length; and during the disastrous winter of 1854–5 he could still refer back to it.[16] The Duke of Newcastle claimed that "as capable, as intelligent and as able a body of commissariat officials as ever accompanied an army in the field" had been brought together to meet the needs of Lord Raglan's force. In reality, it mainly comprised recruits, who had been swiftly and none-too-scrupulously secured and many of whom had absolutely no commissariat experience, or veteran ex-officers like Filder. Some serving commissaries were drafted from the colonies, but Filder complained that they were only assembled "by slow degrees" from stations as widespread as Sierra Leone, Cape of Good Hope and Australia, so the Treasury needed volunteers for the bulk of Filder's men. The original establishment of forty included only a few storekeepers and clerks, for Trevelyan admitted that "we relied upon getting subordinates in the countries where the force was to act". In the event forty-four officers were appointed for an Expeditionary Force more than double the 10,000 forecast, although Filder believed that fifty-four "officers and clerks, exclusive of subordinates" was the minimum requirement. Eventually Filder did get reinforcements from Britain, but their quality may be gauged from one letter to Trevelyan: "I have now more than enough people of one sort or another, but not enough of the right sort. I would rather have one well-trained Commissariat officer than ten police officers" — a reference to the Treasury's selection from the Metropolitan police and Irish constabulary. These, Filder noted bitterly, were "the efficient staff of officers ... nominated to assist him in conducting his duties". He claimed that his "extensive and onerous duties" were always hampered by "an insufficient establishment both of officers and subordinate employees". Sir Charles Trevelyan explained that an Assistant Commissary-General was destined for each division, one Deputy Assistant Commissary-General and one clerk for every brigade, but later admitted that "occasionally" this establishment could not be fulfilled. Lack of manpower remained a constant headache for the Commissary-General. Hence both the numerical strength and the experience of Filder's force were "unsatisfactory". From the vantage point of posterity this hardly seems surprising.[17]

If the Crimean War emphasised defects in the Commissariat's recruitment procedure, it also cruelly exposed the dangers of relying upon the existing contract system: "waggons of the country" and supplies from the theatre of war lost their last shred of credibility, when action took place on a sparsely-populated Tartar peninsula. In accordance with past practice, once the expedition had been agreed the Treasury sent intructions to Commissariat stations in the Mediterranean area, such as Malta and Corfu, to gather supplies and land transport. In March Mr. Calvert, "our excellent consul at the Dardanelles", listed details of supplies in Turkey and, "seven or eight days" before British troops arrived at Gallipoli, Assistant Commissary-General Smith "actually signed contracts with Turkish individuals ... for a supply of every requisite for the army". Contracts were placed throughout Asia Minor, in Malta, Spain and at Trieste for a variety of requirements, including cattle, baggage animals and forage. Yet little over a month after the Allies reached Turkey and before they advanced south of the Balkans, Smith admitted a scarcity of supplies in the field: and in Bulgaria Sir George Brown pointed out that the quality and quantity of bread depended upon the expertise and honesty of individual contractors. With justification Lord Seymour argued that "a good deal of the misfortunes" of the Commissariat could be traced to the contract system, and Filder claimed that uncertainty about the Expedition's destination and strategy prevented forward planning of contractual requirements. Under these conditions there was absolutely no chance of securing the estimated number of animals required in the Crimea for Commissariat use alone.[18]

Much criticism was directed at the alleged inefficiency of Commissariat officers, but a good deal of this may have been ill-founded: the Duke of Newcastle argued that charges of incompetence against Assistant Commissary-General Smith in Turkey lacked foundation, Lieutenant-Colonel Horsford, Officer Commanding the First Battalian the Rifle Brigade, thought his commissary "very attentive" and Sir John McNeill and Colonel Tulloch concluded that commissaries attached to divisions carried out their "purely executive duties" well.[19] Yet the impression endures that the Commissariat simply could not cope. Lord Lucan claimed: "They (the commissaries) were so inefficient that I found it necessary in Bulgaria to give up one of my aide-de-camps exclusively for the purpose of foraging for the cavalry", and McNeill and Tulloch damned with faint praise by writing that commissaries made efforts "according to the measure of their ability and foresight". Captain Somerset Calthorpe and Lieutenant-General Sir George de Lacy Evans were among many others to comment adversely upon Commissariat shortcomings early in the campaign.[20] Attempts to rationalise deficiencies by pleading extenuating circumstances only served to emphasise the paucity of Commissariat arrangements. From Scutari, early in June 1854, Lord Raglan explained that as yet "the organisation of the Commissariat is so much in its infancy"; twenty-five years later Sir George Brown wrote that individual commissaries were "very able and competent men", but that they had been given few subordinate staff to carry out more mundane tasks. Brown argued that a "crippled and half-formed department" was burdened with responsibilities far beyond its normal duties, instancing the need to store camp equipment and distribute "whole ship-loads of London porter". Commissary-General Filder had previously complained that responsibility for Quartermaster-General's stores and hospital stores had been forced upon the Department, and it was charged with provision of fuel to troops in the Crimea, which was outside its normal duties. All this may excuse individual commissaries, but it severely exposed the limitations of the whole system, which was unable to fulfil one of its primary functions — supplying a body of troops in the field. The Duke of Newcastle's condemnation of commissariat efforts on the Sevastopol Heights could be applied more broadly: "The machinery of the Commissariat is undoubtedly defective".[21]

A particular deficiency revealed during the Crimean campaign was the minutely-detailed regulations and lengthy procedures, which bedevilled swift action. Paper abounded. For purposes of later reference, there was justification in the pedantic instruction: "The leaves of all the Bill-books will be numbered consecutively from No. 1 to the end, both on the right-hand top corner of the pages and the left-hand top corner of the counterfoil". The complex procedure connected with the supply of water was less defensible. The Commissariat had the responsibility of providing water for the troops, unless it was done through "wells, tanks, pipes or other works", over which the Ordnance Department held sway. If the chief Commissariat officer thought a works construction more economical, he must apply through the military Officer Commanding to the Board of Respective Officers "for a professional opinion". If that opinion proved favourable, he would again consult the Officer Commanding and report to the Treasury. Meanwhile, the Board of Respective Officers submitted plans and estimates to the Master-General and the Board of Ordnance. However, no expense or decision would occur until the Treasury and the Board of Ordnance had conferred: if they decided upon a change, the Board of Respective Officers would be notified. Accustomed to such a laborious peacetime process, it is small wonder that commissaries found difficulty in adjusting to wartime crises. Lord Panmure argued of the Crimea: "The system by which an army should be provisioned . . . is non-existent". In reality, the system was too rigid, denying initiative to individual commissaries and encouraging them not to issue lime juice, fresh vegetables and even bread because regulations did not specifically allow it. So a Commissariat official objected to Lord Raglan altering the form of requisition for a new greatcoat (a document with two schedules and twenty-four blanks to be filled up in duplicate), as this would lead to abuse: regulations "did not authorise the issue of regimental overcoats more frequently than once in three years".[22] Describing how a detached company near Varna had to requisition for supplies three times in one day due to clerical errors in its returns, the Duke of Cambridge declared: "The forms of the Commissariat Departments are not suited to operations in the field". Sir George de Lacy Evans, taking a broader view, nevertheless reached a similar conclusion: "They were always employed in writing letters to the Treasury and making out accounts in triplicate". The Commissariat Department bore a remarkable resemblance to Charles Dickens' Circumlocution Office.[23]

Above all, perhaps, the Crimean War drew attention to the problems created by civilian commissaries attached to, not under the command of, military officers. Once the railway had been completed from Balaclava to Kadikoi, about one mile nearer to the front line than the Balaclava wharves, Lord Raglan could only request that Commissary-General Filder now use that village as the distribution point for supplies. Officially Filder exercised "the responsible duty of providing all necessary supplies of money, food and transport for the forces under

Lord Raglan's command . . . under the direction of the General Officer Commanding". But "direction" was ambiguous when a comprehensive set of Commissariat Regulations governed Filder's every action and subjected him to orders transmitted from the United Kingdom. A measure of Lord Raglan's frustration concerning this arrangement may be noted in a letter to Lord Panmure: "Mr Filder has been authorised by the Treasury . . . to accept tenders without my previous approval". Early in 1855 first the Duke of Newcastle, then his successor as Secretary of State for War Lord Panmure, gave Lord Raglan "full authority" to remove Filder as Commissary-General in the Crimea, but the practicability of such a manoeuvre was never put to the test. Its legality could, and almost certainly would, have been contested. In practice the system whereby the General Officer Commanding did not control every department with the army was never fully understood by observers, and the custom of dismantling the field organisation once peace arrived was the root cause of the Department's difficulties. As *The Daily News* pointed out: "The Commissariat Department is suddenly patched up to meet the exigency and, like most new instruments, is stiff, unwieldy and liable to derangement". While the policemen, recalled veterans, officials from other government departments and rag-tag of volunteers learnt their roles, the troops suffered — and in many cases died.[24]

Shortcomings in the operation of the Commissariat were not originally identified in the Crimean War: efforts had already been made to deal with many of the problems revealed there. Between 1849 and 1851 Lord Seymour's Parliamentary Select Committee examined Army and Ordnance expenditure, which involved close scrutiny of the Commissariat, and one of its principal recommendations was revision and reduction of the Department's duties. Much of the effect of these conclusions was limited by an energetic counter-attack from Sir Charles Trevelyan, Sir Randolph Routh and James Filder, who all pressed for expansion, not reduction, of Commissariat responsibility. A Treasury Committee, which reported in 1852, also called for reduction in Commissariat responsibility and its establishment, with special reference to the amalgamation of the Commissariat and Naval Victualling departments. Again Commissariat resistance was predictable and successful.[25]

The contract system, which proved so vitally unsatisfactory for Lord Raglan, had been seriously questioned previous to the outbreak of war. Before the Seymour Committee Lord William Paulet drew attention to the way that the Commissariat had been swindled by unscrupulous contractors in Ireland, and a Commissariat Minute was forced to lay down: "The bread supplied under public contract ought not to be inferior to that used in prisons, in workhouses and by heavy labouring men". Yet arguments in favour of contracts being placed and supervised by regiments were countered by Trevelyan, who strongly believed that this arrangement would fail once field operations became necessary. In this he may well have been right, but the matter deserved wider consideration.[26]

One very important issue to be raised was field training for the Commissariat in time of peace. It was not new. In 1806 General Don had called for "realistic field training" for commissaries in peacetime and "a regular establishment" at home. Forty-four years later Sir Charles Trevelyan used virtually the same words in supporting realistic training and the creation of "a small number of Commissariat officers" in the United Kingdom ready to be "despatched to any quarter where their services might be required". The Seymour Committee concluded, however: "It appears on the highest evidence that no training in time of peace will fit a commissary for his duties in the field during war" — and inertia triumphed. A politician, A. H. Layard, a soldier, Sir George de Lacy Evans, and a contemporary writer, E. B. de Fonblanque, all maintained that this omission had disastrous consequences for the troops three years later. Lord Raglan was left to reflect ruefully: "I was right when I told the Committee of the House of Commons that the duties of the Commissariat during peace did not furnish an education for service in the field".[27]

Apathy, reluctance to incur added financial liability and the stubbornness of self-protective individuals only partly explain non-introduction of change, for there were also positive and emotional reasons to encourage inaction. Defenders of the system stated that it had worked in the past, particularly for the Duke of Wellington during the Peninsular War. As Wellington (then Sir Arthur Wellesley) pointed out in his first general order, however, British troops there were operating in friendly territory (Portugal and later anti-French Spain); and moreover with command of the sea the British could move supplies with ease a comparatively short distance across the Bay of Biscay from England. These advantages would not always be enjoyed and certainly did not pertain for Lord Raglan.[28] To support the current system on historical grounds was also to ignore Wellington's own exasperation at Commissariat inefficiency, which caused him to complain that his army was "starving" and "our Commissariat is very bad indeed". Tartly he concluded: "The people who manage it (the Commissariat) are incapable of managing anything out of a country house". Time dimmed the sharpness of the Duke's memory, however, and in later years he was to resist changes in the system. By then he had become more of a politician than a general.[29]

Two additional palliatives were Commissariat achievements in Ireland and at Chobham. During the severe Irish famine of 1846–7, the Commissariat had brought much-needed relief to the hungry in an atmosphere of acclaim. Sir John Burgoyne, a former Chairman of the Public Works Board in Ireland, described the Department's efforts as "the grandest attempt ever made to grapple with famine over a whole country", and Sir Charles Trevelyan maintained later: "Its perfect correctness as a matter of executive arrangement was never questioned". The Chobham practice camp of 1853 produced yet more euphoric praise to satisfy the complacent. Few queried the validity of evidence gleaned on an English summer exercise, during which transport was hired daily, supplies delivered from London and officers returned to their families each evening. So the Duke of Newcastle could confidently announce that Commissariat arrangements made for the Crimean expedition were thorough, and in Turkey James Filder proclaimed satisfaction at the impressive array of live cattle, forage and food procured by his Department. All too soon, no doubt, they and other responsible figures regretted such rash statements.[30]

There were early indications of limitations in the system. Before the War had lasted one month Sir John Burgoyne warned that the supply advantages enjoyed by Wellington in the Peninsular War would not be felt by the Expeditionary Force and, on the eve of departure from the Bosphorus for Bulgaria, Lord Raglan complained of "supine" Turkish attempts to secure baggage animals. Yet in these initial months there was no concerted outburst against the Commissariat nor an apparent sense of urgency to bring about change, possibly because a short war seemed in prospect and transient difficulties comparatively unimportant. During the relative calm of this period, nonetheless, political decisions were taken to change the structure of the Department, for which reasons were to be found far behind the front line.[31]

In the second half of the year criticism of the Commissariat increased to fever pitch and, although arrangements for changes in administration of the Department had already been agreed, it is doubtful whether they could have been carried out in the absence of such a barrage of condemnation. From Varna Raglan was moved to complain that "the word 'difficulty' . . . (is) too much the stalking horse of the department" and to draw attention to inefficient Commissariat activity in the field. Lieutenant Temple Godman wrote of insufficient bread and tar-tasting biscuits, the Commissariat ran short of rice and Richard Airey (then a brigade commander) referred to "unripe fruit and sour milk".[32] Once in the Crimea local supplies became quickly exhausted and terrifying accounts of privation were penned to anxious relatives at home. The Duke of Newcastle reproached Lord Raglan with "numerous complaints . . . (of) men in the trenches being on half and, in some instance quarter, rations". Such evidence caused the Queen acute concern and prompted sweeping attacks on the Department in Parliament.[33]

During the course of the Crimean War, control of the Commissariat was transferred from the Treasury to the War Department. Examples of ineffectiveness at the front had no direct responsibility for this. Although not finally complete until December 1854, the transfer was decided in

May and planned to take place in June, for reasons of administrative convenience and to relieve the Treasury of an executive function strictly incompatible with its wider constitutional role. This move, which tacitly acknowledged that the complicated arrangement of checks hitherto seen as the cornerstone of the administrative edifice no longer remained necessary, was in line with a policy of centralising authority throughout national administration. But the removal of control from one civilian authority to another also suggested that, as the structure of army administration modified, more responsibility was unlikely to devolve on military officers.[34]

The timing of the ultimate transfer of control, December 1854, superficially suggests that deficiencies in the theatre of war led to it. The much-publicised criticism, however, primarily resulted in examination of the operation of the Department by four separate investigating commissions during 1855. On 19 February Sir John McNeill and Colonel Alexander Tulloch were instructed to form a Commission of Inquiry and "proceed to the Crimea in order to inquire into the whole arrangement and management of the Commissariat Department". Additional instructions three days later further directed them to look into "what may have been the sources of supply ... (and) the alleged delay in unshipping and distributing the clothing and other stores" (which, consequently, also involved investigation of the Quartermaster-General's Department). In the House of Commons Lord Palmerston explained that "they would have authority to carry into execution immediately any change or arrangement they might think essential to the public service", though he would not confirm Edward Warner's fear that they could exercise powers of "appointment and dismissal". Two reports were produced and laid before Parliament: from Constantinople on 10 June 1855 and London on 20 January 1856. Both heavily criticised Lord Raglan's personal staff in the Crimea and Commissary-General Filder.[35]

Officers condemned in these reports claimed to have been unjustly attacked and demanded the opportunity to clear their names. In this they were supported by A. H. Layard, who suggested another Commission of Inquiry to consider both the reports and the complaints arising from them. So that "justice should be done to all parties", a Board of General Officers under Lord Seaton was, in consequence, established. Perforce, this Board also examined the work of the Commissariat Department and virtually became another body of investigation.[36] In February 1855, Lord Palmerston decided to send a Sanitary Commission to examine the state of camps at Scutari and in the Crimea. Its task was "to put the hospitals, the port and the camps into a less unhealthy condition than has hitherto existed". In no way was this Commission to interfere with the work of McNeill and Tulloch, nor was it directed at the Commissariat. Inevitably, however, as it was concerned with supplies, it did come into contact with the Commissariat and its comments had some relevance to the Department.[37]

The fourth investigating body was that of the "Select Committee on the Army before Sebastopol (sic)" under the chairmanship of John Roebuck, which Lord Panmure acknowledged had resulted from press and public indignation at the Crimean disasters. Ranging over the entire planning and conduct of the War even while it continued, the Committee attacked ministers, military officers and the administrative system in general. In this, the Commissariat did not escape censure. The Committee concluded that the Expeditionary Force's sufferings were "aggravated by dilatory and insufficient arrangements for the supply of indispensible necessaries" and that "the Commissariat and land transport were all defective". It was unable to discover where "huge quantities . . . of preserved foods", despatched from the United Kingdom, had gone and found it "impossible not to suspect dishonesty". In fact, this report had little effect because it criticised the past, especially the actions of Lord Aberdeen's government which had left office six months previously.[38] The irrelevance of the findings of Roebuck's Committee in the long run may be extended to the other three commissions, which were mainly concerned with operational difficulties of the moment rather than broader issues of military supply.[39]

Of more importance was close contact with the French Army during the Crimean War, which prompted detailed studies of its administration. The position of France on the continental land-mass and its commitment to a European rather than colonial strategy, which allowed heavy reliance on magazines, determined that a British carbon copy of the French supply services would not be feasible. But examination of a supply system organised by a military corps had much to recommend it. Briefed in London and carrying out his investigation in France, Major-General William Knollys reported on the entire administration of the French Army, including the responsibility of the Minister of War, the organisation of his Ministry and that of the Staff Corps (Corps d'Etat Major). He particularly examined the operation of the Intendance Militaire with its sub-divisions of medical staff, administrative staff (supplying, for example, clothing, forage and provisions), military workmen (consisting of carpenters, labourers etc., volunteers from the regular army's ranks with one to two years service, and organised into twelve sections of between three hundred and six hundred men), hospital attendants and transport corps. The latter ('Train des Equipages Militaires') was of particular interest in view of British difficulties in the Crimea. Responsible for all land transport (including hospital ambulances), it was organised into six squadrons, each of four companies with double cadres to allow expansion to eight companies immediately war broke out. During peacetime one company in each squadron remained in France as a depot for training and recruitment, but Knollys noted that in an emergency — though not to the same extent as the British — the French did rely upon securing additional means of transport from local sources.[40]

Ten months after Knollys, Thomas Thackeray produced a two-volume study of the organisation of the French Army, in parts of which he minutely scrutinised the responsibilities of the Intendance and its method of providing supplies and transport. Thackeray pointed out that the Intendance was not in fact fully integrated with the Army, being a corps with its own separate rank structure: in 1856 its five commissioned ranks (corresponding to, but not holding, regular military titles) totalled 300 officers. Although these officers were responsible for the corps' discipline, members of the Intendance were bound to obey any written order from an army commander concerning service within their sphere of duty. Meanwhile in the theatre of war Lord Raglan had also commissioned a report on the French "Corps du Train des Equipages Militaires". This pointed out that its original Napoleonic structure had been modified by ordinances of 1841, 1842 and 1852, and the report's details differed only slightly from those produced by Knollys. Raglan's report claimed five squadrons in peacetime, each with three field companies and one depot company, expanding in war to seven field companies and one depot company, the latter to train recruits.[41]

In addition to these formal studies, a more emotional groundswell of favourable opinion became evident. At Gallipoli Sir George Brown was immediately impressed by French supply arrangements, and Sir John Burgoyne later commented on them with approval.[42] During the first bitter winter, an anonymous writer from "before Sevastopol" claimed that "the French have been all along better off than we have", Captain Henry Clifford believed the French organisation to be much better than that of the British and Sir Charles Trevelyan held that "the superior organisation of the civil departments of the French Army (came from) their constant state of preparation for war". This acclaim was not seriously affected by Somerset Calthorpe's assertion that medical provisions by the Intendance in the Crimea were less than satisfactory. Furthermore, praise for the French prompted interest in other foreign supply systems, resulting in a paper by Commissary-General Sir George Maclean on the Austrian Military Intendance.[43]

The main impact of British supply problems on the Crimean peninsula was to encourage examination of the French system, and details of privation suffered at the front in 1855 had even less direct effect on central Commissariat organisation than that of the previous year. Lord Raglan continued to press for rationalisation of Commissariat responsibilities, Sir John Burgoyne detailed examples of troops burning military equipment in the trenches to keep warm and in March 1855 every brigade detached troops to the Commissariat to prevent a total breakdown of the service.[44] But once spring brought improvement in the weather and the railway had begun to operate from Balaclava, supply problems quickly reduced and, in any case, attention now focused on military action against Sevastopol. By the second winter, the dockyard and its environs south of the harbour had fallen, so danger from enemy bombardment and attack on the Allied lines above Balaclava practically evaporated. Moreover commissaries, who had been so hastily recruited early in the War, were now experienced in their jobs. Hence the reduction in complaints against the Commissariat in the latter part of 1855 should not be taken as evidence that administrative reorganisation had thoroughly cleansed the Department of all evils. Judgement on the performance of the Commissariat in the Crimea during the two successive winters requires careful evaluation.

One positive effect of the Crimean War was removal of responsibility for provision of land transport from the Commissariat and the establishment for this purpose of a military organisation, the Land Transport Corps (afterwards renamed the Military Train). An inescapable fact during the winter of 1854–5 was that, as men went hungry in the trenches before Sevastopol, ample supplies lay near jetties at Balaclava. But there were no means to get them to the lines. Sir John Burgoyne alleged that nine-tenths of all supply difficulties in the Crimea resulted from lack of transport, and McNeill and Tulloch acknowledged that this was a serious factor. Major-General Estcourt, in defending the Staff against charges of incompetence, argued: "The defective state of the Transport Department . . . (led to) the sufferings of the troops".[45]

Inability of the Commissariat to provide sufficient land transport quickly became apparent, while the troops were still in Turkey. Somerset Calthorpe estimated that with 3,000 mules necessary for "ordinary requirements", "only seventy or eighty" were available, and the Duke of Cambridge agreed: "The difficulty of transport is very great". Once in Bulgaria the situation did not improve. Horses were stolen, carts broke down and native drivers absconded to add to existing difficulties, and the situation was considered so serious that a Board of Inquiry convened under Sir George Brown. Operations to relieve the beleaguered Turkish garrison at Silistra would require 14,000 pack-horses and mules, but by mid July only 5,000 had been collected. Fortunately a Russian retreat from the Danube prevented immobile embarrassment. On the Crimean peninsula, after the Allies had settled down to besiege Sevastopol seven miles north of Balaclava, the British land transport deficiency became acute. Henry Clifford noted sharply that the men had "to fetch their own rations on their backs" and that newly arrived transport animals were allowed to die before being put to work. Fury was added to exasperation when the Turks could make 150 mules available to the British, the French supply mule litters for their sick and sixty horses per day to carry up ammunition. Well might Lord

Raglan write tersely that land transport was his "principal want and a most serious one". The impotence of a military commander concerning the Commissariat was heavily emphasised by the fact that he could only officially draw attention to difficulties.[46]

It was scarcely surprising that, as problems escalated, impetus for militarisation of the transport system should increase. Sir John Burgoyne, Major-General Estcourt and Lord Lucan all called for a separate land transport organisation under military discipline, the latter proposing a Muleteer Corps under his direction as commander of the Cavalry Division. Early in 1855, in London, Sidney Herbert called for an overhaul of the entire transport service and the Duke of Newcastle announced: "I am organising a land transport system quite new to the English Service". Shortly afterwards, his successor drew up plans for a military Land Transport Corps.[47] The new organisation experienced considerable recruiting difficulties and not until June 1855 could it make any sort of contribution in the Crimea: indeed, the Corps was not officially raised until 24 June 1855.[48]

The Land Transport Corps, therefore, made very little impact in the Crimea and, if conditions in the second winter had been similar to those of the first, it is doubtful whether it would have provided a better service than the civilian Commissariat. As the War came to a close, it was in the throes of reorganisation under Lieutenant-Colonel E. R. Wetherall with the aim of having 8,000–10,000 men divided into the same number of battalions as there were army divisions in the field, with one transport battalion allocated to each army division. Once the War had ended the Cabinet decided not to continue with this method of reorganisation, but to remould the Land Transport Corps "on a different footing ... (and) to get free from the Crimean Corps". Another Royal Warrant was prepared for "the permanent formation of a land transport corps of our army at home and in the field ... henceforth to be denominated the Military Train". Thus a permanent military transport corps came into being, as a direct result or experiences in the Crimean War and undoubtedly influenced by studies of the French Intendance. Eventually, in 1889, supply and transport responsibilities were again united — in one military organisation, the Army Service Corps.[49]

One feature of reaction to the Commissariat Department during the War was a series of personal attacks on the two principal figures concerned with its operation in the Crimea: Commissary-General Filder and Sir Charles Trevelyan. To some extent they compounded these attacks by their own actions and words. James Beatty, the Chief Engineer responsible for building the Balaclava railway, found that "Commissary-General Filder is a very difficult man to move", Colonel McMurdo, whose Land Transport Corps relied on the Commissariat for forage, exclaimed: "I never in the whole course of my existence met so disagreeable a coxcomb and so utterly impracticable an official as this little viper" and Lord Lucan declared him most unco-operative.[50] Despite a vast amount of evidence to the contrary, moreover, Filder maintained that during the winter he had adequately supplied troops on the Heights. In January 1855 he rejected a French offer to place all "stores and magazines in the East" at his disposal: "We are not now, nor have been at any time, in want of them excepting forage". To this Lord Raglan justifiably appended: "Inquire of Mr. Filder what this means". Significantly, Sir John McNeill and Colonel Tulloch thought that Filder considered it a reflection on his own "skill or ability" if he were "supposed to require advice or assistance".[51]

In particular, John Ball and Lieutenant-Colonel John North attacked Filder for insisting upon the issue of green, unroasted coffee to the troops, who had no implements to grind it with; and even Sir Charles Trevelyan held that Filder made a serious miscalculation over the number of tranport animals required, estimating 6,000 whereas according to Commissariat practice double that number should have been planned. McNeill and Tulloch drew attention to the infamous 278 cases of lime juice which he declined to issue between 10 December 1854 and "the first week in February" 1855, and concluded that he was dilatory too in providing ovens for baking bread. These represented but the tip of a vast iceberg of accusations, which led Lord Panmure to express horror at the "great complaints of inefficiency" concerning Filder, and Sidney Herbert, in alleging the Commissary-General's "great want of energy and resource", to press for his replacement by somebody with "youth and energy". McNeill and Tulloch had already suggested incompetence: "A man of comprehensive views might probably have risen superior to ... disadvantages ... it is unreasonable to expect that every man who may rise to the head of a limited department ... is to display ... inventive resources and administrative capacity of a very high order". Less obliquely, Lord Palmerston dismissed Filder as "wholly unfit" for his post.[52]

Filder consistently protested his innocence and defended himself warmly in both a letter to the War Department in February 1856 and before the Board of General Officers inquiring into objections to the reports of McNeill and Tulloch. He maintained that he had done his best under very trying circumstances and with a minimum of resources at his disposal: he had been misjudged, because the limitations of his powers had not been recognised. Pleading that "neither the Regulations nor the general character of our service give the head of a Commissariat Establishment the unlimited range of discretion", he alleged that the Commissioners had judged him "partly out of a misconception of the extent of my power and responsibility as head of the Commissariat". Further he complained that "a number of alleged instances of improvidence, omissions, mismanagement and even wilful disregard of the best interests of the service . . . (were) given in scattered form" throughout the Reports, although no "distinct charges (were) alleged against me". Not claiming to be "altogether exempt from error . . . (because of) such a mass of difficulties as I have had to contend with", he nevertheless believed his "proceedings . . . to have been in the main correct". Filder protested that no "consideration of mere form or usage" interfered with his duty. He then dealt with specific charges of failing to issue items such as biscuits and lime juice concluding that "although some partial deficiencies of the established allowances of food did unfortunately take place", this was not due to want of effort by his Department and had no "important effect on the health of the troops". Thereupon, he proclaimed that the "injurious quality of the food was for some time incapable of being remedied". Evidently he was oblivious of the contradiction in these latter two statements. He had not been "ordered" to provide lime juice and vegetables, and "as soon as I had the necessary orders" fuel was supplied. But he admitted that "causes beyond my control" created some inadequacy of land transport. The Board of General Officers accepted these arguments and concluded: "We are of the opinion that Commissary-General Filder's conduct in the management of his department was not, and is not, justly liable to the unfavourable animadversion, either expressed or implied, which is conveyed in the Report of the Commissioners".[53]

Filder's superior, Sir Charles Trevelyan, was subjected to similar attack, in particular concerning arrangements for the despatch of supplies from the United Kingdom. Describing him as a "baneful influence", guilty of a "reckless waste of money" and "outrageous audacity" in the use of public funds, Colonel Dunne maintained that "the destruction of our army" resulted from mismanagement of the Commissariat under his direction. There was evidence of inefficient loading of ships in the United Kingdom: supplies were badly stowed and labelled, with the result that vessels frequently returned without unloading. Nor were requisitions speedily met. In January 1855 Lord Raglan noted that "some months ago" Filder had been promised one hay vessel a fortnight from England, but "he has received only one such vessel". It was not until 23 January that roasted coffee arrived. In March 1855 Raglan further complained that Filder had been led to expect a floating bakery and bakers "some months ago", but there was no indication that these had even now left England. Moreover, once the Board of General Officers had cleared Filder of the charges against him, it was bound to blame "the authorities in England" (that is, Trevelyan) for not fulfilling his requisitions.[54]

In answer to a memorandum from the Chancellor of the Exchequer inviting his comments, Sir Charles replied to the charges against him. Fundamentally, he disagreed with the Board's comments that deficiencies in land transport were caused by lack of forage. Provision was sufficient until the hurricane of 14 November, and subsequent shortfalls were "caused by bad roads, exposure, and fatigue after the hurricane, and by the helplessness and exhaustion of the native drivers and horse-lifting". He went on to assert that Filder's "real or supposed" difficulty with sea transport was the basic reason for his troubles and that Quartermaster-General Airey's evidence before the Board of General Officers, that "the Commissary-General could not venture to bring the animals (from Varna) to Balaclava because he had no forage for them", was unsupported by documentary proof. But Trevelyan's protests were revealing. He admitted that much of Filder's correspondence was ignored and that the Treasury only acted when "later letters . . . became precise, pressing and urgent". It is difficult to imagine a more "precise" letter than that of 13 September 1854 which clearly requested 2,000 tons of hay, delivery of which took nine months. Quite what made a letter "pressing and urgent" Trevelyan did not reveal, although he went on to claim that the Treasury was "entirely free from the blame implied in the report of the Board of General Officers . . . even if the want of forage had been the proximate cause of the failure of the land transport". By Trevelyan's own admissions, such a contention is difficult to support. He stood condemned by his own words.[55]

In practice neither the protestations of Trevelyan and Filder nor the favourable conclusions of the Board of General Officers could obliterate the enduring picture of incompetence. Inevitably the fact, that civilians were responsible for supply services which failed Lord Raglan, strengthened arguments in favour of military ancillary organisations for the Army. A Royal Warrant of October 1858 eventually laid down the military nature of the supply system, by ruling that commissaries should henceforth be drawn from commissioned army officers and subordinate officials be volunteers from the ranks.[56]

Apart from the Land Transport Corps, however, there is little evidence that problems on the Sevastopol Heights or the failings of Commissariat officers during the War led to the form of the Department, which developed within three years of the Peace of Paris. None of the arguments for change put forward in the War were new; and, indisputably, the major decisions concerning overall direction of the Department had been taken before any British soldier set foot on Russian soil or even serious privation had been suffered in Turkey. Certain financial readjustments also occurred without reference to the conflict. Lord Panmure made clear that the transfer of the auditing of Commissariat accounts from the Treasury to the War Department owed nothing to the War: "The revision of all accounts, and the due enforcement of all regulations for controlling that expenditure, can nowhere be so efficiently conducted as in the office where those regulations are framed, from which the sanction for all military expenditure emanates, and where the responsibility for it ultimately rests". This move formed part of a quest for administrative symmetry.

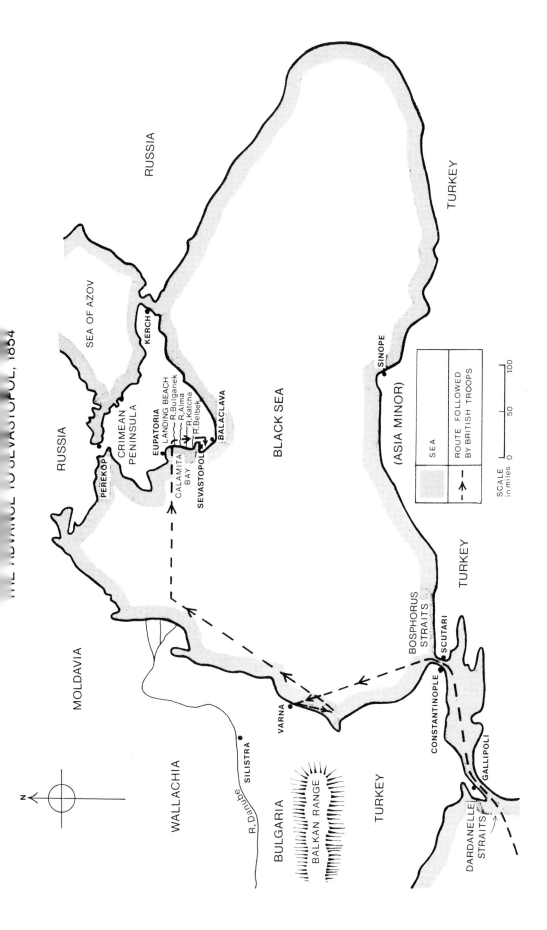

THE ADVANCE TO SEVASTOPOL, 1854

RUSSIA

RUSSIA

SEA OF AZOV

KERCH

CRIMEAN PENINSULA

PEREKOP

EUPATORIA

LANDING BEACH
R.Bulganek
R.Alma
R.Katcha
R.Belbek

CALAMITA BAY

SEVASTOPOL

BALACLAVA

BLACK SEA

MOLDAVIA

WALLACHIA

R.Danube

SILISTRA

BULGARIA

BALKAN RANGE

VARNA

TURKEY

BOSPHORUS STRAITS

SCUTARI

CONSTANTINOPLE

GALLIPOLI

DARDANELLE STRAITS

TURKEY

(ASIA MINOR)

SINOPE

TURKEY

SEA

ROUTE FOLLOWED BY BRITISH TROOPS

SCALE in miles
0   50   100

N

THE SIEGE OF SEVASTOPOL, 1854-1856

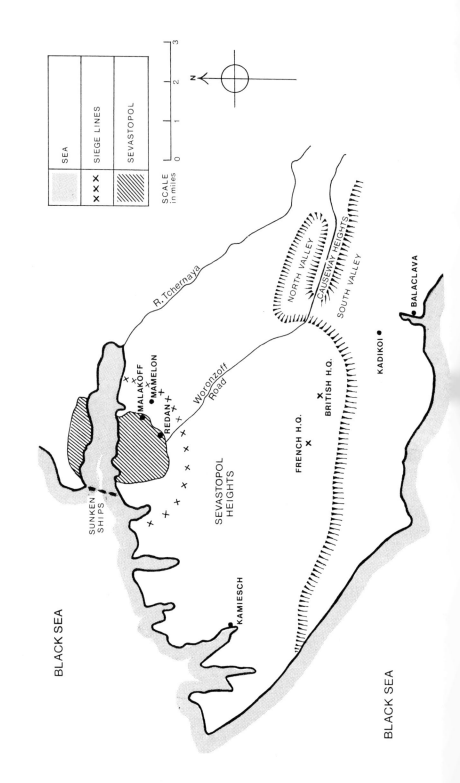

BLACK SEA

BLACK SEA

SEA

SIEGE LINES

SEVASTOPOL

× × ×

SCALE
in miles

0 1 2 3

N

R. Tchernaya

NORTH VALLEY

CAUSEWAY HEIGHTS

SOUTH VALLEY

BALACLAVA

KADIKOI ●

BRITISH H.Q. ×

FRENCH H.Q. ×

Woronzoff Road

MALAKOFF

MAMELON ●

REDAN ●

SEVASTOPOL HEIGHTS

SUNKEN SHIPS

KAMIESCH ●

Nor was the militarisation of the Commissariat a straightforward case of cause and effect. It owed something to experience in India, as well as study of other armies and lessons from the Crimea.[57]

The Ordnance

The Ordnance Department was the worst managed department in the country.
(William Williams M.P., 1855).[58]

The Ordnance Department experienced even more drastic reorganisation during the Crimean War. Like the Commissariat it had not previously escaped censure, yet in April 1854 the Duke of Newcastle expressed satisfaction with it. Fourteen months later his successor as Secretary of State for War, Lord Panmure, announced that change in the Ordnance had become inevitable. Apparently only departmental inefficiency in the opening phase of the war could have caused such a transformation in government policy. In reality, as with the Commissariat, the reasons behind reconstruction were more complex.[59]

With records going back to 1455, the Ordnance predated the War Office and the standing army by two centuries. At its head was the Master-General of the Ordnance, a title first associated with Lord Dartmouth in a royal warrant of 25 July 1683, although in 1513 Sir Sampson North had been known as "Master of the King's Ordnance". By the nineteenth century, the procedure for appointing a Master-General had been established: letters patent were issued by the Crown, but in practice the post was filled by the Prime Minister after Cabinet approval. Lord Anglesey first unsuccessfully approached the King and eventually secured the office through the Prime Minister, George Canning, in April 1827. Lord Fitzroy Somerset was offered the appointment by Lord Derby and clearly understood that he would hold in only while he retained the Government's confidence: "I cannot in the present state of the parties but view my tenure of the Ordnance as most precarious", he wrote; and the Duke of Newcastle later confirmed: "The principal appointments of the Ordnance have hitherto been removable with the Government of the day". The post itself, however, was not political: when Lord Hardinge became Master-General in February 1852, he accepted on the understanding that he would not need to support anti-Peelite policy, and Lord John Russell agreed that the Master-General was not appointed for his political views.[60]

That the Master-General normally sat in the Cabinet until 1828 does not invalidate this contention, for his main purpose there was to offer specialist military advice. Before 1793 the C-in-C was rarely in the Cabinet, after 1795 never in his official capacity: on only two occasions in the period 1782–1828 was the Master-General of the Ordnance excluded.[61] He was not included in Wellington's Cabinet in 1828 because the Prime Minister could proffer military opinions and, whether in or out of office, the Duke continued to do so until his death twenty-four years later. But permanent exclusion of the Master-General was not intended. In February 1852 Lord Derby omitted Lord Hardinge from the Cabinet for political reasons: "You have rightly interpreted my abstaining from offering you the Cabinet . . . I could not offer so important an office to a political opponent". By 1852 it was possible to appoint Hardinge without a Cabinet seat, because the practice had been interrupted for a lengthy time, and, moreover, Wellington was still alive. The latter argument did not apply when Fitzroy Somerset (Raglan) succeeded Hardinge. Although a former Member of Parliament, he did not gain Cabinet status. No Master-General has, therefore, in practice done so since the fall of Lord Goderich's brief ministry in 1828.[62]

The Master-General of the Ordnance was usually a distinguished, senior officer, who was required to act in twin capacities: strictly as a military officer and, secondly, as overlord of the civilian Ordnance Department.[63] In his military role, the Master-General commanded the Ordnance forces (commissioned and non-commissioned ranks of the Royal Artillery, officers of the Royal Engineers and other ranks of the Corps of Royal Sappers and Miners), which comprised a military body distinct from infantry and cavalry under the C-in-C's command. The Ordnance Corps had its own uniform, promotion structure, Paymaster-General, hospital and transport services. The Master-General also commanded the Royal Military Academy, Woolwich, which trained Ordnance cadets, and from 1847 the pre-Woolwich school at Carshalton House, Croydon, entry to which was via his nomination.[64] Responsible for the discipline and deployment of Ordnance forces at home and abroad, he acted in conjunction with the C-in-C in preparing the defence of the United Kingdom. Under the Master-General, the Inspector-General of Fortifications was effective head of the Royal Engineers and the Deputy Adjutant-General similarly over the Royal Artillery: commanders of Engineer and Artillery detachments at home and abroad reported regularly to these two officers.

In his military capacity the Master-General also supervised construction and maintenance of fortifications throughout the British Empire. Under certain exceptional circumstances, general officers could authorise immediate construction, but the Master-General's written authorisation must still be secured. Without express Treasury authority, the Master-General could spend up to £500 on repairs, although for normal expenditure he was subject to Parliament through the Ordnance Estimates.[65] For advice on military matters, he referred to a number of specialist committees, such as the Select Committee of Artillery Officers and the Select Committee on Small Arms instituted respectively in 1805 and 1848; and his immediate subordinate, the Lieutenant-General of the Ordnance, acted as his deputy in command of the Ordnance forces.[66]

In his second role, through the Board of Ordnance, the Master-General controlled the civilian Ordnance Department, which provided certain supplies for both the Army and Navy. The Board, dating with certainty from Elizabeth I though not formalised until Charles II's reign, originally comprised five members: Lieutenant-General of the Ordnance (its only military officer, who presided in the Master-General's absence), Surveyor-General, Clerk of the Ordnance, Prinicipal Storekeeper and Clerk of Deliveries, with the Master-General at its head. A Treasury Committee of Inquiry noted in 1853: "The Master-General had an independent and superior authority and might at any time override the decisions of the Board or make orders without them", although in practice he did not exercise this right in purely civilian matters. Regulations governing the Board's business were detailed: financial transactions, for instance, required the authorisation of three members; and to deal with its weighty volume of corre-spondence the Board had the assistance of its own Secretary and the Secretary to the Master-General.[67] Two of the Board's officers, the Clerk of the Ordnance, who prepared the Annual Estimates, and the Surveyor-General were political nominees and, as members of that body, independently responsible to Parliament for their duties. In 1831 the office of Lieutenant-General was discontinued and that of Clerk of Deliveries abolished. Five years later the Treasurer's office (not held by a Board member) was dispensed with, leaving the Clerk of the Ordnance responsible for finance, Principal Storekeeper in charge of equipment and Surveyor-General with supervisory responsibility over expenditure. Once the Board was reduced to three, the signature of only one member was normally required on official documents.[68] Then in 1850 the Surveyor-General surrendered his financial duties, so that the Clerk of the Ordnance now had charge of cash transactions and the Principal Storekeeper all store account business, forfeiting personal charge of stores at the Tower to the Local Storekeeper. As a consequence of the latter arrangement, the 1853 Treasury Committee recommended that he should henceforth be known as "Comptroller of Stores", although to avoid legal complications "Comptroller of Stores and Principal Storekeeper" might be more appropriate — a style officially adopted on 19 January 1854. Lord Panmure, in describing the Board's duties at the beginning of the War, wrote: "The Clerk of the Ordnance prepares the annual estimates for Parliament. He controls and brings to account the entire cash receipts and expenditure of the Ordnance Department. He records all appointments, civil and military; and generally in financial matters affecting the Ordnance Military Corps, he acts in the same capacity as the Secretary at War for the C-in-C ... The Principal Storekeeper is charged with the provision and custody of Ordnance carriages; small arms ammunition and stores of every description to meet the demands of the service, naval, military and civil, recording and

controlling the entire receipts and expenditure thereof." William
Monsell, the Clerk of the Ordnance, claimed that the arrangement,
whereby individual Board members supervised particular areas of
business, led to a lack of "central control", because they tended to
concentrate on these alone. When he spoke in mid 1855, however,
Monsell was attempting to justify expenditure incurred in destroying
this system.[69]

Nevertheless, the responsibilities of the Ordnance were undeniably
wide and diverse, and the 1853 Treasury Committee concluded: "The
functions of the department are of a miscellaneous character". Charged
with "issuing all kinds of warlike stores" to the Army and Navy, together
with clothing for the Ordnance Corps, reserve forces and colonial
troops, the Board also supplied greatcoats for the entire Army.[70] In
addition, bread, meat, fuel, light and forage were provided for troops in
barracks in the United Kingdom (though in camp this became the
province of the Commissariat), and various stores were furnished for
military prisons, convict establishments overseas and, in special cases,
the East India Company.[71] The Department managed a certain amount
of property, whose annual rent totalled over £53,000 in 1854, produced
large-scale and detailed geographical surveys of the United Kingdom
and, due to its reliance upon contractors, had inspectors to supervise
production of small arms in private firms. Certain factories, such as the
one producing powder at Faversham, were directly controlled by the
Ordnance, which also owned tracts of military land, like Sconce Point,
Isle of Wight. Although stores and equipment for overseas destinations
were carried by the Admiralty, the Ordnance had its own vessels for
inshore transportation of ammunition. In accordance with its responsibilities it was called upon to secure a variety of supplies for the Crimean
army: "boots and shoes, haversacks, swords and scabbards" . . . "(an)
armourer's forge and chest of tools" . . . "waterproof clothing and
waterproof articles", apart from artillery weapons, small arms,
ammunition and other military necessities.[72]

Upkeep of fortifications and barracks at home and overseas
constituted an arduous duty for the Ordnance, with which the Barrack
Department under the Deputy Inspector-General of Fortifications
dealt. Lord Anglesey claimed full responsibility for this function,
arguing strongly against interference by the Secretary of State for War
and the Colonies, and at home the C-in-C could only express concern to
the Board about the state of defences at Pembroke. Once it had regained
full control of barracks in 1822, the Ordnance guarded its charge
jealously. Ordnance personnel were active in another strictly non-
military sphere, too. Until the mid nineteenth century there were few
qualified civil engineers, so officers found themselves in demand for a
number of civilian tasks, ranging from canal building and road
construction to expert advice: increase in the Ordnance Estimates for

1846–7 was explained because the services of Engineer officers were "now called for in every quarter for civil employment as well as military". In the space of two years, for example, Sir John Burgoyne served on four separate bodies investigating the sanitary arrangements for London, and the Ordnance officially surveyed conurbations under the provisions of the Public Health Act.[73]

In fact, the Ordnance Department greatly extended its duties in the years after 1815. Control of barracks within the United Kingdom was followed by responsibility for supplying all troops within them, and by 1848 the Ordnance dealt with 233 stations in the United Kingdom alone. In April 1849 the Ordnance supervised 594 barracks throughout the world, which accommodated 111,946 officers and men, and the spread of Ordnance responsibility may be gauged from the eighty-four matters of authorised expenditure processed on a single day, 22 March 1854, involving locations as scattered as Portsmouth, Guernsey, Malta, Bermuda and Western Australia. The interim report of Lord Seymour's Committee on Army and Ordnance Expenditure, 12 July 1849, acknowledged that the Ordnance had acquired certain duties from other departments and "many entirely new charges have also arisen from the increase of our colonial possessions, and from new systems of defence, both by sea and land, of military prison discipline and military schools". It noted that since 1835 the Ordnance had been given responsibility for further stations in Australia, South Africa, Canada, New Zealand, Gambia, Hong Kong, Honduras, St. Helena, Cape Coast Castle and Nova Scotia. Inevitably, the cost of the Department rose steeply — £2,992,143 in the 1849 estimates, compared with £1,959,000 in 1828 — although the number of departmental pesonnel did not show a marked increase: 504 civilian officers and clerks in 1820 became 530 eight years later, and in some areas the number of officers actually declined.[74]

A basic difficulty with the Ordnance, however, was that its civil and military functions could never be fully separated and rapid extension of departmental responsibility exposed embarrassing weaknesses in its method of operation. This was apparent before 1854. The contract system became one point at issue. The Ordnance did not have the capacity to produce all necessary supplies, and contracts were therefore concluded with private concerns, of which small arms manufacturers represent one example. Before the Crimean War this practice had already proved unsatisfactory: in April 1853, for example, complaints about defective muskets were recorded. The quality of bread from Ordnance contractors gave rise to adverse comment, too; and William Shaw wrote to Fox Maule (later Lord Panmure), Chairman of the Parliamentary Select Committee on Army, Naval and Ordnance Stations: "In consequence of the contract system, the quality of the cloth supplied has most materially deteriorated, so that now the soldier is supplied with a coat, which fails to protect him effectively either from the cold or wet". The Clerk of the Ordnance maintained that the contractor's offer usually fell "below the merchant's price of the article", but Shaw, hinting strongly of corruption, stated that high prices were being paid for inferior goods, which were subject to "the most trifling" examination. A further complication was that, like the Commissariat, the Ordnance moved only ponderously through the by-ways of bureaucracy. "Under circumstances of peculiar and pressing emergency" a Governor or Officer Commanding a colony could in writing order the Commanding Engineer to erect a military building. But, as soon as possible, he must communicate his reasons for, and full details of, the operation to the Secretary of State for War and the Colonies, who would forward them with his comments appended to the Treasury. In turn, that august institution would communicate with the Master-General. Meanwhile, the Commanding Engineer transmitted precisely the same information through the Inspector-General of Fortifications to the Master-General. Official authorisation for the expenditure would be granted through the same channels in reverse. When 'circumstances' were neither 'peculiar' nor 'pressing', the process tended to be particularly lengthy and often, for financial reasons, unsuccessful. No clear amendment to this procedure occurred when war broke out, so if the Expeditionary Force required permanent buildings the same process had officially to be followed. Practised in the routine of peacetime, the Ordnance was not prepared for war, as the 1853 Treasury Committee hinted: "If war were to occur, the pressure upon it would be augmented in a tenfold degree".[75]

Overlap of responsibility between Ordnance and Commissariat departments was observed both by the Seymour Committee in 1851, which described "unnecessary duplication", and in the report of the 1853 Treasury Committee. Lord Grey called for amalgamation of certain departmental responsibilities in the colonies in February 1854, and Mr. A. Drew, an Ordnance storekeeper with sixteen years' "eyewitness to its bad organisation", claimed: "The Department is anything but purely Ordnance, having custody of Arms and Ammunition for the whole Service, whether Cavalry, Infantry or Artillery", together with considerable financial duties. Drew revealed that in Dominica both the Ordnance and Commissariat maintained two officers, plus labourers and clerks, in separate buildings, with each set of staff handling cash and stores. He agreed with Grey that amalgamation of responsibility should take place.[76] Inability to distinguish military and civil functions at all levels in the Ordnance added to other difficulties. Manufacturing depots, like Faversham and Enfield, and the coastal delivery vessels were normally controlled by military officers and staffed by civilians. In a sense this pinpointed the central problem of the Ordnance Department: in character it was neither completely military nor civilian. Yet while it existed apart from the War Office, and the Master-General commanded his own force independent of the C-in-C, the administration of the British Army could never be wholly satisfactory.

Identification of weakness was infinitely more simple than remedial action, in the presence of financial stringency and political apathy. Before 1854 attempts to introduce reform were unco-ordinated and inconsistent. Sir Daniel Lysons seized upon malfunction of equipment during the Canadian disorders to attack the Ordnance on a minor point of issuing ex-Peninsular rockets; Lord Howick sought to bring the Ordnance under the Secretary at War and later criticised the Corps' system of promotion by seniority as certain to produce old, inactive generals. In April 1837 Sir Rufane Shaw Donkin, Surveyor-General of the Ordnance, acknowledging that the Department's civil business might be brought under the War Office, proposed that the Artillery be transferred to the C-in-C; four years later Sir Charles Napier and Captain Pechell both pressed in Parliament for a naval officer to head the Board of Ordnance; and in 1850 Fox Maule, calling for reorganisation, stated: "Whatever the Ordnance office may have been it is now notoriously a clog upon the military Service". As the Duke of Newcastle pointed out, there were a number of suggested reforms from a variety of people, who rarely agreed on aims. An organised campaign with clear intentions did not exist, and "recommendations ... (were) in many respects entirely opposite to one another".[77]

Defenders of the Ordnance could thus pick off their critics in detail with relative ease. Sir Henry Hardinge, when Secretary at War, and Frederick Peel countered the call for a naval officer over the Board by arguing that even if, as Napier claimed, "many of the muskets went off half-cocked" a naval officer was no better qualified than "a military man" to guarantee improvement of supplies. And attacks against the contract system lost credibility in the fact of evidence by an army agent before the 1833 Select Committee on Army and Navy Appointments that it worked satisfactorily. Furthermore, the Ordnance appeared to be progressive: it instituted an improved examination for clerks, set up its own committee to examine departmental efficiency and assertions by the Clerk of the Ordnance concerning advances in organisation and production of equipment on the eve of the Crimean War brought only minor dissent. William Monsell, in fact, stressed that the Ordnance structure, with internal sub-divisions, was preferable to that of the Admiralty, which he believed to be over-consolidated.[78]

The Crimean War encouraged support for military change and brought about crystallisation of the main issues concerning the Ordnance. It provided ample evidence of the Department's inability to fulfil its supply activity under pressure. At the front Sir John Burgoyne admitted that lack of ammunition caused temporary interruption in siege operations, and Sir Thomas Hastings' contention, that many complaints by the troops about poor quality equipment were ill-founded, appeared perverse in the light of mounting evidence to the contrary. The Duke of Newcastle agreed that initially insufficient shells were available for the Expeditionary Force and that only Captain Boxer, the Additional Firemaster at Woolwich, by "his great ability, great scientific knowledge and great energy . . . saved the Ordnance Department from disgrace". And early in the conflict Colonel Dunne uttered implied criticism by querying why in a Supplementary Estimate "so small a sum was required for gunpowder? £8,250 would only provide sufficient gunpowder to fire away in one battle".[79] Specific complaints centred on supplies to the troops and ranged from flimsy entrenching tools, rusty arms and leaky boots to threadbare tents. By early 1855 criticism of the Department had become intense and George Muntz, objecting to a request for further money to develop the Enfield factory, alleged: "Last year the Board of Ordnance made good none of their promises and in every important instance they were obliged to admit they had been deceived in their calculations". Disagreement in London between the Lieutenant-General of the Ordnance and other Board members about respective civil and military duties and distribution of patronage did not improve the Department's tarnished image.[80]

Accusations of inefficiency against individuals within the Department aggravated the situation. The Clerk of the Ordnance was criticised for not being "very candid in his statements", and Colonel Dunne, rejecting Monsell's explanation of inefficiency concerning the Lancaster Shot Factory, spoke yet more pointedly: "Many of the disasters in the Crimea had been occasioned by the same improper interference, and he warned the Honourable Gentleman that if he persevered in this course, the army would have no confidence whatever in his conduct of this department". Monsell hardly helped matters by insisting, despite strong evidence to the contrary, that "after a searching inquiry . . . generally speaking" clothing already sent out to the troops was "of excellent quality". In the Commons, William Williams indirectly attacked Sir Hew Ross, by maintaining that "the Ordnance Department was the worst managed department in this country" and adding that if the head of the department had been at his desk instead of "3,000 miles off . . . many thousands of our men, as well as the honour and character of the country would have been saved". Major-General Jonathan Peel referred to Ross's "want of judgement and temper" and the fact that he was "imperfectly acquainted" with the constitution of the Department over which he presided. Moreover, when Ross was originally appointed to be Lieutenant-General of the Ordnance on Lord Raglan's departure for Turkey, Colonel Maule believed that his appointment would cause "unpleasant feeling" at the Ordnance Board, preferring Lord Seaton to act in Raglan's place. Lord Aberdeen overrode this objection, though the suspicion remained that from the beginning Sir Hew might not have been a good choice. Condemning "the mismanagement and misconduct of the officers of the Ordnance", Charles Newdegate went on to attack George Lovell, the Ordnance Inspector of Small Arms, for awarding a prize to a musket design, which had been officially rejected by his own department.[81]

Quite apart from the alleged or real incompetence of individuals, in the heat of battle the Ordnance could not function adequately, and its arrangements for weapon production were especially ridiculed. Early in 1855 George Muntz revealed that only 50,000 out of 90,000 rifles contracted for during 1854 had been delivered and, in the meantime, the price of bayonets had risen from 5/6 to 7/6. He then described how a Birmingham manufacturer had received a letter from the Board of Ordnance demanding an explanation for non-delivery of goods, which had been lying in Ordnance stores for a month. Independently, Sir Joseph Paxton explained that the Ordnance could not erect military huts at Aldershot in the promised six months, as neither the necessary materials nor transport were available. Whereupon Lord Seymour bitingly concluded: "If he were desirous of giving an instance of the mismanagement of a public department, he could not adduce a more striking case than that of the Board of Ordnance", and Charles Newdegate complained that delay and muddle caused by the Ordnance Department had cut the production of Birmingham small arms manufacturers by half. Calling for "every exertion possible" to aid the troops in the Crimea, in reply Lord Palmerston pleaded that the House should "rise superior to these miserable quibbles", though he revealed that failure to secure the required number of rifled muskets from British sources had forced the Ordnance to deal extensively with Belgian and American companies. Privately, he reinforced the impression of departmental incompetence by upbraiding Sir Hew Ross, because the Board of Ordnance had provided the wrong pattern and so slowed down production in the United States.[82]

There were examples, too, of the complicated Ordnance system causing serious difficulty during the War. Sir Thomas Hastings, Comptroller of Stores and Principal Storekeeper, prompted by the Secretary at War in June 1854 placed a large order for winter clothing, which the Clerk of the Ordnance subsequently cancelled because neither he nor the medical authorities had been consulted. For five weeks this procedural wrangle between two Board of Ordnance officers remained unresolved. In August, the Admiralty at length learned that the consignment was ready for shipment, and the Ordnance considered its duties over. The clothing was despatched in October on *The Prince*, which foundered in the Black Sea during the following month with the loss of its entire cargo. On another occasion, Lord Grey drew attention to the case of Price's Patent Candle Company, which proposed lighter "candle stoves" for the troops' use. The idea was put forward by the company "before Christmas", but by 22 January 1855, after being referred to three officers in the Department, Messrs. Price had gained no satisfaction, merely being informed that the matter was "under consideration". While the wheels of bureaucracy ground relentlessly and slowly, the troops suffered and died.[83] So Lord Raglan could request huts for the Crimean hospitals on 5 December 1854, and a month later the Duke of Newcastle could inform him that the Board had been authorised to "enter into contracts" and that "no time will be lost" in sending out articles, which had not even been completed. And in April 1855, but then only after a further urgent plea, the Board "approved" requisitions for stores sent from the Crimea five months previously.[84]

In practice, such evidence of inadequacies in the system had very little impact on Cabinet deliberations leading to fundamental reorganisation of the Ordnance: wider issues of administrative control and convenience provided the root cause for change. Although details of the reform were not formally given until May 1855, considerable discussion took place during the preceding fifteen months and they may well have been agreed in principle before some regiments even set sail from England. Two episodes concerning Ordnance appointments early in the War suggested that something was afoot. For almost six months the vacant posts of Secretary to the Master-General and Surveyor-General of the Ordnance intermittently occupied the Government's attention. On 19 March 1854, Lord George Paget was considered for the latter position and, although Lord Aberdeen later wrote that "probably" he would not continue the office (as the Clerk of the Ordnance and Principal Storekeeper could cope adequately), the problem remained obstinately unsettled. In mid July Lord John Russell noted that no decision had been reached, but soon agreed that the appointment of Secretary to Master-General should be abolished and, although retained, that of Surveyor-General would no longer be held by a Member of Parliament. Effectively, the Board of Ordnance had been weakened.[85]

The second indication of possible change occurred over revival of the office of Lieutenant-General of the Ordnance, necessary because the Master-General (Lord Raglan) had been given command of the Expeditionary Force. Considerable, and at times acrimonious, debate took place about the selection of Sir Hew Ross for the post in preference to Sir John Burgoyne, senior to Ross and currently Inspector-General of Fortifications. Colonel Maule, the retiring Surveyor-General, expressed reservations within the Ordnance and Sir John himself made known his displeasure. On being assured by the Duke of Newcastle that "the only motive is to secure to the State the advantage of your valuable assistance with the Army in the East", which would be impossible if he were tied to the Board of Ordnance in the United Kingdom, Sir John withdrew his opposition and Ross was at length appointed on 29 April 1854. Perhaps the most significant aspect of these exchanges is to be found in the Government's defence put forward by the Chancellor of the Exchequer, W. E. Gladstone. He reasoned that, if Sir John had been appointed, he might have received "a very left-handed compliment" by being placed in a position "from which he might in consequence of other changes have been soon removed". This was the clearest portent so far that plans for reconstruction of the Ordnance might be close to fruition.[86]

Distinct from these issues, there were other signs throughout 1854 that change was on the way. Three days before Lord Raglan received his formal appointment as commander of the Expeditionary Force and while discussions about the vacant Ordnance post and the appointment of Ross were under way, Lord Hardinge, C-in-C at the Horse Guards, agreed with Lord Grey that "alteration and improvement" were required in the Ordnance, but warned of a need for "the utmost care and attention". At the end of May Lord John Russell observed more specifically that "it may probably be found that the office of C-in-C and Master-General of the Ordnance ought to be united"; and within a month, perhaps knowing that more sweeping measures were under consideration, the Ordnance itself proposed a partial take-over by the War Department. The Clerk of the Ordnance wrote to the Duke of Newcastle: "It is probably better for us voluntarily to put ourselves under you than to be ordered by you to do so", then listed relatively minor adjustments in procedure to give the Secretary of State some oversight of Ordnance stores and equipment. He followed this with a plan for retention of the Secretary to the Master-General, restyled "Military Secretary to the Board of Ordnance", with all Ordnance papers routed through his office. No doubt fully aware that division of responsibility within the Department was a principal criticism, William Monsell claimed that this scheme "would be a great step towards that unity in the civil departments of the Ordnance without which I do not think that it can ever be prompt and efficient". Neither suggestion found favour and, in reality, Monsell may have been probing to discover the exact nature of rumoured alterations.[87]

Hints at change continued. Another Cabinet Minister, Sidney Herbert, in describing the separate Ordnance Corps as "a great evil", urged that all regular troops should come under the C-in-C, and Colonel Dunne promptly seized on his words to claim that they foreshadowed separation of civil and military functions of the Ordnance. A month later, Gladstone proposed a major Ordnance reorganisation, to make it responsible to the Treasury for finance and "to the War Minister in respect to the military part of its duties". Before the close of the year Karl Marx reflected a growing body of opinion by describing the post of Master-General as "a lamentable relic of the times when science was considered unsoldierlike": apparently at least some of the Cabinet subscribed to this view. Possibly failure to reorganise the

Ordnance during 1854 resulted from the six-month delay in transferring the Commissariat from the Treasury to the War Department, and the difficulty of effecting a second administrative upheaval at this stage of the War.[88]

Once the Duke of Newcastle had finally attained control of the Commissariat, discussion about the Ordnance gained momentum. This may be explained by accusations of inefficiency levelled against Lord Aberdeen's government and its eleventh-hour efforts to retain power. Early in January 1855, the Duke of Newcastle informed Sir Hew Ross of a government decision to rename the Select Committee of Artillery Officers as "The Ordnance Select Committee", and to introduce into it civilian members "so as to give the Government the advantage of obtaining other than strictly military opinion upon questions of a mixed scientific and practical character". Despite objections from Ross and the Director-General of Artillery, Newcastle insisted on this increased civilian involvement in Ordnance affairs and consequent extension of War Department control over it. Meanwhile William Monsell, writing to Newcastle, had referred to "when you begin to consider the reorganisation of the Ordnance", and a scheme put forward by Lord John Russell envisaged immediate abolition of the Board of Ordnance. On the very day that demise of the Coalition was arranged, Lord Grey once more pressed for amalgamation of the Ordnance and other military departments under the Secretary of State for War.[89]

Once Palmerston had taken office as Prime Minister, impetus for Ordnance reform gained rapid pace. Five days after kissing hands he informed the Queen that the Cabinet had decided to end the Ordnance "as a separate and independent establishment". It intended to transfer "to the commander of the forces (the C-in-C) the discipline and patronage of the Artillery and Engineers, placing at the head of those corps an adjutant-general of Artillery, to be in the same relation as the adjutant-general of the army to the commander of the forces; and placing the civil departments of the Ordnance under the direction and control of the Secretary of State for the War Department": Lord Panmure had been instructed to undertake preparations to this effect. Writing from the Crimea at this time, Sir John Burgoyne showed no knowledge of these plans, about which W. E. Gladstone enthused: "Lord Palmerston told me last week, that he hopes to break up the Ordnance Department — a measure towards which my desires have long pointed". During the next two days Panmure spoke of bringing all civil administration of the Army under one minister, with discipline under the C-in-C, and he drew up a confidential memorandum for the Cabinet with full details and an explanatory diagram for the complete reorganisation of the Department, "placing the purely military branch of the Ordnance forces under the C-in-C, and the civil branches under the Minister of War". Almost certainly unaware of this detailed plan, nevertheless Sir Hew Ross drew Lord Raglan's attention to Panmure's Parliamentary statement, which suggested to him that the Government "holds in contemplation the long-threatened changes in the Ordnance Service". Early in March the Prime Minister publicly revealed that "the Government was going to reorganise the Ordnance Department to improve its organisation", and the Clerk of the Ordnance said that "within a few days" he would "explain certain alterations about to be made in the Ordnance Department".[90]

However, as yet no precise details had evidently been circulated to the Cabinet, although Palmerston's statement to the Commons in March suggests that general discussion had taken place among its members. In April, the Solicitor to the Treasury concluded that draft Letters Patent to revoke the appointments of the members of the Board of Ordnance and others "vesting the administration and government of the Army and Ordnance in the Secretary of State for the War Department" were legal, and that it would be in order to use the Great Seal with them. In the first week of May, Sir Charles Trevelyan declared: "The office of Master-General should be abolished", and Panmure produced four Cabinet confidential memoranda. Two of these, on 1 and 4 May, described the history and duties of the Board of Ordnance; that of 2 May criticised its "slow, jarring and cumbrous machine", which led to delay "when a day is of the greatest importance" and by whose patronage "many inefficient old men are kept in offices for which they are altogether unfit". Panmure wanted abolition of the Board of Ordnance, the civil duties of the Ordnance to come "under a civil head" and the C-in-C to assume the military duties of the Master-General of the Ordnance, whose post would be abolished. A day later he circulated the detailed plans, which had been drawn up in February, and on 7 May Panmure wrote to Raglan telling him that he was about to propose "the consolidation of the Civil Departments of the Army". In this, the first official indication to the Master-General that changes were imminent, without further explanation he advised that the Board of Ordnance would find them "unpalatable". Four days afterwards Lord Palmerston announced that his government proposed "to remodel the Ordnance, to abolish the office of Master-General of the Ordnance, and to abolish also the Board of Ordnance as a separate establishment", with the troops coming under the C-in-C and the civil business under the Secretary for War. The rationale for these changes was to be discovered not in operational shortcomings, but the many arguments propounded before the War.[91]

One week after Palmerston's announcement, Panmure addressed the House of Lords on the proposed reorganisation, although, because the appointments of the Master-General and other Board members were revocable by the Crown, Parlimentary sanction was required only for the transfer of Ordnance lands to the Secretary of State for War. The

Government planned "to abolish the Master-General and the Board of Ordnance altogether": Ordnance troops would henceforth come under the C-in-C and the Secretary of State for War gain "supreme direction of, and be responsible for, the administration of all the business of the department" previously carried out by civil members of the Board of Ordnance. "A Chief Officer" would be appointed to put into effect the Secretary of State's "views and instructions", supervise the whole civil administration of the Army and, as a Member of Parliament, be directly responsible to the House of Commons. The duties of existing Ordnance officers would be amended and new posts created as necessary. The *Inspector-General of Fortifications* was to be responsible to the C-in-C for the "planning of fortifications and drawing up schemes of defence", but for "building ... erection ... purchase of land and the like" he would answer to the Treasury. Sir John Burgoyne saw "no difficulty" in this arrangement. The *Director-General of Artillery* would advise the Secretary of State "in all matters connected with the 'matériel' of the artillery department", arm the Inspector-General of Fortifications' defence works, be conversant with the nature and state of all artillery throughout "Her Majesty's domain" and sit 'ex officio' as president of the "Scientific Committee". The *Naval Director of Artillery*, a naval officer connected with the Ordnance and responsible for all naval artillery, would "in future . . . (be placed) in connection with the Director-General of Artillery".

Three new posts were intended. Recalling that when once sitting on a Parliamentary Select Committee he found military storekeepers ignorant "of taking stock upon approved commercial principles" and that it was "almost impossible" to discover what military stores were in the country, Panmure said that an "entirely ... civil office", *Superintendent of Stores*, would be established. "This is a department of no small importance", he continued, which would answer to the Secretary of State "for the entire conduct of the store-keeping ... of the Ordnance" and must be run on strictly commercial lines. To avoid future criticism of the contract system, Panmure determined to find a good "commercial gentleman" to act as *Superintendent of Contracts*, responsible for the making and fulfilment of "all contracts". Thirdly, to replace the Board of General Officers, he planned a *Superintendent of Clothing*. Under the Secretary of State, this officer would supervise patterns, examine all clothing designed for the Army and ensure its correct transportation and issue. All these officers would soon be brought "under the same roof as the Secretary of State".

In addition, it was proposed that the Ordnance "departments of manufacture" (such as Woolwich and Enfield) should come under the Secretary for War. Towards this end, two new officers would be appointed: a *Superintendent of Ordnance* at Woolwich responsible for the manufacture and issue of ordnance, and a *Superintendent of Gunpowder*

Works to supervise the quality and purity of all governmental and contracted powder. The duties of three existing officers were also to be more clearly defined and widened. The *Superintendent of the Carriage Department* would be responsible for the construction of all naval and army gun carriages, waggons for ammunition, land transport and ambulance work, and all military machines; the *Superintendent of the Laboratory* would supervise all ammunition and "combustible material" for the Army and Navy; and the *Superintendent of Small Arms* oversee all Ordnance-manufactured and contracted small arms. These latter five officers would be serving artillery officers detached for five years from their regiments, to put them beyond the discipline of commanding officers without prejudice to their promotion prospects.

Panmure insisted that these changes would produce a far more economical system, but the emphasis of his final justification is particularly interesting. He was at pains to point out that the war effort would not suffer adversely: necessary adjustments had indeed been made because the time was convenient, not because the military situation demanded them. Lord Ellenborough, followed by Lords Grey, Monteagle and Hardwicke, rose to complain that "too great a mass of business detail" would overwhelm the Secretary of State. But, in fact, no serious Parliamentary challenge developed. The offices of the Master-General of the Ordnance and the entire Board of Ordnance had been destroyed with ease for, although the title of Clerk of the Ordnance remained, that official became the Secretary of State's "chief officer".[92]

The changes outlined by Panmure were very swiftly carried out. Five days after his Parliamentary statement, the Secretary of State for War warned Sir Hew Ross that the Government intended immediate action, and on 28 May he and Sir Thomas Hastings were officially informed that their appointments would be terminated. Already, however, the War Department had assumed control of Ordnance patronage, *The United Service Gazette* had published details of the forthcoming Order in Council and Panmure had justified himself to Raglan on the grounds that henceforth speedier action would be guaranteed.[93] On 24 May Ordnance clerks began transferring to the War Department and, a week later, Panmure re-emphasised that an annual saving of £2,584 would be achieved by the reorganisation. The final version of Order in Council, revoking the Letters Patent, was drawn up on 1 June and the next day Panmure took charge of the civil business of the Ordnance, although the Order was not formally signed until 6 June.[94] Two months later the Clerk of the Ordnance claimed that the new arrangement was working well, now that areas of responsibility were clearly understood: "Every department which had military duties to perform was under a military man, and every civil department under a civilian". Legal formalities, giving the Secretary of State for War authority over Ordnance lands, were completed with royal assent to the requisite bill on 14 August 1855.[95]

The United Service Gazette praised "the admirable measure of reform . . . in doing away with the Ordnance as a Separate Department . . . as it was well known that the late Board of Ordnance was extravagant in its outlay of public money and was not altogether free in doing so from the influence of nepotism and partiality". Such forthright criticism went virtually unchallenged, and the lukewarm reaction of the Department's supporters in Parliament on 18 May proved unextraordinary. Not surprisingly Lord Raglan showed himself strongly opposed to the measure in writing to Panmure: "I believe that the change will be the reverse of beneficial to the public". Like Ellenborough, he argued that the Secretary of State could not properly discharge his responsibility in both the War and Ordnance departments, so that "confusion and dissatisfaction may be expected to arise". Moreover, transfer of the Ordnance Corps to the C-in-C was "an imperfect measure", placing officers in "the disagreeable position of having two masters", the Minister of War and the C-in-C. The Secretary of State made little effort to answer Raglan's points. He claimed that "every man's tongue was against the department" and concluded: "The change at the Ordnance is effective and I am sorry to hear that you anticipate so much confusion from it". At a distance of 3,000 miles and with more pressing matters to occupy him, the Master-General could hardly mount a telling counter-offensive, particularly as information about possible change reached him only spasmodically and usually through military, not political, channels. He was reduced to complaining to his son that "the overthrow of the Ordnance . . . is a sad blow" and reiterating his belief that the Secretary of State would not efficiently handle the increased business.[96]

From Sir Hew Ross, head of the Ordnance in Raglan's absence, spirited defence might have been expected. But he exerted very little influence outside his own office, and the circumstances of his appointment as Lieutenant-General of the Ordnance suggest that he received the position because no embarrassment would be felt if he subsequently lost it through reorganisation. Predictably, therefore, when he uttered a forceful opinion it was to Lord Raglan: "I am astounded . . . that any gentleman new to a great office should consider himself equal to discharging the duties of Master-General, Minister of War, Minister for War and Commanding in Chief (sic) . . . Great confusion must issue . . . There never was such folly". With certainty, three months before Panmure's Parliamentary statement, he knew something of the proposed changes, but evidently he eschewed an aggressive, rearguard action. If the politicians chose him for his pliable qualities, they could not have been disappointed. More distinguished and potentially more influential than Ross was the C-in-C, Lord Hardinge. Sir John Fortescue has credited him with an energetic defence of the Ordnance, but apart from praise in Parliament for its performance and similar observations to Lord Raglan, his alleged efforts on behalf of the Ordnance have gone unrecorded. Possibly his campaigns were conducted in private and, once defeated in political argument, he considered it his duty publicly to support the Government: a statement to Richard Airey, "decisions of Her Majesty's Government must not be obstructed by the C-in-C", gives weight to this viewpoint. However Fortescue's claim is unsubstantiated by independent evidence, so the fact of Hardinge's efforts must remain unproven. Like Ross, after the event, he addressed a fretful obituary to the Crimea: "I feel confident that the present concession by the abolition of the Master-General — and the substitution of civil for military authority — will not work well". Perhaps his feelings were tempered by the prospect of enhanced personal prestige through acquisition of the Ordnance Corps for his Horse Guards' demesne.[97]

Other senior Ordnance officers did speak out. The Principal Storekeeper, Sir Thomas Hastings, argued that a system "which places the great manufacturing military departments in the hands of a civilian ignorant of military and naval requirements cannot work well". But Hastings' judgement had to some extent been discredited, when he claimed that Birmingham small arms manufacturers could only produce 25,000 muskets in 1854, whereas they achieved twice that number. And he, too, tended to direct his comments to Raglan. William Monsell, as the Department's spokesman in the Commons, made several attempts to defend it against particular charges of inefficiency, without advancing a cogent case in opposition to the proposed reorganisation. His first impulse on learning about it was to resign. Once he had been dissuaded from this course, he no doubt drew comfort from the fact that he would become the Secretary of State's "chief officer". Absence of comment from the Inspector-General of Fortifications, Sir John Burgoyne, may be explained by his position as a serving officer: he would have considered interference unwarranted and unprofessional. With neither influential politician nor high-ranking officer prepared to back it resolutely, the Ordnance Department expired with scarcely a whimper.[98]

Nonetheless, a lengthy history could not be destroyed by the stroke of a pen. As a nod towards tradition, the designation "Clerk of the Ordnance" remained for a short while, though it proved less easy to manage subordinate staff steeped in Ordnance service. The Secretary for War inherited 153 clerks in the eight departments of the Ordnance Office in Pall Mall, in addition to 119 he already controlled, and attempts by the Deputy Secretary at War (Sir Benjamin Hawes) to prune this unwieldy mass met with only limited success.[99] Some evidence exists, too, that the reorganisation did not immediately silence complaints against the Department at functional level. At the end of

1855 many old flintlocks remained in Ordnance stores, several regiments in the Crimea still used the 1851 pattern Minié and new fortifications at Harwich were armed with mere twenty-four pounders. Early in the following year, a lack of muskets existed in Canada, and in July 1856 Lord Hardinge admitted that difficulties of procedure and responsibility concerning the construction of military works remained unresolved. Initial troubles in such a broad measure of reorganisation were inevitable and, in view of the military circumstances of the moment, surprisingly few.[100]

Lord Panmure's changes were indeed bold and far-reaching, but their origin owed little to events in the east. The anomalous position of the Ordnance had long been evident; and, as with other contemporary administrative reorganisations, the main contribution of the War was creation of an atmosphere in which such readjustments were acceptable. In this instance, absence of the departmental head from London represented a special bonus for reformers. Undoubtedly, reconstruction of the Ordnance was mooted by the Government in spring 1854, for which problems in the field could not have been responsible. How far these plans progressed at the time is uncertain. In July 1854 Sir Hew Ross rather vaguely condemned "the ruinous principle of amalgamation" to Raglan, which might have referred to transfer of the Commissariat to the new Secretary for War or indicate that he knew of projected Ordnance changes. If the latter were true, it would not be inconsistent with the impression gained from other sources at this time. Furthermore, when introducing his plans to Parliament, Panmure claimed that they were the product of consideration over a lengthy period.[101]

This may not have been pure rhetoric. Several of Aberdeen's ministers continued to serve under Palmerston and, perhaps, Panmure owed more to their experience of deliberations in the Coalition Cabinet, of which he was not a member, than he cared to admit. Whether difficulties connected with transfer of the Commissariat from Treasury to War Department did prevent Ordnance reorganisation under Aberdeen, and whether activity towards it in January 1855 was an indication of what might have been achieved then rather than the death throes of an Administration, must be a matter of conjecture. For, fashioned in a bygone age, the independent Ordnance was an anachronism. On 31 December 1856 the last entry was recorded in the Minutes of the Board of Ordnance. It concerned the maintenance of privies in Ireland.

V

Military Command
The Commander-in-Chief

The Commander-in-Chief [is] the natural and recognised protector of the soldier under all circumstances . . . the situation [is] not a political one.
(General Lord Hill, 1831).[1]

Utterly separate and distinct from the Master-General of the Ordnance, another military officer, the Commander-in-Chief (C-in-C), was involved in the administration of the Army: from 1795 his Headquarters became established at the Horse Guards, Whitehall. Prior to that date, the post of C-in-C had been intermittently filled, which led to uncertainty about the exact parameters of its responsibility, especially in connection with civilian government ministers. So in the nineteenth century, the C-in-C's office enshrined a certain enigmatic quality.[2]

The Earl of Arundel first held the office in Charles I's reign, but thereafter an appointment was usually made only in time of crisis. The fact that its title varied suggested lack of permanence: Captain-General, General on the Staff and General Commanding-in-Chief were at times used in place of C-in-C. The earliest surviving letter-book of the C-in-C was dated 1765, which might indicate an intention to retain the office permanently, but in 1789 the decision was taken not to appoint a C-in-C in peacetime. Not until four years later, therefore, on the outbreak of war with France, did Lord Amherst become C-in-C: in practice, the office was then occupied continuously both in war and peace. The extraordinary length of the French wars may have affected this development; and during their twenty-two years the C-in-C grew to be an accepted feature of military administration.

In a haphazard fashion, he acquired political acceptance, a personal staff and additional responsibility. In 1812 the C-in-C was formally recognised by Parliament, when he received his pay through the Annual Estimates not the Extraordinaries. Lord Amherst immediately secured transfer of the Adjutant-General, Quartermaster-General and their departments to him from the Secretary at War; two years later his successor, the Duke of York, won the right to appoint both these officers and, shortly afterwards, completed his personal staff by making a serving officer Military Secretary. Control over all regular forces in the United Kingdom was given to the Duke of York and he assumed, too, most of the duties of the Board of General Officers. In 1799 questions concerning discipline and military regulations were routed through the Adjutant-General's office, though not until six years later did all army discipline, except that of the Ordnance Corps, effectively come under the C-in-C. These developments, and the disappearance of a separate Irish establishment with the Act of Union, did much to clarify the C-in-C's responsibility, although unresolved disputes over their areas of current authority resulted in acrimonious exchanges between the War Office and Horse Guards well into the nineteenth century.[3]

The C-in-C received his appointment by letters patent to the command "during our Pleasure of all and singular our Land Forces employed or to be employed in Our Service within Our United Kingdom of Great Britain and Ireland". But his responsibility went beyond this. He supervised "the general distribution of Her Majesty's troops throughout the Empire ... all questions regarding the supply to troops of government stores, camp equipage etc ... all reports upon vessels intended for the conveyance of troops". To assist him in these duties, the C-in-C had his personal staff and an establishment of civilian clerks, which in 1809 totalled thirty-two, eleven years later twenty-one and by 1854 had fallen to fourteen. This reduction came partly through political attacks on military expenditure: in 1843 Sharman Crawford objected to annual expenditure of £17,000 on the Horse Guards' staff — a figure, which remained fairly constant for the next four years.[4]

Within the general scope of his duties, in the United Kingdom the C-in-C commanded regular infantry and cavalry and, when embodied, reserve forces. His authority in this respect was fully acknowledged by the War Office, hence he organised the disposition of troops within Great Britain and Ireland, arranged the inspection of reserves and Chelsea pensioners and controlled permanent staff of the Militia. The C-in-C co-ordinated national defences against invasion: so the Queen asked him for a summary of British defensive capability in 1852 and *The United Service Gazette* strongly favoured Lord Hardinge's appointment to the post, because of his known interest in coastal fortifications. But the C-in-C had neither executive control over Ordnance troops nor over the functions of the Ordnance Department; and the Duke of Wellington once rebuked a commander of forces in the Leeward Islands for impinging upon Ordnance authority.[5]

The C-in-C's responsibility for army discipline meant that he controlled training establishments within the United Kingdom, so Lord Hardinge negotiated a permanent training site at Aldershot and insisted on regular musket practice at Hythe.[6] The Judge Advocate General acted as the C-in-C's adviser in matters pertaining to Military Law, and would have been consulted, for instance, about the C-in-C's reaction to damage to property by troops in Brighton in 1844 and his restrictions on military duelling. More routine matters demanded constant vigilance. The state of Devonport garrison claimed the C-in-C's attention, charges to troops for "schooling" and "the alteration of their clothing" were limited; Wellington simply referred to standing orders in rejecting Lord Cardigan's claim, as Commanding Oficer, to have all regimental business referred to him while on leave and Lord Hardinge formally disciplined Sir George Brown for remarks attributed to him in *The Morning Advertiser*. There was, too, considerable Horse Guards' correspondence on the subject of military uniforms, and the C-in-C showed marked interest in the performance of military weapons.[7] Under the umbrella of discipline came promotion. The C-in-C needed to approve all purchase transactions, granted commissions without purchase himself and laid down the requirement of examinations for an officer's first commission and promotion. In the eighteenth century field commanders could promote independent of other authorities, but Wellington found himself unable to do so, and Lord Raglan might only recommend officers for promotion to Lord Hardinge.

Two particular duties connected with expeditions and overseas stations fell within the C-in-C's province. He nominated troops and reinforcements to go abroad — the Duke of York did this for Portugal in 1826 and the C-in-C normally arranged colonial reliefs — and had the power to allocate officers to senior and staff appointments without reference to the commander in the field. The Duke of Wellington discharged numerous broadsides about unwanted officers foisted on him by the Horse Guards, and a potentially embarrassing situation occurred in the Crimean War. Hardinge appointed Major-General Schoedde to be Military Commandant in the Bosphorus, unaware that Raglan had already assigned Lord William Paulet to that post. Reserving his right to do so, the C-in-C did not overrule the field commander in this instance; and James Estcourt appreciated that, if he wished to secure a senior staff appointment with the Crimean expedition, he must cultivate the Horse Guards.[8]

Apart from the East India Company and Ordnance forces, the C-in-C was therefore responsible for the professional state of readiness of the Army, though there were limitations on him within these bounds. The C-in-C's connection with expeditionary forces was very restricted. Once operational, their officers answered to the Secretary of State for War and the Colonies, not him: in the Crimea, Sir John Burgoyne emphasised that this constituted a practical, not theoretical, procedure. Lord Panmure, for instance, informed the commander in the Crimea, by then Sir William Codrington, that the posts of Quartermaster-General and Adjutant-General in his army were not to be merged, and Lord Hardinge could only privately suggest to Raglan "a portable Railway for yr (sic) heavy siege guns — In heavy sands, or broken ground, the assistance may be great, as proved in Agriculture". In practice, too, how far the C-in-C actually selected senior officers for an expedition independent of its commander, depended very much on the personalities of the officers involved: certainly many of those seeking preferment actively lobbied Lord Raglan, not Hardinge. The C-in-C's executive power was in other respects limited: for example, he could express concern about excessive discharges granted to troops in India, but acknowledged that only the presidential governor might in practice deal with the situation.[9]

The burden of the C-in-C's responsibilities, despite these areas of undoubted limitation, was such that one person could not possibly deal with it effectively. Thus, in reality, the bulk of routine business devolved upon three personal assistants and their staff. Each of these assistants was a military officer, appointed and liable to dismissal by the C-in-C, the most influential being the Military Secretary. In the past, this post had been occupied by a civilian clerk, but the Duke of York appointed a field officer, whose annual salary rose from £182 in 1795 to £2,500 in 1807, when it became equivalent to that of the Deputy Secretary at War. The position was in no sense political and, when Sir Herbert Taylor entered Parliament in 1820 while Military Secretary, the Prime Minister instructed him not to interfere in military matters in the House of Commons, where the Secretary at War represented the Army. All confidential correspondence to and from the C-in-C and all communications with other government departments (including the East India Company) passed through the Military Secretary. Henry Torrens thought that no subordinate Crown office involved so much "labour, importance, variety of matter and incessant confinement", and to his former Military Secretary, Richard Airey who had been appointed to command a brigade, Hardinge wrote: "You will find the labours of the Brigade not very onerous after those you so ably fulfilled here". The volume of written work involved in the post was immense, and his long sojourn in this capacity at the Horse Guards prompted Raglan to view senior posts of responsibility as a handwriting exercise. Nevertheless, the office holder wielded considerable influence, which acquired a certain aura of omnipotence because it defied explicit definition. There was more than a suspicion that, as Wellington's natural powers declined in the final decade of his life, Lord Fitzroy Somerset exercised increasing control in the distribution of patronage. How much direction over the Army was exerted by the Military Secretary during this period, however, must remain a matter of conjecture. If short of complete, it was nonetheless considerable.[10]

The second personal assistant was the Adjutant-General. The protracted threat of resignation by Sir George Brown from this office in 1853, because he could not work with the Duke of Wellington's successor, underlined close association of the post with the C-in-C.[11] The

Adjutant-General's particular area involved military discipline. In this capacity, having taken legal opinion, he advised the C-in-C on courts martial, arranged for the passage of troops going overseas, dealt with problems of inter-regimental transfers and was concerned with the establishment of regimental schools. The Adjutant-General, taking note where necessary of the Board of General Officers, supervised the selection and inspection of all military clothing except that issued by the Ordnance and the provision of arms for all regiments: in the Crimea, Major-General Escourt corresponded with the Adjutant-General in London about arms and ammunition, and Lord Hardinge stated that the issue of Miniés to Sir George Cathcart's division was "an Adjutant-General affair".[12] His responsibilities in these matters also extended to reserve forces (Militia, Yeomanry and Enrolled Pensioners), and all military commandants in the United Kingdom and abroad submitted regular reports to the Adjutant-General. Scotland had a Deputy Adjutant-General in Edinburgh, whereas Ireland and every foreign station had its own Adjutant-General: all these officers were responsible to the Horse Guards. So, too, were the Assistant Adjutant-Generals of military districts in the United Kingdom, who were appointed on the Adjutant-General's recommendation.[13]

Directly answerable to the C-in-C for the efficiency of the Army, the Adjutant-General's duties were arduous and, like the Military Secretary, he found himself virtually tied to a desk. Writing to Brown, Sir George Cathcart commented on his appointment: "I by no means relish the thought of imprisonment with hard labour, which is a condition inseparable from the appointment of Adjutant-General". To some extent this was due to the "great variety of details", with which the Adjutant-General's department had been progressively forced to cope since coming under the C-in-C; and a full explanation of which Sir John Macdonald, when Adjutant-General, could not provide. Sir Harry Calvert had expanded the department during the French wars: only the Adjutant-General and his deputy staffed it in 1792, but by 1808 sixteen subordinates had been acquired. Although Macdonald admitted that in the post-war years, despite colonial expansion, the business handled declined, the establishment of this Horse Guards' department increased: by 1836, it comprised four officers, plus subordinate clerks, and ten years later its cost had risen to almost £13,000 per year.[14]

The duties of the third officer, the Quartermaster-General, were less demanding. With responsibility for the march, embarkation and disembarkation of troops, he controlled the siting of encampments and the accommodation and billeting of troops. So he superintended the defensive plans of camps and barracks, assumed an overall interest in the maintenance of military establishments and a particular duty for the defence of Great Britain. He supervised all military science and formed Information and Survey branches with a Military Plans and Papers

Department. Like the Adjutant-General, the Quartermaster-General had three officers with subordinate staff to assist him at the Horse Guards, but the annual cost of his department was half that of his colleague's.[15] Similarly, too, there was a Deputy Quartermaster-General in Edinburgh and Assistant Quartermaster-Generals in the United Kingdom districts, required to submit monthly returns to the Horse Guards.

Some aspects of the Quartermaster-General's position were less clear than those of the Adjutant-General. He issued movement orders only on the authority of the Secretary at War, and in this sense he served two masters. Nor were his duties concerning defence planning, barracks and fortifications ever satisfactorily distinguished from those of the Master-General of the Ordnance and his Department. For his interests in military science he raised a corps, which virtually rivalled the Royal Engineers, and for the erection of field and defence works (such as the Military Canal at Hythe and the Martello Towers) he formed his own Staff Corps. Another anomalous duty also fell to him. If troops were used in support of the civil authority to quell disturbances, the Ordnance Department produced the supplies, which the Quartermaster-General officially distributed. In consequence he acquired responsibility for the issue of military equipment at all times, and Officers Commanding stations requisitioned military supplies from the Quartermaster-General at the Horse Guards, which he in turn obtained through the Ordnance Department. In practice normally he acted in a supervisory role and left the Ordnance to issue the equipment.[16]

Whenever a major expeditionary force was raised, it duplicated the structure of the Horse Guards' staff: Commander-in-Chief, Military Secretary, Adjutant-General and Quartermaster-General. There were complications, however. The commander of the expedition was directly responsible to the Secretary of State for War and the Colonies (not the C-in-C in London) and, although he commanded the immediate loyalty of his three assistants, the Adjutant-General and Quartermaster-General depended for military supplies upon the parallel departments in the Horse Guards. Wellington had disputed this disjointed system in the Peninsular War, but had not purged it. Hence the Horse Guards did retain a measure of control over the expedition through the military needs of these two departments.

Only superficially was the arrangement of personal staff recreated in the field, for their precise duties varied with the different demands of individual campaigns. Yet certain similarities of function were recognisable. Lord Raglan's nephew, Lord Burghersh, refused the post of Military Secretary as he was "not very fond of writing", the Adjutant-General held responsibility for men and discipline and the Quartermaster-General for the camp and equipment. Each division then had its own Assistant Quartermaster-General and Deputy

Adjutant-General, but their duties were not clearly defined. Major A. R. Godwin-Austen has shown that no worthwhile instruction in field duties occurred at the Senior Department of the Royal Military College after 1820, and in the Peninsular War duties had varied according to the personality of the officer involved. No written instructions existed, as Lord Seaton explained to his son when he took up his staff appointment with Raglan's Third Division, and Richard Airey wrote to the Quartermaster-General in London for guidance four months after his own appointment as Quartermaster-General in the Crimea. He received an unhelpful reply and a copy of the evidence of Lieutenant-General Sir William Gordon before a House of Commons' Select Committee in 1820.[17]

Despite limitations on his absolute control of the infantry and cavalry overseas, the C-in-C undoubtedly commanded troops within the United Kingdom and exercised considerable influence outside it. His political position, not least in the context of constitutional propriety, was therefore of special importance. The Cabinet clearly decided upon the appointment of a C-in-C and even had influence on his exact title. When Prime Minister, Wellington offered Lord Hill the post with the address "Senior General upon the Staff", because "some of the government" objected to "Commander-in-Chief" as he ranked comparatively low in the seniority list. Political responsibility for the appointment was underlined when, on Wellington's fall from power, his successor Lord Grey expressed the "earnest desire" that Hill should continue at the Horse Guards and, when he retired from office in August 1842, Hill's letter went to Sir Robert Peel, then Prime Minister. Although Peel wished Wellington to resume as C-in-C, he acknowledged that Cabinet approval must precede any offer, and when Sir Robert's government resigned Wellington admitted that his future depended on the incoming Administration.[18]

Nevertheless, the C-in-C was not a politician and he was not expected to play a political role, other than to offer military advice when requested. An attempt to remove Lord Hill from the Horse Guards, because his political opinions did not coincide with those of whig ministers, failed — lack of political influence in the post being recognised. Both Wellington and Hardinge emphasised that the C-in-C must avoid any hint of political opposition to the Government. Lord Hill, however, almost reversed this argument: if the appointment were not political, then the C-in-C need not always support the Government. This view, expressed privately, was never put to public test. Interpreting the situation in yet another way, at first Wellington could not understand the need to resign as C-in-C, when he became Prime Minister in 1828. As the Horse Guards' appointment was military, he believed that the two posts could be combined, until persuaded otherwise.[19]

The importance of the Army, its involvement in maintaining internal order and securing colonial expansion, raised several issues concerning civil-military relations. In this, the influence and attitude of the Court presented a special, complicating factor. Prince Albert showed deep interest in the Army and Lord Derby certainly discussed Wellington's successor at the Horse Guards with him in some detail. Constitutionally, there was no need to do this with the Prince, who had no recognised authority nor political standing; but Derby's action, based perhaps on no more than passing politeness, encouraged royal arguments that the Horse Guards represented a peculiar constitutional element. Derby was at Balmoral on 16 September 1852, when news of Wellington's death arrived. He then evidently considered the matter of successor with Prince Albert, who contrived to convey in later correspondence that his choice of Lord Hardinge had prevailed over Derby's preference for the Duke of Cambridge. Almost certainly, Derby was merely reiterating Cabinet reasons for a decision which, in view of the Duke's age, would have already been taken in principle.[20]

Court interest in the Army was not confined to Prince Albert, for Queen Victoria, whose father the Duke of Kent followed a military career, claimed: "I was always taught to consider myself a soldier's child". Historical precedent was quoted in the attempt to demonstrate that the C-in-C had an unique position completely divorced from politics — an argument which, since 1689, had no basis in fact. In this context, the term "Commander-in-Chief" itself gave rise to some confusion. In the past it had been reserved to the Sovereign who, when not actively directing a campaign, delegated his duties to a Captain-General. After the Restoration, this practice had not been continued and Lord Palmerston pointed out that in 1745 both a Captain-General (the Duke of Cumberland) and a C-in-C (General Wade) had been appointed: variations in the exact title of the C-in-C served further to confuse the issue.[21] As government ministers sought to exert constitutional control over the Army and the Crown adhered to an historical view of that officer's function, friction developed. Hence when the Duke of Wellington refused to serve as C-in-C under George Canning, George IV reputedly said: "I shall keep the command of the Army in my own hands till my friend Arthur recovers his temper", informing Wellington that "the command of the Army is still open, and if you choose to recall that resignation . . . you have my sincere permission to do so". On his accession, William IV intimated similar opinions, and Prince Albert countered a proposal by Lord Grey for a Civil Board under the House of Commons to control the Army as destructive of "the prerogative of the Crown".[22] This royal viewpoint was not altogether irrational, nor in any way unconstitutional. For one of its main aims was to keep promotion and appointments in the Army outside the theatre of party politics. This danger, rather than irresponsible royal use of the armed forces, represented the more likely possibility in the mid nineteenth century. Both Lord Melbourne and the Prince advanced fear of such a development, in expressing concern about extension of Parliamentary control over the Army.[23]

Certain incidents caused particular tension. Lord Cardigan's conduct on Easter Sunday 1841 led to pressure from the Cabinet for his removal from command of the 11th Hussars, with a successful counter-attack by the Duke of Wellington and Lord Hill on the grounds that flogging on the Sabbath was not illegal under the Mutiny Act and Articles of War; and, after evidence of its opposition, the Horse Guards was "informed of the proposals for limited service" in 1847. In this latter instance, the limitations of the C-in-C in a policy decision were underlined.[24] Indeed, the whole question of the C-in-C's political involvement was aired over his position in the Cabinet. During the Second Rockingham and Shelburne ministries of 1782, General Conway sat in the Cabinet as C-in-C, so did Lord Amherst from January 1793 until February 1795. When a royal prince, the Duke of York, followed Amherst to the Horse Guards it was constitutionally undesirable that he should sit in the Cabinet; hence, the C-in-C's exclusion resulted from an accident of birth rather than a question of principle. The Duke of Wellington, therefore, served at the Horse Guards when exclusion of the C-in-C from the Cabinet had become accepted, and his reason for supporting the practice ran very close to that of Prince Albert and Lord Melbourne for protecting the Army from Parliamentary interference. Wellington argued for exclusion because the C-in-C "ought not to be supposed to have any political influence as a bias on his mind — most particularly upon the subject of the promotions of the Army". The subject was further examined at some length by the House of Commons in February 1843. Lord John Russell drew attention to Wellington's resignation as C-in-C when he became Prime Minister in 1828, and the fact that, while he lived, there was no justification for any other officer to advise the Government on military matters. Sir Robert Peel "apprehended that there was no constitutional rule against the tenure of a seat in the Cabinet by the C-in-C", explaining that neither Sir David Dundas nor Lord Hill had been "political characters". He concluded that both the C-in-C and the Master-General of the Ordnance might sit in the Cabinet, but the matter was not pressed: with Wellington now at the Horse Guards, moreover, at this time no clash of opinion occurred as he supported the politicians. Four months later Reginald Blewitt queried the Duke of Wellington's position in Peel's Cabinet, as Minister without Portfolio, while C-in-C. Peel treated Blewitt with disdain, though he eschewed a direct answer to his probing: "The Duke of Wellington refrains from meddling with matters with which he has no concern, and over which he has no control and perhaps the Hon. (sic) Gentleman himself might have profited by the example". While Wellington survived, major controversy seemed unlikely; and, in fact, his attitude and the unwillingness of his successor, Lord Hardinge, to become politically involved avoided potential conflagration.[25]

Another issue of latent conflict was still-born by Wellington's adherence to the spirit of the constitution, in discounting direct military intervention in politics. For he appeared to distinguish between country and government, when explaining his opposition to Canning: "I stated repeatedly ... that I should support the Government whenever their Measures were calculated to promote the Honour or Interests of the Country". Expressed by an influential military figure, with his power and views, this distinction could have proved embarrassing, if not constitutionally dangerous. Yet the very statement of this position, together with Wellington's known personal devotion to the monarch, possibly encouraged the Court in its determination to see special royal control over the Army. Later, amid his traumatic dealings with government ministers about the Crimean winter disasters, his disciple, Lord Raglan, seemed to make a similar distinction and reach similar conclusions. That Wellington and Raglan, as well as Lords Hill and Hardinge, did not exploit this situation was no guarantee of inactivity by later officers. In the mid nineteenth century, however, stringent brakes on military expenditure and decreasing capability of the Crown for independent political initiative were more effective safeguards of the constitution than the opinions of individual Commanders-in-Chief.[26]

One dispute, involving the respective duties and responsibilities of the C-in-C and one civilian minister, the Secretary at War, continued relentlessly throughout the first half of the century. Before the appointment of Lord Amherst in 1793, the Secretary at War had controlled the Army. Thereafter, despite Parlimentary regulation of the post, up to the outbreak of the Crimean War the civilian minister believed himself superior to the C-in-C. Altercation between Horse Guards and War Office could not therefore be avoided. In 1810 Sir David Dundas, then C-in-C, observed that the Secretary at War was subordinate to him, in much the same way that the War Office had been subordinate to the Crown before 1793: the Minister's only functions were to ensure that the Law between the civil and military populations was duly observed and army accounts properly balanced. Lord Palmerston, currently Secretary at War, supported by the Cabinet vehemently protested that as controller of military finance he had the right to issue orders to the Army. Eventually in May 1812 the Prince Regent, while broadly upholding Palmerston's viewpoint, ruled that the Secretary at War should show the C-in-C orders prior to their publication: in case of dispute reference must be made to the First Lord of the Treasury, the Chancellor of the Exchequer and the Secretary of State for War and the Colonies. Tempers were thus stilled and blushes deadened, but the main difficulty had scarcely been tackled.[27]

For two periods in 1827 there was no C-in-C, and the Secretary at War issued orders to the Army. In January, after the death of the Duke of York, the King attached a note to a draft General Order, that it should be "submitted previous to its being given out in orders to the Secretary at War, as he is now responsible for those duties attached to the C-in-C". Five months later, the Duke of Wellington resigned as C-in-C when George Canning became Prime Minister. Palmerston, still at the War Office, informed the Lords of the Treasury that "the principal part of the duties attached to that appointment have according to the ancient custom of my office devolved upon me as Secretary at War", and that he had taken immediate steps to ensure the smooth running of the Army. All these events suggested, however, was that the Secretary at War became responsible for the Army, while a vacancy remained at the Horse Guards. They did nothing to clarify the situation when both a Secretary at War and a C-in-C held office.[28]

Four years later trouble arose over the control of pensioners. Lord Hill, when C-in-C, protested at a letter from the Secretary at War, Watkins W. Wynn, claiming that any petitions concerning pensions should go direct to him not the Horse Guards. Hill argued that "the C-in-C (is) the natural and recognised protector of the soldier under all circumstances", referring to "the trust reposed in him by the King" and practised by "illustrious men who have preceded me". Wynn replied that he could "not imagine that it can be the Intention of His Majesty's Government . . . that an Establishment should be kept up in one office for the purpose of discussing and disposing of Public Business" handled by another. But, significantly, neither Wynn nor Hill could prove his point by reference to conclusive regulations. The same problem arose the following year between Lord Hill and Sir J. Cam Hobhouse; and, similarly, nothing was solved.[29]

Disagreement over command of the Army occurred once more following Wellington's death in September 1852, and before his successor had been appointed. William Beresford, the Secretary at War, cited the correspondence of 1827 to the Prime Minister, Lord Derby, and secured recognition by both the Adjutant-General and the Quartermaster-General of his control over the Army. The Adjutant-General, Sir George Brown, agreed that the Secretary at War was "the responsible adviser of Her Majesty and, therefore, any question involving advice should be submitted to the Sovereign through him", and that the Adjutant-General merely "watched over . . . the detailed arrangements of the proceedings of the army" under the Secretary at War's authority. Colonel Richard Airey, Deputy Quartermaster-General, accepted that "all questions upon which it has been the custom to take the orders of the C-in-C will be submitted with the same view to the Secretary at War". Both memoranda were counter-signed "approved" by Beresford. At least the Secretary at War's responsibility in the absence of a C-in-C seemed to have been established. But Brown appended a note to another memorandum on the Adjutant-General's duties, claiming that this situation only constituted an "understanding" between the parties.[30]

Moreover, while the relative positions of the War Office and the Horse Guards remained at the centre of the controversy, debilitating guerrilla warfare was in evidence between the two departments. Occasionally it advanced to a strategic confrontation over minor issues, such as the foundation of regimental savings banks or officers' applications for travelling expenses. Both major and minor encounters combined to create mutual antagonism.[31] The spasmodic resurrection of con-stitutional dinosaurs, who tried to extend the C-in-C's powers against an unsympathetic political backcloth, further polluted the atmosphere. Disagreeing with Lord Howick's administrative proposals in 1837, Sir Hussey Vivian suggested that the C-in-C should head all the military departments of the Army and, together with his civil and military secretaries, be included in the Government. On the day of Raglan's appointment to the expeditionary command, a correspondent to *The United Service Gazette* complained about "interference from civil departments" with the Army and called for the C-in-C to be given full, unrestrained control over it.[32]

Events during the Crimean War demonstrated clearly both the limitations and the scope of the C-in-C's powers, but they also clarified some disputed issues. Lord Hardinge claimed that "the Horse Guards have completely established the right not to be interfered with in Promotion and Discipline", and certainly he exercised a strict hold over these areas. When Lord de Ros retired as Lord Raglan's Quartermaster-General, the C-in-C promoted Richard Airey to take his place and, similarly, made Harry Jones a major-general on his appointment as Commanding Royal Engineer with the Expeditionary Force. Although the Prime Minister recommended to Queen Victoria Raglan's promotion to field-marshal, the C-in-C actually conferred the rank and Raglan could only suggest to Hardinge that Sir William Codrington be promoted major-general. Shortly after taking office as Prime Minister, Lord Palmerston declined to interfere in promotions.[33] Discipline, too, remained a strictly military responsibility. Lord Hardinge formally gave Lord Raglan his instructions as commander of the Expeditionary Force, emphasising that reports on discipline should be submitted to the Horse Guards, and he dealt with a variety of disciplinary matters throughout the War. He authorised troops in Raglan's army to wear moustaches, refused Lord Lucan's request for a court martial following the Light Brigade débâcle and ruled against the provision of servants for medical officers from the ranks of effective soldiers. So returns on the state of regiments in the Crimea were made to Hardinge, and to him Queen Victoria addressed her anxiety about reported laxity of discipline at the front.[34] Within the general limits of his disciplinary responsibility, the C-in-C was concerned with staff appointments to the Expeditionary Force. He decided that regulations would not permit addition to Lord Lucan's staff and, when seeking a post on the staff to regularise his presence in the Crimea, Sir John Burgoyne wrote to Hardinge, who subsequently confirmed the appointment. The C-in-C continued to use his powers of patronage, appointing, for instance, both Raglan and Sir George Brown to regimental colonelcies and selecting nominees for the Order of the Bath.[35]

Lord Hardinge, in accordance with the C-in-C's acknowledged responsibility, detailed troops for the Expeditionary Force and, later, sent out reinforcements to it. Two days after the Cabinet decision to despatch 10,000 men to Malta, he announced the composition of the First Division and promised that of the Second and Third divisions "in a day or two". Early in 1855, when a Depot of Drafts at Malta was agreed, he allocated the regiments for it and for additional drafts to the Crimea, as they were voted.[36] The C-in-C offered professional advice to the Government. He successfully recommended to the Cabinet Lord Raglan for his appointment and the Duke of Cambridge as a divisional commander, but he declined to support Sir George Brown as Second-in-Command. Hardinge believed that Brown did not "possess those qualities of judgement, temper, skill and foresight" necessary for that post in an Allied force containing French and Turks, and consequently Brown was not offered the appointment.[37] The influence of the C-in-C in the business of appointments was recognised by the Duke of Cambridge, who noted in his diary: "Very busy all the day at the Horse Guards with a view to being employed with the Army to go to Turkey". Indeed, Hardinge's advice was sought on the appointment of Sir George Cathcart to command the Fourth Division, who should succeed Sir James Simpson as the Crimean army's commander and on the idea of splitting the Expeditionary Force into two corps. When the Duke of Newcastle formed an *ad hoc* board to consider military matters early in 1855, Hardinge attended two of its three meetings, later that year took part in two Councils of War at Windsor and on occasions went to meetings of both the full Cabinet and the War Committee of the Cabinet.[38]

But the C-in-C only gave advice to the Cabinet and other political bodies when requested to do so, and he did not challenge overall political direction and responsibility for the Crimean War. Raglan answered for his conduct of the campaign to the Secretary of State for War, not the Horse Guards, and certain decisions concerning the War were shown to be outside Hardinge's jurisdiction. When the Government undertook to move reinforcements to the east at the expense of home defence, the C-in-C could but protest in vain, and Newcastle revealed later that he showed Hardinge only selected despatches.

Embarrassed by the Parliamentary brouhaha over Lord Lucan's recall, Hardinge feebly acknowledged his political impotence: "I can do nothing in resisting any measure brought forward by the Government and approved by the Crown". In relatively minor instances, too, the C-in-C accepted political inferiority: he received sickness reports from the front, only by courtesy of the Secretary for War, and, after remonstration from the Duke of Newcastle, Hardinge rescinded the appointment of Lord George Bentick to command the garrison at Portsmouth.[39] Recognising his restricted field of manoeuvre, Hardinge carefully offered only private advice to officers in the Crimea, for fear of offending political sensitivity. So he tactfully suggested reorganisation of the Quartermaster-General's department to Airey and explained in the House of Lords that he had strictly avoided advising Raglan, in accordance with custom, in case an opinion contrary to that of the Government created "embarrassment and difficulty". Because he recognised, and practised, his limited authority, Hardinge held that the administrative changes of mid 1854 did not affect the C-in-C.[40]

Lord Hardinge's conciliatory opinions in reality conveyed a less-than-accurate impression of departmental peace: for, behind the calm façade, violent in-fighting occurred. Unconnected to similar strife with the War Office, wrangling over the relative powers of the C-in-C and Secretary of State for War resembled a putrid sore, and Lord Panmure admitted that this dispute alone was of "magnitude ... (and) importance". Renewed calls for a military officer to become Secretary of State for War, even combining this function with that of C-in-C, were counterbalanced by Lord Palmerston's insistence that the Secretary for War could, in matters "of sufficient importance", effectively overrule the C-in-C concerning staff appointments. This image of inter-departmental pugilism was somewhat marred by Lord Hardwicke's complaint that "a civilian", Panmure, answered questions in the House about the Army with the C-in-C "acting as his tutor" at his side. Yet Hardwicke's conclusion seemed not unreasonable: "This was a bit of machinery which he ventured to say would not work". For the Duke of Newcastle (lately Secretary for War) soon destroyed any illusion of blissful co-existence between equals, by his evidence before the Sevastopol Select Committee: "There is nothing to compel me to submit anything to Lord Hardinge, because in all matters connected with the war the Secretary of State for War is supreme"; and in May 1855 Lord Panmure received a supplementary patent, in an effort to settle outstanding differences.[41] In practice, this solved nothing. Within a month Hardinge revealed that, in the aftermath of Ordnance reorganisation, fearing exposure of the C-in-C to undue political pressure, he had asked for "the line of demarcation between the Secretary of State and the Commander-in-Chief (to) be carefully defined." Panmure re-emphasised his department's constitutional superiority by noting that the Secretary of

State, but not the C-in-C, could signify the Queen's pleasure to a third party. Possibly in search of a truce, Hardinge wrote to Panmure about the Minister's willingness "to place the most liberal construction on the duties of the C-in-C", though he qualified these words by adding that "for the most part" the respective duties were "well marked out". Panmure's response was not entirely pacific: five days later, he underlined the need for the Secretary of State to approve recommendations for major military appointments before they were submitted to the monarch. To this, however, Hardinge raised no objection and followed this procedure, when seeking Richard Airey's appointment as Quartermaster-General at the Horse Guards.[42]

Dissatisfaction with this uneasy state of affairs persisted, and it was not confined to the two departments concerned. In the closing months of the War, the Earl of Derby initiated a lengthy debate by moving in the Lords: "That an humble address be presented to Her Majesty for a copy of any Document in which the respective duties of the Secretary of State for the War Department and the C-in-C of Her Majesty's Forces are limited and defined". Admitting that precise delineation was impossible, in reply Panmure referred to the 1812 Minute in Council, which laid down "a very broad line of demarcation" and basically relied upon sensible consultation between the C-in-C and Secretary of State in troublesome cases. This, he claimed, had worked "most satisfactorily". But he went on to state emphatically that ultimate responsibility lay with the Secretary of State, as "there is no act of the C-in-C, however small or however great, that does not constitutionally come within the revision of my department". Derby's motion was defeated and next day the Secretary of State wrote to the Queen, "that this important question of Your Majesty's C-in-C will be set at rest and fully recognised for the future". Optimism of such a final solution was not expressed by him to Major-General Codrington, commander in the Crimea: "I think we have settled that question for some time". For the Queen's assertion, a year earlier, that the C-in-C's duties "rest entirely on tradition and are in most cases ambiguous and undefined" retained more than a grain of truth.[43]

Indeed, the Court's anachronistic efforts to perceive a special relationship between Monarch and Army contrived further to muddy the constitutional waters, parallel with the Horse Guards' struggles against the War Department and War Office. When the Duke of Newcastle proposed a permanent consultative board of military and civilian members in January 1855, Queen Victoria sought to trade her approval for a more satisfactory definition of the C-in-C's duties, with the implication that the C-in-C would enjoy a measure of independence from close political control. On the formation of Lord Palmerston's government, the Queen objected to the appointment of Frederick Peel as Under Secretary of State for War, because his inexperience "may

cause serious embarrassment and further exposure to successful attacks
the already much-threatened maintenance of proper authority of the
Crown over the Army". Four months later, the Court seized upon
changes in the function of the Board of General Officers to propose that
all reports affecting military discipline should in future emanate from
the Horse Guards, arguing: "Civil Heads of Department . . . are
continually changing and must chiefly aim at giving satisfaction to this
or that party in the House of Commons". Pinpricks of the royal gnat, if
lacking in consistency, thus proved persistent. In Autumn 1855, Prince
Albert complained about the dangers of placing too much control of
military affairs in transient political hands, and the period surrounding
Lord Derby's Parliamentary motion, early the following year,
prompted a barrage of nervous reaction. Referring to the "serious
difficulty" and "ferment" created by publication of the second report
from Sir John McNeill and Colonel Tulloch, Lord Panmure obliquely
recorded: "High personages are fearful lest this opportunity be seized to
get the administration of the Army placed, as the Admiralty, under the
control of Parliament". In response to a royal attempt to prevent
political consideration of the C-in-C's position, Palmerston told
Panmure: "I must try to explain to her (the Queen) that no Department
paid by money voted by Parliament . . . can be kept out of discussion in
Parliament". The Queen's disinclination to abandon her prepared
position was illustrated shortly after the War ended, when a successor to
Lord Hardinge came under discussion. Agreeing that the Duke of
Cambridge should go to the Horse Guards, she demanded that the
appointment be communicated by the Prime Minister, not the
Secretary of State for War, and that she should also write to the Duke.
The Queen then added: "The office is not a subordinate one of the
class of those appointed to by the head of a department, and has at all
times been recommended by the Prime Minister. Lord Derby wrote
to Lord Hardinge and the Queen knows this to have been in strict
accordance with former precedents, which the Queen wishes to have
adhered to."[44]

Queen Victoria's entrenched resistance involved not only the relation
of Monarch with Army, but also the triangle of responsibility between
Crown, War Department and Horse Guards. Little had been clarified.
The situation was further complicated by yet another demand for the
C-in-C's inclusion in the Cabinet and, in Hardinge's words: "Her
Majesty's command . . . that I should for the future remain in the
Presence Chamber, the same as the Cabinet Ministers, in all Court
Ceremonial and on State occasions". Moreover, there seemed little hope
of reaching a satisfactory understanding, so long as the C-in-C could
speak of being "at war" with a government department.[45]

Even more confusion evolved from piecemeal references to a number
of the issues by political figures of different standing and varying

responsibility. Before the War had lasted a fortnight, Lord Grey attacked the Crown's views on Army control. He declared as "unsound" the concept that the Army should remain exclusively under the C-in-C and that interference with this arrangement would be "unconstitutional . . . (and) an invasion of the Royal prerogative". Further, he maintained that there was "no distinction that I am aware of between the military or any other branch of the executive authority of the Crown", which could only be exercised through government ministers. If it were therefore being argued that the Crown should exert "personal power" over the Army which did not apply to other departments, the notion was unconstitutional. If, on the other hand, it were proposed that the C-in-C should be completely independent of Parliament, it would be "neither convenient for the public service nor very safe for the C-in-C", as that officer could not defend himself in Parliament. The C-in-C was, and ought to be, answerable to Parliament through a responsible minister. No speaker disagreed with Grey's conclusion, which in broad terms re-iterated his repeated call over the past twenty years for administrative consolidation. But it was not particularly helpful, as the C-in-C dealt with more than one minister: at times, the Home Secretary, Secretary for War and the Colonies and, until his effective abolition in February 1855, the Secretary at War.[46]

This particular foray produced no real effect, and Grey continued to direct ranging rounds at the Horse Guards. Two months later, at the time of the creation of a separate Secretary of State for War, he discharged a more dangerous salvo. Writing to Henry Drummond, he declared: "What is most necessary is the abolition of the office of C-in-C", because that officer's powers were unsatisfactory and limited: "To have a General Officer with authority over the whole army at home and abroad, without pecuniary authority or responsibility is an arrangement so radically vicious that it never can work as it ought to do". This particular viewpoint was circulated and certainly discussed in Cabinet. Sir Charles Wood, President of the Board of Control, agreed with Grey that greater administrative consolidation was required, but warned him that "most of the Cabinet are against what you consider essential, the abolition of the C-in-C". He forecast "great con-sternation" at Court, if the proposal were pursued, and anticipated little support for it in Cabinet. Two days later Wood confirmed the impossibility of achieving abolition at this time: "All the world are against abolishing the C-in-C and I doubt whether anybody in the Cabinet would agree to it except myself — the Queen would not have agreed and (neither would) Aberdeen, Russell, Palmerston, Graham or Newcastle".[47]

The concept lay fallow for some months until reactivated during the political crisis of January 1855. Once more Grey advocated dismantling the C-in-C's department, redeploying administrative responsibility to the Secretary for War and leaving the C-in-C only in command of troops in the United Kingdom. In fact, he was prepared to dispense with the actual title of C-in-C, as the appointed general's task would have become so pared. The C-in-C's main function at present, he claimed, was to ride at the head of troops on ceremonial occasions and his "duties might perfectly well be performed without his ever putting a red coat on his back". Predictably, with the fate of Lord Aberdeen's government hypnotising politicians, Grey enjoyed no more success then than seven months previously, although W. E. Gladstone added disarray to the jigsaw of confusion by describing the C-in-C as "all but a Minister". Later, in the Spring, the Duke of Cambridge produced a memorandum, rather vaguely suggesting that a course of action be planned by a minister with the C-in-C organising deployment and discipline of the troops involved. This roughly followed the arrangement in use for expeditions, but provided scant assistance in resolving perennial difficulties in time of peace.[48]

The debate in May 1855 about Lord Panmure's plan for the reorganisation of the Ordnance presented another opportunity for focusing attention on the Horse Guards. Grey complained that Panmure's proposals for "the consolidation of the civil departments of the army" left the C-in-C "precisely in his present position". He therefore suggested that in future all the C-in-C's business be conducted through the Minister of War to eliminate the controversial claim of direct access to the Sovereign, which he enigmatically described as "an anomaly of recent date": in this suggestion, he was supported by Lord Hardwicke. Grey had put forward this idea before and it remained unworkable, so long as the C-in-C answered to more than one minister. Panmure in rebutting it, however, succeeded in further confusing the issue: "He could not believe that it would be at all expedient to place the C-in-C, as head of the army, under the control of a civilian".[49]

The Court was quick to see in Panmure's measures a reduction in the powers of the C-in-C and a further subordination of military interests to civilian control. The reorganisation included appointment of a Superintendent of Clothing, responsible to the Secretary of State for all questions of uniform, in place of the Board of General Officers. So the C-in-C in this comparatively minor instance lost a measure of direct control. Although Queen Victoria signed the warrant setting up this new clothing authority, she thought that all matters of dress and discipline should still be submitted to her by the C-in-C. Furthermore, the Board of General Officers had hitherto advised the C-in-C upon uniform patterns, which he then put before the Sovereign. Prince Albert maintained that this particular function had not been abolished and the Superintendent of Clothing exercised only a general oversight in the matter. He held also that there was an implication that, hereafter, the Secretary of State would summon all Boards of General Officers (for whatever purpose) instead of the C-in-C. This he considered unacceptable. Like the Queen, he insisted that all clothing correspondence and suggestions should reach the Sovereign through the Horse Guards.[50]

From these views of the Queen and Prince Albert Lord Panmure demurred, thereby revealing that, whatever he had meant by his remarks in answer to Lord Grey and Lord Hardwicke, it was not that the C-in-C should be independent of ministerial control. He held that the C-in-C could gather a group of officers to proffer advice, but only the Secretary of State might assemble a paid board. Panmure then demolished the Court's case by re-stating an accepted constitutional fact: only through the Secretary of State could the Queen's pleasure be signified and the C-in-C was unable to do this. In further support of this contention, he submitted a memorandum in July 1855 arguing that "appointments to military command at home and abroad ought to be concurred in by the Secretary of State before they are formally submitted for Her Majesty's approval". But nothing constructive had been achieved by any of these exchanges, other than to demonstrate just how unclear was the entire range of royal, ministerial and military responsibility. Furthermore, extension of his power to cover the Ordnance troops strengthened the hand of the C-in-C and encouraged the Court to resist the mythical assault of civilian politicians on its military stronghold. In this sense, the situation had acquired additional complication.[51]

Yet, almost imperceptibly, the Crimean War years proved important in the development of the C-in-C's office. His military duties were confirmed: he continued to control troops in the United Kingdom and deploy them in its defence, discipline and the distribution of units overseas remained his unquestioned province. Control over promotion and patronage was secure, and he fulfilled his nominated role in connection with the Expeditionary Force: he arranged drafts and reinforcements, dealt with staff appointments, promoted and rewarded and gave military advice when required. Some aspects of his duties undoubtedly caused problems, and little advance appeared to be made in solving various constitutional disputes between him, the Crown and government ministers. Certainly, bickering did not subside in the immediate post-war period. Queen Victoria noted that the Duke of Cambridge, Lord Hardinge's successor at the Horse Guards, "spoke of the bad system of the Government in not telling him *beforehand* (sic) what is intended to be done, merely taking decisions, which he could not always carry out", and the Queen herself complained: "I fear the Cabinet have been dabbling in military affairs again ... for which they are eminently unfit". Neither Cambridge nor the Queen appreciated that their protests were founded on sand.[52]

Only days before a truce effectively brought the Crimean War to a close, Lord Hardinge declared: "I am not aware that the duties of the C-in-C have been in any degree restricted by the recent changes in the composition of the War Department". This was strictly true, but the politicians had already prevailed over military opinion and immeasurably increased their hold over the Army. The Duke of Cambridge received a letter of service signed by the Secretary of State for War, not letters patent. Moreover, as if to underscore his subordinate position, Cambridge was designated "General Commanding-in-Chief", not "Commander-in-Chief". Later Cambridge agreed: "The Secretary of State would, in the constitutional form, advise Her Majesty to take his opinion, and not that of the C-in-C", so, as Sir James Graham pointed out, admitting "the supreme control of the Secretary of State over the Army". Cambridge at length recognised what had become evident five years earlier, despite Hardinge's contrary impression and the Queen's myopia. Constitutionally, it was imperative that the Horse Guards should be brought without question under political direction. Possibly a more vigorous C-in-C than the aged Hardinge could have positively advanced the influence of his office, at a time when the Government lacked military advice from the front. But, through his former experience in Cabinet office, he knew the dangers of inadequate resistance to the contemporary tide of administrative consolidation impelled by responsible ministers. Reaction based upon royal prerogative and military independence, however stout, would have rested on dubious precedent and, at best, could merely have decelerated progress. At worst, ill-judged action might have encouraged support for Grey's drive towards abolition of the C-in-C's office or, conceivably, have damaged the prestige of the Crown. In neither case would the Army or the country have gained benefit.[53]

VI

Ministerial Responsibility
Secretary at War and Secretary for War

The Secretary at War and the Secretary of State for War and the Colonies were the government ministers most intimately concerned with army administration. Frequently both sat in the Cabinet: constitutional practice decreed that the latter, as a Secretary of State, should always do so, but the Secretary at War was not ever-present. Long before hostilities with Russia, disputes arose between the ministers themselves and between each of them, the C-in-C and the Master-General of the Ordnance, which pressure at times of stress harshly illuminated. During the Crimean War, arguments were advanced for re-examining ministerial duties, especially following establishment of a fourth Secretary of State: change could then be achieved in the guise of administrative rationalisation and military benefit. Before seals had hardened on the Peace of Paris, the office of one of the two ministers had, in effect, been removed from the political scene.

The Secretary at War

> ... a sort of barrier between the military authority of the Officer in command of the Army and the civil rights of the people. (Lord Palmerston, 1811).[1]

By the mid nineteenth century, the Secretary at War exercised a wide degree of responsibility in connection with army administration. The Duke of Wellington complained: "The C-in-C cannot at this moment move a corporal's guard from hence to Windsor without his approval", and Sir Henry Hardinge observed: "The duty of a Secretary at War is to be responsible for all military transactions to this House (of Commons) and the country".[2] Like other authorities involved in the administrative process, and especially the C-in-C, the Secretary at War had accumulated duties and responsibilities in a piecemeal fashion. Hence his powers could never be accurately defined, and considerable interdepartmental controversy resulted. Not unreasonably, C. M. Clode has described him as "that ambiguous official" and Sir John Fortescue as "that rather mysterious functionary".[3]

The War Office establishment can be traced with certainty to 28 January 1661, when William Clarke, Lord Albemarle's personal secretary became "Secretary at War to all the forces raised or to be raised in England and Wales". Nine years later, on Albemarle's death, the post of C-in-C was left vacant, and the Secretary at War assumed greater responsibility for the Army. When Matthew Locke became Secretary at War in 1676 he was known as "Secretary to the Forces", all warrants and orders hitherto signed by the C-in-C were now issued by him; and the commission of his successor, William Blathwayt, read virtually the same as that of all later holders of the office. Because his appointment proved continuous, and that of the C-in-C spasmodic, the Secretary at War enlarged his power during the reigns of William III and Anne by filling military appointments and exercising control over discipline. When there was no C-in-C, the Secretary at War commanded the Army, corresponding with Officers Commanding at home and abroad and dealing with all matters of discipline. Even when a C-in-C held office, he retained extensive military responsibility.[4] Because the volume of work at the War Office had so increased, in 1778 a Deputy Secretary at War was assigned to it: thereafter, this post became permanent with its holder chosen by the Secretary at War. In 1798 the Deputy Secretary at War's annual salary stood at £2,000 and nine years later rose to £2,500. By then the French wars had brought much additional labour to the War Office, especially as its control of military finance had been regularised by Parliament in 1783. This function had undoubtedly been retained when Lord Amherst took charge of military discipline and command of the Army ten years later. But the respective duties of military officer and civilian minister were never properly divided. Initially, a permanent commander at the Horse Guards was not planned, so the Secretary at War found himself something of an administrative schizophrenic. He retained enough military interest, possibly in anticipation of full resumption of power over the Army at a future date, for him not to be wholly civilian: in Palmerston's words, "as a Staff Officer he has now only a nominal existence" — nominal, but not altogether negligible. Failure to deal decisively with the Secretary at War's continued aspirations to military command led to protracted altercation.[5]

The fact of the Secretary at War's administrative power could not be denied. In 1836 Lord Howick wrote: "The duties of the Secretary at War have, at different periods, been subject to much variation, (but) at present they chiefly consist in preparing and submitting to Parliament the Army Estimates, in checking the details of military expenditure and in attending to the execution of military law", a conclusion with which Lord Seymour's Select Committee on Army and Ordnance Expenditure broadly agreed fifteen years later. The Secretary at War was the Army's spokesman in the House of Commons. It was in this capacity that he introduced the Annual Estimates (those for 1846–7 covered eighteen separate votes and totalled £6,082,091) and in 1842, for example, explained an increase of fourteen battalions in the previous four years as necessary for security operations in Canada, India, Australia and China. Similarly he discharged responsibility for the annual Mutiny Bill and defended its provisions: in 1842, for instance, military flogging came under heavy Parliamentary fire. He also introduced amendments to it: in 1846 Sidney Herbert successfully sought to close a legal gap, by which some mutineers and deserters had escaped punishment.[6]

The Secretary at War's introduction of these two measures signified Parliamentary recognition of his two major administrative functions concerning the Army: Finance and Law. His financial responsibilities were detailed in the War Office's *Warrants and Regulations concerning Military Finance* (1841): travelling allowances, grants for servants, purchasing of discharges and supervision of clothing regulations all came under him. He controlled the pay and allowances of reserve forces and paid military pensions. In his financial capacity he authorised military rail travel and extraordinary rations to dependants, he dealt with claims for losses on active service and he checked regimental accounts. So the Secretary at War regulated allowances to the Life Guards for clothing and remounts—ridiculed as "a mere petty, paltry and dirty economy" —and was required to determine regulations for pay and bounties under the 1852 Militia Act. He authorised expenditure on buildings for "the Pensioner Establishment", extraordinary payment to Ordnance officers at Chatham and improvements to military prison cells; he formally approved staff pay, and hence that of Lord Raglan and Sir John Burgoyne in the Crimea.[7] A myriad other financial details occupied his attention. He approved the cost of white cap covers, examined the Horse Guard's case for an increased establishment of clerks and ruled on a commanding officer's ability to withhold troops' pay. But he could not interfere in matters of private finance and, although responsible for the payment of non-effective pensions, did not deal with pensioners' superannuation and allowances nor provide for widows of pensioners.[8] Despite his wide authority in military finance, he was not therefore omnipotent. In accordance with constitutional practice, the Army Estimates needed Parliamentary approval and War Office accounts were scrutinised by the Treasury's Board of Audit. In fact, the Secretary at War authorised expenditure, but could not initiate it; and he had no concern with stores. The conclusion by the Seymour Committee nicely summarised this role: "The Secretary at War is responsible to Parliament for all questions connected with Army expenditure".[9]

The Secretary at War exercised similar authority concerning Military Law. In addition to introducing the annual Mutiny Bill, he prepared the Articles of War and ensured that both were enforced. With no legal department of his own, the Secretary at War relied on either the Judge Advocate General or the Solicitor to the Treasury for expert advice; and he was responsible for the conduct, as distinct from the arrangement, of courts martial. In his legal capacity, the Secretary at War dealt with a number of different questions. When at the War Office, Sir Henry Hardinge answered a Parliamentary challenge about the imprisonment of two officers for more than eight days without court martial, contrary to the 107th Article of War, by pointing out that any officer could be kept under arrest by order of the C-in-C; and he laid down that no pension was permissible for the widow of an officer killed in a duel. On other occasions the Secretary at War concerned himself with matters from billetting soldiers in Ireland to the sale of alcohol in military canteens on Sunday.[10] In his legal role, Lord Palmerston viewed the Secretary at War as a barrier between the civil rights of the people and the potential power of the Army. Hence William Beresford investigated the charge by Sharman Crawford of military interference with an election in Enniskillen.[11]

Partly as an extension of his legal duties, but mainly because he represented the Army in the House of Commons, the Secretary at War also handled questions connected with military discipline. Edmund Roche complained that a soldier of the 5th Fusiliers had died on parade in Ireland from apoplexy brought on by "over-drinking" and Sir Henry Hardinge promised to look into the incident; Fox Maule answered a question about the use of soldiers' knapsacks and later grappled with queries on the lieutenant to captain promotion examination due for introduction in July 1852. In after years, reflecting on his time at the War Office, Maule (then Panmure) said that ninety-nine out of a hundred questions, with which he had been called upon to deal, concerned discipline not finance.[12]

As the area of British colonial territories grew in the first half of the nineteenth century, the Army's commitment thereby increased and the volume of business passing through the War Office expanded. Palmerston foiled attempts to reduce the salary of the Deputy Secretary at War post Waterloo, emphasising the heavier work load, and, although below the combined establishment of some 200 held in the Whitehall and Duke Street departments during the French wars, the War Office staff remained substantial: in 1836 it totalled fifty clerks, a number which rose to seventy-two in November 1852 and eighty-six two years later. Writing in 1854 the Deputy Secretary at War, Benjamin Hawes, revealed that following the 1852 Act of Parliament enrolment of the Militia alone occupied six full-time clerks, and a serious backlog of work was only cleared between 1851 and 1854 by the addition of nine clerks.[13] Quite separately from the Militia commitment, the Secretary at War's duties had multiplied. Parliament made him responsible for the payment of all out-pensioners, both military and naval, supervision of the new Corps of Schoolmasters fell to him and, as a result of interest shown by successive office holders, a watching brief had been established over soldiers' welfare. Hawes therefore referred to the "widely extended" obligations of the War Office "sprung from the improvement in the condition of the Soldier, Military Libraries, Military Schools, the very extensive topic of Prison Discipline at Home and Abroad, and not least the transfer of the Payment of the Out Pensioners 85,000 and the organisation of the Chelsea Pensioners". The volume of correspondence soared from 94,112 letters in 1851 to 112,352 two years later. When Sidney Herbert moved to the War Office in 1845, he found the labours less arduous than those he left at the Admiralty. On re-assumption of the Secretary at War's post seven years later, he discovered his tasks very much increased, though only more important matters were referred to him by his clerical establishment. The extent of the Secretary at War's work even barred desirable reform. In 1851 the Seymour Committee wished to abolish the system of army agents, but was partly deterred from doing so as neither the Secretary at War nor the Paymaster-General would be able to cope with a resultant increase in financial business.[14]

And far-reaching though the private empire of the War Office had spread, the Secretary at War found himself tantalisingly short of full executive power. He existed in something of a political limbo. For with such wide responsibility in military administration, he was not a Secretary of State and his important policy documents needed a Secretary of State's counter-signature. Owing to his close connection with command of the Army before the appointment of a permanent C-in-C, he did not sit in Cabinet until July 1794, and then his place was not assured. Between 31 May 1828 and 29 December 1852, of the fifteen Secretaries at War only seven were in the Cabinet, and among these Edward Ellice and Fox Maule gained admission some time after they took office. Lord Palmerston, who relinquished the War Office in May 1828, was a member, his five successors were not; the following eight, with the sole exception of Sir Thomas Freemantle, were included, so was Sidney Herbert who went to the War Office in December 1852. Granting of Cabinet rank depended more on the personality of the office holder than the importance of the War Office. Fox Maule waited five years after 1846 before gaining entry, on the excuse that the Cabinet was "more than usually full": in reality, with mainly junior ministerial experience, he was serving probation. Before the Crimean War there was, therefore, no clear policy about this matter, in which royal influence held little sway. As Lord Aberdeen planned his government, to no avail the Queen wrote: "The Secretary at War ought properly to be left out of the Cabinet for the well-working of the Army".[15]

Proliferation of the Secretary at War's duties and his incomplete constitutional power brought him into collision not only with the Horse Guards, but with other government ministers. The unedifying battle between War Office and Horse Guards, temporarily halted by the

Prince Regent's Minute in Council of 1812, was openly re-engaged in the two brief interregna in 1827 and once again in 1852, when no C-in-C existed. During the first of these periods, Palmerston exacerbated the situation by appearing at a review in military uniform, and during the second Prince Albert, referring to the earlier correspondence, declared: "I consider Lord Palmerston's letter (of 1811) as a mere attempt to arrogate supreme power for his Office, which rests on no foundation". Possibly influenced by Court distrust of Palmerston, the Prince's comment should be read in conjunction with that from Queen Victoria three months before seeking to exclude the Secretary at War from the Cabinet: recognition of such War Office control would weaken the Crown's mythical hold over the Army. Curiously, and almost simultaneously, Colonel Richard Airey remarked on Benjamin Hawes' prickly manner at the War Office in commenting to Sir George Brown: "Entre nous he is afraid of his old friends thinking that he is lowering the prerogative of the Secretary of War's Department, and yielding to the dictation and guidance of the Military Authorities at the Horse Guards". Such sensitivity was neither Hawes' preserve nor exhibited solely in dealings with the Horse Guards. When Secretary at War, Lord Howick hastened a testy missive to the War Department, demanding to know why a regiment had been moved from Halifax, Nova Scotia, into Canada without prior reference to him.[16]

The unsatisfactory nature of the Secretary at War's political position resulted in endeavours to rationalise, and extend still more, his duties. Both the Richmond and Howick royal commissions wanted the powers of the post defined and expanded, and the Secretary at War made independent attempts on his own behalf. Queen Victoria opposed Sir George Grey's suggestion that in future only the Secretary at War should sign the commissions of army officers, tartly concluding: "The Secretary at War speaks in his Memorandum of his responsibility to Parliament with respect to allowing Appointments to go on; the Queen apprehends that his responsibility does not extend beyond the appropriation of the money voted by Parliament for the use of her Army". Four years later Prince Albert, identifying another attempt by the War Office to gain power, similarly wrote: "The Secretary at War has no authority whatever except over money". Three weeks before the Crimean War commenced, Sidney Herbert, arguing that the Army was more economically managed than the Navy through the Secretary at War's financial powers, wanted them extended to the whole of the Ordnance. These manoeuvres were in vain; the doomed office secured no reprieve.[17]

As yet, its expiration was not widely foreseen. The Secretary of State for War and the Colonies, occupied with administration of extensive colonial possessions, delegated to the Secretary at War much of his military business, which inevitably built up as the War progressed. In practice, the War Office supervised the hospital services (for whose effectiveness at least one later commentator has castigated Sidney Herbert), organised the despatch of Florence Nightingale and her nurses to Scutari, was involved in the formation of the ill-fated Ambulance Corps and controlled the Purveyor's Department in Turkey.[18] Sidney Herbert, when out of office, claimed that his interests in these matters were mainly financial, but in Parliament James Whiteside acknowledged the Secretary at War's responsibility for medical arrangements at the Front, and Herbert himself had accepted military volunteers from Chatham for service as orderlies in the Scutari hospitals. Moreover, the Secretary at War arranged for clerical reinforcements to join the Purveyor's Department.[19]

As the War opened there were few bad omens for the War Office, which seemed destined to discharge a truly vital role in army administration. Lord Grey took the opportunity to resuscitate one of his best-loved schemes. Proposing a board system for the Army similar to that of the Admiralty Board, he suggested that, if this were unacceptable, the Secretary at War should have "the functions of his office altered and enlarged". Before the end of the month Lord John Russell had once more doused this project with icy discouragement. He objected to transferring part of the Secretary of State for War's powers to the War Office and, with splendid disregard for reality, maintained that the Secretary at War "receives his orders from the C-in-C". Russell went on to describe utter confusion in army administration and to propose three possible solutions: the Secretary at War should gain full control of army affairs and become a fourth Secretary of State, a Military Board under the Secretary of State for War and the Colonies should be established or, thirdly, the Secretary of State should himself assume overall control of the C-in-C, Secretary of War, Ordnance and Commissariat Departments. In a letter to Lord Aberdeen, the Prime Minister, he favoured the latter solution, which would reduce the power of the Secretary at War. A further memorandum on the last day of May re-emphasised this preference, but with an important modification: the Secretary of State for War and the Colonies was to control the C-in-C, Ordnance and Commissariat Departments, but the Secretary at War would "retain his present function". Nothing came of Lord John's proposals, although reduction of the Secretary at War's responsibility had now been broached and seriously discussed. Of more significance was the fact that ministers treated the question as one of administrative efficiency without reference to experiences in the War. Six days later, yet again Grey returned to his favourite theme. He wanted "an Army Board, presided over by a Cabinet Minister of the same rank as the First Lord of the Admiralty, and composed principally of officers of the Army". If this could not be achieved, the task should be fulfilled by the Secretary at War with "four or five additional subordinate officers of the same rank as the present Deputy Secretary at War". It all remained a pipe dream.[20]

For the opening months of the War had exposed two serious political problems. With the Secretary of State for War and the Colonies (the Duke of Newcastle) immediately responsible for conduct of the campaign in the Lords, the Secretary at War needed to answer for his actions in the Commons. Looking back on this period Sidney Herbert, with a hint of self-excuse, complained: "Though I had no authority in the management of the war, I was supposed to have". It might be argued, however, that if the Secretary at War could not adequately speak about military administration in time of war, the justification for his office required careful examination. In the second place the inevitable weight of material, which now occupied the Secretary of State for War and the Colonies, determined that a fourth Secretary of State, concerned only with "War", should be created. Once this occurred, early in June 1854, the War Office could expect to come under political attack. Within days Lord Hardinge disclosed that the incumbent was aware of potential danger: "Sidney Herbert is uneasy — the Secretary at War will never again have a seat in the Cabinet — his position is greatly reduced in importance".[21]

Before that month closed, Lord Dudley Stuart reasoned that a Secretary at War was now unnecessary. Shortly afterwards Sir John Pakington, declaring the position "anomalous", expressed surprise that the Secretary at War's office should continue. Sidney Herbert leapt to his own defence. He contended that the Secretary at War's position did not revolve around responsibility delegated by the Secretary of State, but primarily involved financial duties deputed by the Treasury. The Secretary at War was important in ensuring "economy and efficiency in the administration of the Army" and not "useless", as Pakington declared. Most emphatically, the post should not be abolished; and, furthermore, both the Secretary for War and the Secretary at War ought to sit in the Cabinet. With this vigorous counter-attack Herbert staved off immediate peril, as he had apparently done before: Lord John Russell asserted that exclusion of the Secretary at War from the final version of his plan for administrative reorganisation in May had been forced on him by opposition from Sidney Herbert.[22]

The matter was not seriously re-opened for another four months. Early in November Russell gave notice of hostile intent: "I have come to the conclusion that you cannot frame the Estimates for next year on the basis of having both a Secretary of State and Secretary at War". A fortnight later he unequivocally wrote: "I do not think a Secretary at War can be maintained together with a Secretary of State for War", claiming that "Sidney Herbert has, in the fairest and handsomest manner, said nearly the same thing". His main argument was that their duties overlapped to the point of confusion, and he went on to suggest that the office of Secretary at War be abolished with the Secretary of State moving to the Commons. This plan would result in both abolition of the Secretary at War's office and removal of the current Secretary of State (Newcastle), who was in the Lords. To meet the latter contingency, Russell proposed that Lord Palmerston should become Secretary of State for War. Hence his "reform" seemed based less on administrative necessity than political intrigue, aimed at ousting the Peelite Newcastle from office.[23]

Aberdeen professed shock at Russell's latest stratagem, which he found "so unexpected". Within three days he had recovered enough to pen a cogent reply. Agreeing that the two offices "cannot be maintained together ... as at present constituted", he nevertheless believed that a Secretary of State always in the Commons would be "objectionable in principle and might be inconvenient in practice". During the Napoleonic Wars, the Secretary at War had sat in the Commons, with the Secretary of State in the Lords, so the situation was not unique. Aberdeen believed that Russell's proposal implied censure on Newcastle and would be resented by Cabinet colleagues, but the main point of disapproval must be that the combined duties of Secretary for War and Secretary at War would be too onerous for one man. He therefore concluded: "I do not perceive the immediate necessity for the abolition of Herbert's office".[24] Lord John refused to be silenced and repeated his original arguments, adding an objection to the Secretary at War moving the Estimates because in wartime the Secretary for War should have full "authority to control other Departments". To this Aberdeen replied in turn that he could not "honestly recommend" such a change, because it was "not absolutely necessary ... (and would) only tend to weaken the Government". Naturally Aberdeen was concerned with maintenance of the coalition, fearing its disintegration if other Peelites resigned should Newcastle lose office. Russell remained dissatisfied, and informed the Prime Minister that he "must propose to the Cabinet that the office of Minister of War should absorb that of Secretary at War and that the office should, for the present at least, be held by a member of the House of Commons".[25]

Within a week Russell knew that he had failed. Popular clamour about conditions for the troops in the Crimea was now demanding more attention from ministers, but a more fundamental blow for Russell's hopes occurred when Palmerston supported retention of the War Office under the Secretary at War. Like Aberdeen, he thought the combined work too much for a single minister. Not surprisingly, given pre-occupation with the war effort, potential difficulty over removing Newcastle and the disapproval of Aberdeen and Palmerston, the Cabinet rejected Lord John's proposals as "quite untenable". Prince Albert wrote that "the universal feeling of the Cabinet seemed to be one of indignation ... at Lord John's conduct", for apparently he made it clear that his primary objective was not administrative reform, but removal of Aberdeen from office.[26]

However, the Secretary at War's post did not long survive. Despite his defence three months earlier, almost certainly calculated on the strength of known opposition to Russell's scheme and with one eye directed towards support for himself in the impending political storm, Lord Palmerston did not appoint a Secretary at War to his government in February 1855. Before the omission could be finalised, Sidney Herbert had to be placated with an alternative Cabinet post. On 4 February Palmerston announced his intention, by writing to Herbert: "I want to merge the office of Secretary at War in that of Secretary of State for War. Will you take the Home Department?" On the following day, after an interview at which Palmerston formally kissed hands, Queen Victoria wrote: "Lord Panmure will go to the War Office, or be Secretary for War, the offices of Secretary for War and at War being ultimately consolidated". Immediate uncertainty ended when, on 7 February, Herbert opted for the Colonial not Home Office, leaving Palmerston free to give Panmure the War Department. Nevertheless, even after the new Cabinet had been completed, the fate of the War Office remained undecided, for Palmerston told the Queen that the Secretary at War's office had been left vacant "pending consideration as to whether and how that office might be consolidated with that of the Secretary of State for the War Department".[27]

The United Service Gazette quickly welcomed this development: "We take it for granted ... (that) this is the first step towards that amalgam and concentration of many authorities in one, which has been so long desired". But no perceptible moves were made to consolidate the War Office and War Department, and correspondence with the former continued, to which the Deputy Secretary at War attended. In August 1855, Augustus Stafford complained that the "radical changes ... had not (been) defined with sufficient distinctness", demanding to know whether the Secretary of State for War was to continue as Secretary at War indefinitely.[28]

In the event abolition of the office did not formally occur until May 1863, though no separate Secretary at War was appointed after the fall of Aberdeen's government. Disasters at the front had very little direct effect on its disappearance, the wheedling of self-interested politicians during the first week of February 1855 was of greater significance. Sidney Herbert and Lord John Russell were the key figures in this five-day verbal ballet. Once Herbert had accepted another Cabinet post, the way lay open for reorganisation. As the Duke of Newcastle declined to serve under Palmerston, fear that rearrangement of appointments would adversely reflect on him, and so cost the new Prime Minister Peelite support, evaporated. But Palmerston was virtually bound to include in his Cabinet the whig leader Russell, who seems likely to have bargained support for partial acceptance of his reform plan of November 1854 — without the Secretary of State for War in the Commons. Although Russell's precise rôle may be in doubt, sufficient evidence exists to indicate that the destiny of the War Office was determined by political considerations in London, only tenuously connected with winter experiences in the Crimea.[29]

The Secretary of State for War and the Colonies

> The lamentable results which have attended our present expedition . . . [are] solely to be attributed to the want of proper control by a single Minister over every Department of the Army. (Lord Panmure, 1855).[30]

Historically the junior Secretary of State, like other holders of that office, the Secretary of State for War and the Colonies received his appointment by letters patent. After 1782, there were two Secretaries of State, for Home and Foreign affairs, with the former managing the War Department. In 1794, the year after war with France began, William Pitt created a separate Secretary of State for War, despite opposition from Henry Dundas, the first holder of the appointment. Dundas argued that as "all modern wars are a contention of purse . . . the Minister of Finance (the Prime Minister) must be the Minister of War" and that a War Minister could not "superintend the detail of the execution of operations", which constituted a firm Cabinet responsibility. He did, however, take the office, to which four years later responsibility for the colonies was added. The Secretary of State for War and the Colonies had been born. His duties were never closely defined, which caused the embarrassing, politico-military exchanges between War Department, War Office and Horse Guards of the future. Indeed, to later eyes the very origin of the post was steeped in obscurity. When Prime Minister and questioned by Queen Victoria, Lord Melbourne could not pinpoint the year of its creation, venturing 1793 and, only after consultation with the librarian at Holland House, correcting this to 1794. Even then he believed that the new minister immediately assumed control of "Colonial and Military Affairs".[31]

The Home Secretary's retention of control over reserve forces in the United Kingdom and his interest in national defence detracted from the new Secretary of State's military responsibility. Addition of colonial business further hampered his ability to deal efficiently with the Army, for which the appointment of a second Under Secretary of State in 1809 could not compensate. After 1815 expansion of overseas territories brought an unprecedented weight of correspondence to the Secretary of State's table, so that, at a time of rising tension in the Near East between 1852 and 1854, thirteen out of sixteen boxes in the Newcastle Papers refer to colonial business.[32]

Despite practical difficulties in their execution, however, many of the Secretary of State's military duties were clear. He controlled colonial reserve forces, such as the Gambia Militia and Maltese Fencibles, supervised out-pensioners overseas, appointed and corresponded with military commanders in the colonies.[33] Foreign campaigns were conducted under his direction, which Henry Dundas had thought both unwise and impracticable, so the Secretary of State for War and the Colonies enjoyed political oversight of all line and reserve troops outside the United Kingdom, except those in the army of the East India Company. Through him proposals for the annual army establishment, military recommendations for the Order of the Bath and important command appointments were submitted formally to the Crown, and the organisation of any force proceeding abroad was ultimately subject to his approval. In theory, though not in practice, he was obliged to consult neither the C-in-C nor Master-General of the Ordnance on these matters. Indisputably, he was the minister who discharged the major responsibility for army administration.[34]

As the Duke of Newcastle emphasised before the Sevastopol Select Committee, commanders of an army abroad invariably corresponded with the Secretary of State not the C-in-C at the Horse Guards and, in practice, the War Department's responsibility for the conduct of the Crimean expedition was accepted. When conditions for the troops fell short of expectation, Newcastle found himself reproved by distraught relatives, and throughout the campaign both he and his successor, Lord Panmure, fully exercised his authority. In the Queen's name, Newcastle appointed Lord Raglan "to command the army ordered for service in Turkey in support of her Ally", stating unequivocally that "your correspondence will be conducted direct with me". Aiming to leave Raglan "free to act according to conscience", he nevertheless continued: "I do not claim for myself freedom from responsibility for what you may do". Quite independently, Lord Hardinge underlined this accepted position in Parliament and privately to Richard Airey.[35]

Although Newcastle might claim to allow Raglan certain freedom of action — "much must necessarily be left to the free exercise of your own judgement and decision on the spot" — he issued comprehensive instructions from the beginning, showing his determination to exert actual, not theoretical, supervision. Raglan was instructed to go to Unkiar Skelessi, leaving 5,000 troops at Gallipoli under Sir George Brown, and from there to send forward troops to prepare "lines of defence in front of Constantinople between the Black Sea and the Sea of Marmara". He must "consult" with the French "upon all occasions" and Omar Pasha (the Turkish commander) so as "not to interfere with his operations". Vice-Admiral Dundas, in command of the British fleet, would "co-operate . . . so far as the means at his disposal will enable him to do so". Similarly, strict instructions were issued to Brown, who commanded the British advance contingent, to remain at Gallipoli. So Sir George refused an urgent plea from the British Ambassador (Lord Stratford de Redcliffe), in view of Russian successes on the Danube, to move to Constantinople, "seeing that I am under specific instructions" from the Duke of Newcastle. Throughout the War, the Secretary of State maintained a sharp watch on the state of the British force by ensuring that regular returns, concerning everything from sickness to clothing, were transmitted to him.[36]

Supervision of the campaign meant constant attention to strategy in the field. In this the Secretary of State did not shirk his duty, however irksome his vigilance might appear to military officers. Newcastle quickly made it plain that the latitude afforded to Lord Raglan would be in tactical not strategic matters. On the same day that Raglan was officially appointed to command the Expeditionary Force, Newcastle also sent him a secret despatch, which laid down that his "first duty" should be the defence of Constantinople. But if no positive Russian threat to it developed, he was to prepare offensive operations with the aim of taking Sevastopol and destroying the enemy fleet. In preparation for the latter contingency, he should make "careful but secret inquiry into the present amount and condition of the Russian Force in the Crimea and the strength of the Fortress of Sevastopol". In this document, alternative plans for Allied strategy were examined: from the beginning, therefore, offensive action against the Crimea had been contemplated. Less than a fortnight later, referring to this private letter, Newcastle pointed out that Russian columns had come to a halt along the Danube and pressed for an Allied advance to Varna in Bulgaria. "We must endeavour to do what is both militarily and politically right", he argued, and this advance would impress the Turks. Early in May Newcastle became more ambitious in declaring that the British should move north of the Balkan range with Varna on their right. It is against this background of advice, and especially the secret despatch of 10 April, that the Cabinet communication of 29 June 1854, transmitted by Newcastle to Raglan, should be read. Now that the Russians had retreated across the Danube, the War took on "a new character", and the contingency plan of April must be put into effect. Due to health risks, the Allies should not follow the enemy through the Dobrutscka swamps, but invade the Crimea before enemy troops could reinforce it via the Perekop peninsula. If "upon mature reflection" Raglan ruled against the invasion it might be postponed, but the Government would "regret" this, and the Cabinet emphasised that a "safe and honorable (sic)" peace was impossible without reduction of Sevastopol. The Government's strategy involved four elements: an attack on Sevastopol; occupation of the Perekop peninsula to deny reinforcements for the Crimean garrison; a naval blockade of the Sea of Azov; and Turkish action in the Caucasus. A private letter to Raglan by Newcatle expressed his own complete agreement with these plans and personal determination that the project against Sevastopol in particular should succeed. Tactical arrangements, however, were left to Raglan.[37]

Troop dispositions, which could affect strategic capability, were subject to the Secretary of State's approval. Those carried out after the Battle of Inkerman were formally sanctioned by Newcastle; and early in the new year Palmerston acknowledged the War Department's responsibility in this respect by suggesting to the Secretary of State certain redeployments in the Crimea. On the same day Newcastle proposed reorganisation of the entire Allied dispositions before Sevastopol, because French forces there were double the number of British. Hours before John Roebuck's Parliamentary motion effectively brought down the Coalition, Newcastle noted that his plans for reorganisation had not envisaged General Bosquet's solution of French occupation of the extreme right of the Allied line, leaving the British a rocky perch in the centre. During the political turmoil which followed, this latter development could not be avoided; but Newcastle's successor, Panmure, similarly kept a weather eye on strategic matters. In March 1855 he expressed concern at the slow progress of the siege, success of which was "by no means certain", and proposed more widespread activity to attain victory, particularly a combined Allied attack on Kerch. A month later he revealed that the French Minister of War, Marshal Vaillant, also entertained doubts as to the outcome of continued bombardments of Sevastopol and that the British and French governments were seriously considering field operations in the near future. Panmure backed the French Emperor's plan for three Allied armies: one to stay on the southern heights before Sevastopol, the second to skirt its eastern suburbs and link with a third advancing south from Eupatoria to complete investment of the naval port. Early in June, repeating a telegraphic message of four days before, he wrote: "No time should be lost in making a movement against the enemy ... either by the Chernaya (sic) or by cutting off the enemy's communication with Simpheropol". In the Crimea neither men nor equipment were available for such an ambitious venture, which owed more to the political needs of Napoleon III than military commonsense. The project for field operations in Spring 1855 showed the Secretary of State's concern with strategy: it also demonstrated the futility of military planning from a distance of 3,000 miles.[38]

The Secretary of State for War practised his authority over the expedition in other ways. He overruled Lord Raglan's vehement protests and allowed Lieutenant-General Beatson to raise a force of 4,000 Turkish irregular cavalry. Lord Panmure stressed that he had the power to dismiss Raglan's personal staff without the Field-Marshal's approval, required the expeditionary commander to explain Allied lack of progress against Sevastopol and took Raglan to task because "your Lordship's reports to my Department are too scanty". Queen Victoria, with justification, complained that despatches were sent to the Crimea before a copy had been submitted to her, and Newcastle believed that, had he been permitted to visit the front while Secretary of State, "the authority of the office ... (and) overruling power" would have "put many things right". Newcastle's optimistic assessment of his own battlefield ability was, perhaps fortunately, not put to the test, but his ultimate control could not be doubted. It was not unreasonable that Lord Hardinge should congratulate him on the success of Allied landings at Calamita Bay.[39]

The Secretary of State's power was not unbridled, although Lord Howick concluded that he had "an authority in all matters relating generally to the Army". Constitutionally, he was unable to act independently of the Cabinet, which did not always endorse his advice. Newcastle submitted Hardinge's recommendation that Raglan be appointed to command the Expeditionary Force, but made his own disapproval clear, as Raglan lacked "experience of the personnel of the army". Evidently Newcastle's Cabinet colleagues disagreed with him, for three days later he informed the Queen that "the Cabinet warmly approved the appointment of Lord Raglan to command the expedition now preparing for the East". Two years later Lord Panmure was taken to task for announcing in the Lords that the pay of troops in the Crimea would be doubled, without having previously "uttered a syllable" to the Prime Minister or the Cabinet, despite a "standing rule" to the contrary. As Palmerston pointed out to the Queen, such independent action "by ministers presiding over departments" would result in "the administration ... (becoming) an anarchy, and the affairs of the State would fall into confusion". And over the press the Secretary of State had no control. Perturbed by the revelation of detailed military information in newspaper reports, Newcastle might only approach the editors of all morning papers for their co-operation in the national interest. To John Delane, he wrote: "I fear the heavy loss of general officers at Inkerman may be attributed to the information conveyed by the correspondent of *The Times* that the white plumes were worn not by Commissariat officers, but by generals". Held responsible for the conduct of the campaign, the Secretary of State nevertheless lacked any means of controlling press reports about it.[40]

Such was the acknowledged extent of the War Department's control over the Army, however, that even before war broke out demands were made for a military figure to be appointed Secretary of State for War and the Colonies. Put forward in the press, notably by *The Times* and *The United Service Gazette*, they did not visibly abate during the War and were based upon a fear that civilian ministers, with inadequate appreciation of the profession of arms, could never properly direct troops. Specific mention was made of France, where the Minister of War was normally a senior serving officer, and more oblique references appeared to countries where "generals were preferred to civilians". The Duke of Newcastle's handling of arrangements for the expedition appeared to justify these comments. He ordered the embarkation of 4,000 troops at Malta for the east, admitting no "accurate information" of the number of vessels available for their transportation; and, similarly, he "hoped accommodation under roof may be procured for the large portion, if not the whole of the 10,000 men" despatched to the island in February 1854. Practical problems of transport and supply seemed utterly foreign to the minister, whose lack of military experience led him to underestimate difficulties in the field. When pressed for material to build winter quarters, he replied that the capture of Sevastopol would solve the problem. But these incidents only suggested Newcastle's inadequacy: they did not prove that all civilians made poor Ministers of War. In fact, in the context of constitutional development and civil-military relations, at that time a military Minister of War would have been unacceptable.[41]

The Secretary of State's concern with "War" and "the Colonies", more especially as responsibility for the latter had shown such marked increase, meant that supervision of the Army devolved on the Secretary at War, as the Seymour Committee recognised. While no major expeditionary force was in being, serious problems did not arise, and the inability of the Secretary of State fully to deal with military matters was largely disguised. The expedition to Turkey posed searching questions and brought several difficulties more sharply into perspective. Six weeks before the official declaration of war, regiments began to sail for the Mediterranean and Whitehall swarmed with officers seeking employment in the coming fray. Political attention, therefore, began to centre on the War Department. During the Parliamentary debate of 2 March, Sidney Herbert called for closer co-operation between administrative authorities, and Lord John Russell also indicated support for reform. A fortnight later Lieutenant-Colonel Mundy was appointed as an additional Under Secretary of State to handle all the War Department's military correspondence. Lord Grey remained unconvinced that the administrative machine could satisfactorily organise the campaign, which now seemed unavoidable, and took the opportunity to initiate further discussion of the subject, concentrating on responsibilities of the Secretary of State. Early in April, Lord Aberdeen feared Grey's "intention of bringing forward plans for the better administration of the army". Although Aberdeen admitted that "some reforms may probably be requisite", he deplored hasty action: "It will be necessary to be cautious in giving any encouragement to these projects". Prince Albert was less phlegmatic. In an interview with him, Grey declared that the only way to improve army administration would be to establish "a Civil Board ... under the control of the House of Commons". The Prince viewed this as a threat to "the prerogative of the Crown" and urged the Government to take it "seriously". However in essence Grey's plan was hazy, and during the interview he gave the impression of emotional wildness: in Prince Albert's words, "he continued eagerly to decry the present system, the gross ignorance of Military men, their incapacity to reform the Army and his hope to bring forward facts which would startle the world". Lord Grey's intemperate language was not, for him, extraordinary and it indicated a basic incapacity for clear thought and political timing, which had hitherto marred his reform efforts. Prince Albert's remark, as Lord John Russell sought to form a government in 1846, appeared valid: "In or out of office he (Grey) seemed to be made a difficulty".[42]

Aberdeen's warning of his impending action proved both timely and accurate. In Parliament, on 7 April, Grey moved for the production of "certain papers" to show "what changes, if any, have been made in the department of the Secretary of State for War and the Colonies", believing that these papers would reveal the urgent need for "much greater" change. He continued by yet again calling for administrative consolidation, emphasising that the Secretary of State's "paramount authority" over the Army was limited by independent Treasury control of the Commissariat. It was "physically impossible", however, for one man to deal with colonial and military matters, maintaining that the Duke of Newcastle had agreed that "under the existing system the Secretary of State for War and the Colonies could not possibly give sufficient attention to all his duties". The logical conclusion to these arguments would have been a proposal to divide responsibility for "War" and "the Colonies", with Commissariat control transferred to a Secretary for War. But once more, Grey became a victim of his own personality. After a long digression about his experiences when Secretary at War, he suggested that the responsibilities of the Secretary of State for War, C-in-C, Secretary at War, Master-General and Paymaster-General be gathered "into one great office ... (under) a principal Secretary of State". This would put the responsibility for estimates and expenditure under the same roof. The appointment of an additional Under Secretary of State (Mundy) had been "altogether inadequate to meet the difficulty" and would only "mitigate the evil ... (not) remove it". He positively rejected the elevation of an existing officer to this post. Referring to the Admiralty, he favoured a similar board system for the Army, with a Minister of War in place of the First Lord of the Admiralty.

Although this was a variation of a well-worn theme, Grey had thus put forward a worthwhile plan. Instead of closing his speech then, he proceeded to cloud the issue. Arguing that the Admiralty system eliminated the potential difficulty of board members with equal status, he pointed out that the First Lord was a Cabinet Minister, but not a Secretary of State: at home, in war or on colonial duty, the appropriate Secretary of State directed naval operations. As this arrangement had proved satisfactory, Grey supported it for the Army and opposed creation of a fourth Secretary of State to deal with military affairs: this explained why, earlier in his exposition, he had not proposed division of "War" and "the Colonies". Grey seemed incapable of leaving the House with a simple proposition. Such a board might be "objectionable". If so, the Secretary at War "with the function of his office altered and enlarged" could become the fourth minister. In anticipating an objection that this would transfer control of the Army to the House of Commons, which some would perceive as "unsatisfactory . . . an invasion of the Royal prerogative", he pursued another diversion, this time into the realms of political theory and constitutional practice. In this the administrative aspirations of the Crown and the office of the C-in-C figured prominently. At long last, after covering thirty-three columns of Hansard, he moved his address.[43]

At root Grey had proposed an alternative: an army board, similar to the Board of Admiralty, with a Cabinet Minister at its head or, with shades of his Commission's report seventeen years previously, a Secretary at War with enlarged powers. Unfortunately he had grossly befogged the central issue by fringe excursions into the memoirs of an ex-War Office minister and the theory and practice of war, the latter with examples going back some 200 years and all liberally spiced with extravagant condemnations of the present administrative system. It was therefore comparatively simple to detract from Grey's actual proposals. Rising to reply, the Duke of Newcastle concentrated on refuting suggestions of current administrative confusion and attacking points of detail. Turning, like Grey, to history for support, he referred to the conclusion of various commissions and committees, even quoting the Duke of Wellington's approval for Treasury control of the Commissariat. In fact, Newcastle devoted a considerable passage of his speech to defending the Commissariat and only after an extensive preamble did he briefly look at Grey's proposals. Because Grey did not go into the idea of a fourth Secretary of State "at any length", he too would not "enlarge upon it". The concept of a more powerful Secretary at War he rejected as an "unconstitutional arrangement", for the reasons which Grey feared, and a board would merely be "cloaking and avoiding" the responsibility of departmental heads. He drummed up military reinforcements against the board by suggesting that a civilian head might distribute army patronage and require distinguished officers to act as his subordinates: once more, the name of Wellington was produced to emphasise the full horror of this possible humiliation. Although *The United Service Gazette* applauded Grey's efforts, in practice absence of lucidity on 7 April determined that no immediate action would be taken to deal with the Secretary of State's crushing burden of work. Perhaps the most interesting aspect of these exchanges was the miniscule attention paid to division of his labour and the prospect of appointing another Secretary of State exclusively for the Army.[44]

For this matter very shortly afterwards preoccupied government ministers. On 24 April Lord John Russell described the administrative system as "defective" and called for "control over the military departments (to) be made more general and more effective" in the cause of "more rapidity and unity". He rejected extension of the powers of the Secretary at War and also a board system, proposing that responsibility for "War" and "the Colonies" be divided. During the first week in May Russell complained that the Prime Minister had not put these views to the Cabinet, emphasising that for the scheme to be viable support from Palmerston and Sidney Herbert was necessary. Almost simultaneously, *The Times* urged creation of one responsible War Minister and repeated that call later in the month. Evidently Russell's promptings persuaded Aberdeen to discuss the matter in Cabinet, and towards the end of May several of its members produced favourable memoranda on the subject. Crucially, Sidney Herbert favoured one Secretary of State to supervise the whole of army administration, and Palmerston evidently did not disagree.[45] On 28 May Aberdeen informed the Queen that the Cabinet had discussed the possible appointment of two separate Secretaries of State and that, when it was raised in Parliament the following day, Russell would agree that the subject was under consideration. The Prime Minister added pessimistically: "This will not satisfy the Military Reformers, but it would remove the evil which really exists and would probably prevent any serious pressure". Two days later separation had been decided. Aberdeen explained to the Queen that it had been "rendered indispensable by the accumulated labour of the present time" and if carried out quickly would forestall "any desire of further changes for some time to come". He wrote in a similar vein to Lord John Russell. One day later Lord John produced a detailed memorandum on his views concerning the proposed change and agreed with Aberdeen that it might be "unjust" to remove the Duke of Newcastle from the War Department. Two problems now remained to be solved: after legal advice, the practical means of accomplishing the plan, and which ministers would fill the War and Colonial offices.[46]

Almost inevitably, due to their prolonged nature, knowledge of these discussions could not be confined to Cabinet members; and agitation during the first week of June, not least by the persistent Grey, to some extent embarrassed the Government. In the Commons Henry Drummond questioned Lord John Rusell "respecting the intention of the ministers to place all the military resources of the kingdom under one individual", which, he later claimed, met with applause from both sides of the House. Then, and in private correspondence, Russell conveyed an impression that the Government intended no action. Drummond, therefore, sought Grey's advice about a resolution calling for one man to head "the Military Department of the Empire". In this post he would prefer a military figure (possibly Lord Raglan or Lord Seaton), but if a civilian proved unavoidable, he should have two Under Secretaries of State, one for military business (such as the stationing of forces), the other for civil (like provision of clothing). Drummond wanted responsibility for the Militia, Yeomanry and internal defences of the country to come under the new minister, envisaging abolition of the posts of Secretary of State for War, Master-General of the Ordnance, Paymaster of the Forces and Judge Advocate General. He did not accept that such a reorganisation would be impossible in time of war, for only "the clerks who have hitherto managed these matters should be placed under the new minister for military affairs".

Grey did not eschew this opportunity to re-state his opinions. He replied to Drummond: "Our Army never will be properly managed until the administration of its affairs is simplified by the consolidation of the various departments among which this branch of the public business is now divided". He went on to complain that the C-in-C, Secretary at War, Master-General of the Ordnance (with the Board of Ordnance) and Commissariat Department were "all independent of one another" and the system could only work effectively if brought "under one head in one office". Grey rejected division of responsibility for "War" and "the Colonies" as a solution to the problem of separate administrative authority, and he argued that the Army would more willingly submit to a board of military men than a single civilian minister. He therefore favoured "an Army Board, presided over by a Cabinet Minister of the same rank as the First Lord of the Admiralty and composed principally of officers of the Army", but, in default of this, the Secretary at War "with four or five additional subordinate officers of the same rank as the present Deputy Secretary at War" should assume overall control.

None of this was new: in fact, the words were almost precisely those used by him to Parliament in April and his scheme relied heavily upon the recommendations of the Richmond and Howick commissions twenty years before. In one respect, however, Grey had shifted his ground in the past two months. He now saw the Secretary of State for War and the Colonies as the minister with oversight of his proposed board. Grey then revealed that he was unaware of the speed with which events were proceeding. For he cautioned Drummond against precipitate action, advising him to make no further move until the next session of Parliament to enable "a little more time to enquire into the subject". Long before that time government measures had pre-empted him.[47]

Even as Grey and Drummond were exchanging letters, the Cabinet's plan for reform was finalised. No doubt fearing trouble from them and anxious to act before Cabinet support could melt away, early in June Lord Aberdeen wrote: "It will be necessary speedily to settle the mode in which it is to be carried out", revealing that neither a precise measure nor timetable for its introduction had been settled. Six days later,

Aberdeen told Prince Albert that merely a division of the office of Secretary of State for War and the Colonies was intended, without "creation of any new power". Privately, the Prince lamented that the proposal had been "carried without a definite plan, leaving everything to the future". On the following day, in Parliament, Lord Derby referred to "the important changes now supposed to be in the contemplation of the Government, in the creation of a new office of Secretary of State for the War Department, separate from that of the Secretary for the Colonies", asking for a definition of the proposed new minister's duties. Apart from a short statement that "the functions of the Secretary of War will be those which are at present exercised by the Secretary of State for War and the Colonies in the War Department", and that he would have "nothing whatever to do with control of the finance department" of the Army, Aberdeen was "not prepared" to give a definition. But he did reveal that the division "will be carried into effect before the next meeting of the House".

Hoping, even at this late stage, to affect details of the change, Lord Panmure and Lord Derby rose in succession to make a number of points. Panmure had "no desire to see things done hastily: but if the office of Minister of War is to be established, the officer who fills it must have a department as well as a name". He should take charge of all army finances, the Commissariat and the Militia, and "the Ministry of War (should be) a department that will exist in time of peace, as well as in time of war, and that will, at all times, have control over everything connected with the military administration of the country". Derby queried whether, if the Minister of War had no control over finance and patronage (still exercised by the C-in-C), he would merely be a wartime office holder. Aberdeen declined a specific reply, seeking refuge in evasion. The new office would "add to the efficiency of the public service"; and "as for what may happen in time of peace, the noble Earl will, perhaps, have the goodness to wait until time of peace" before asking that particular question.[48]

Events outside the debating chambers decreed that Aberdeen could not be more forthcoming, even had he wished: government agreement over the new appointment proved very difficult to achieve and legal restrictions a complicating factor. When offered the Colonial Office, Sir George Grey made his acceptance conditional on the understanding "that the creation of a 4th (sic) Secretary of State is not to be the final change in the Administration of the army, but only the first step towards a consolidation under one head of the various departments concerned in the conduct of Military Affairs". Aberdeen claimed not to understand "exactly" what Sir George meant by "consolidation", but did state that any further change in military administration must be undertaken by the new Secretary of State for War, when finally appointed, and after Cabinet discussion. Disturbed by Grey's reaction, the Prime Minister first asked Russell if he would take the Colonial Office; then, on his refusal, suggested Lord Granville. Lord John countered by pointing out that, if Newcastle retained the War Department, both Secretaries of State would sit in the Lords which "would not be fair on the House of Commons". The next day, when Aberdeen faced Derby and Panmure in Parliament, Russell disclosed that the law officers had ruled against a new office holder sitting in the Commons.[49]

In the event Sir George Grey became Secretary of State for the Colonies in the Commons, and on 10 June 1854 a fourth Secretary of State came into existence; though the fears of Prince Albert and Lord Panmure were to some extent realised. The Duke of Newcastle, the Secretary of State for War, received no clear definition of his duties and later claimed to have had no office of his own until December. Two days after the Order in Council, he left the Colonial Office building and the following day complained to Lord Raglan of the "confusion of change of office", so that it was "impossible to give you any instructions" — perhaps an apt illustration of the casual manner in which this entire administrative exercise was conducted. *The United Service Gazette* showed considerable displeasure at the net result, suspecting a simple addition "to the number of officials through whose routine the public duty is perplexed and retarded", and Karl Marx concluded: "The only merit of the change is the creation of a new ministerial place".[50]

Contrary to Aberdeen's hopes, the measures seemed merely to whet the appetite of military reformers. Once a minister responsible solely for military affairs had been created, it followed that all relevant responsibility should accrue to his office. Within a month indications of further administrative rumblings could be detected. *The United Service Gazette* linked its criticism of the reorganisation with a renewed call for a military Minister of War, and Lord Grey wrote of "the new arrangement of the War Department, which I believe will do more harm than good". Early in July a plan to transfer the Militia from the Home Secretary to the Secretary of War was opposed by Palmerston, who argued that the Militia must be retained as a civilian bulwark against the regular Army. This argument could only be valid if the Army were politically irresponsible or control of the Militia passed out of civilian hands, rather than from one Secretary of State to another. Possibly Palmerston's opposition went no deeper than a reluctance, as Home Secretary, to see the prestige of his office marginally reduced by surrender of this control. Nevertheless, the Prime Minister agreed with him and no transfer took place. Shortly afterwards Lord John Russell took the opportunity in Parliament to review the whole spectrum of military administration. Noting a history of investigatory commissions and committees on the subject, he recalled that since establishment of the fourth Secretary of State, demands for administrative consolidation had only slightly receded. Considering whether "other changes with regard to the military departments" should be carried out, he referred particularly to demands for unity of all military departments under one Secretary of State. He reaffirmed that the Government had divided responsibility for "War" and "the Colonies", because it was "physically impossible . . . to keep these offices united". But he adamantly refused to countenance more upheaval "in time of war".[51]

One minor change did occur in the autumn, however, with the appointment of a second permanent Under Secretary of State for the War Department. The Duke of Newcastle noted that, when the fourth Secretary of State was created, the Treasury had agreed to two Under Secretaries of State: a military field officer to be permanent, "being necessary . . . for the transaction of business incidental to the present war and the conduct of the general Military Correspondence", and a second Under Secretary, "being required to undertake the Charge of the Civil and Miscellaneous Correspondence and to superintend and to be at the same time responsible for the discipline and management of the internal routine of the Establishment". This was approved by an Order in Council of 1 July, and Parliament agreed that the permanent Under Secretary of State should be a military officer, but ruled that the second be civilian, temporary and possibly a Member of Parliament liable to lose his post with a change of government. Under these circumstances nobody would fill the second under-secretaryship, and the Duke of Newcastle asked that it also be made a permanent post. He further argued that this development was necessary, "with the desire of making prospective and early provision for the completion of the final arrangements of this Establishment and especially for the removal of the Commissariat business from the superintendence of the Treasury to the control and supervision of the Secretary of State for War". It is possible that Newcastle's line of argument contained exaggeration to achieve effect, in view of his later claim that at this time he could not take over the Commissariat due to lack of office accommodation. Nevertheless, the Treasury acceded to his request, an Order in Council formalised the matter and on 23 November 1854 Mr. H. Roberts became the second permanent Under Secretary of State for the War Department.[52]

Meanwhile, despite his Parliamentary opposition to further War Department change in July, Lord John Russell again began dabbling in administrative reform, initiating his lengthy correspondence with Lord Aberdeen about extension of the Secretary for War's powers over all military departments including the War Office. Russell justified himself by referring to "the general efficiency of the public service . . . (and) the immediate requirements of the great war in which we are engaged", thus neatly reversing his previous argument that no additional changes could take place while the War lasted. Aberdeen opposed the scheme, especially the contention that the Secretary of State should always sit in the Commons, and rejected Russell's suggestion that Palmerston should displace Newcastle: in view of Palmerston's imminent replacement of Aberdeen, ironically Aberdeen held that the "laborious and complicated duties" of an enlarged War Department would be beyond such an old man. Russell met Aberdeen's objections in detail, suggesting that Sidney Herbert might become Paymaster-General and referring to the "vigour of his (Palmerston's) mind and body". He would compromise on none of his proposals, emphasising that Parliament had a right to expect final settlement of the Secretary for War's duties, which had remained indeterminate since June 1854. Maintaining that the present system allowed the Secretary of State's intention to be thwarted by other departments, he argued that the public good must be the overriding factor in all questions of political responsibility. Underlining need for a vigorous War Minister, he concluded his letter to Aberdeen on 28 November with something of a bizarre flourish: "A Cabinet is a cumbrous and unwieldy instrument of carrying on war — It can furnish suggestions, or make a decision upon a measure submitted to it, but it cannot administer". Aberdeen forbore to take up this point, contenting himself with a plea on behalf of the common weal. Interestingly, he based his opposition to permanent location of the Secretary for War in the Commons, not purely on the grounds that a suitable peer might thus be disqualified, but because in certain (unspecified) circumstances appointment of a military man might be desirable. Queen Victoria declared herself "perfectly horrified" by all this and, eventually, the Cabinet rejected Russell's proposals. Lord John was most unwilling to permit the matter to rest, but allowed himself to be persuaded by Lord Panmure that "the present was not a fitting time for his proposed changes". He reserved his option, however, to reintroduce the subject at a more opportune moment, which did not augur well for future administrative stability.[53] And within a short time, added mystery surrounding the origin and duties of the separate War Department came to light. In again pressing for production of all the relevant papers, Lord Grey "presumed" that an Order in Council had divided responsibility for "War" and "the Colonies". The Duke of Newcastle, in reply, claimed that no Order in Council had been issued: "The alteration had been effected by a somewhat similar document, a Declaration in Council", and "provisional" agreement had been reached between the two Secretaries of State as to their respective duties. Early in 1855, however, Lord Derby referred in the Lords to establishment of the War Department by an Order in Council of 10 June 1854 and Newcastle, who spoke immediately after him, did not contradict this, even though the area of discussion — the Secretary of State for War's responsibility and the office space at his disposal prior to December 1854 — was virtually the same as that covered earlier with Grey. Lord John Russell had evidently not been unjust in pointing to impenetrable mist engulfing the subject and suggesting that Parliament "would expect after six or seven months of deliberation a final arrangement of the War Department".[54]

While negotiations for a second Under Secretary of State and discussion of Russell's proposals were in progress, considerable attention was also devoted to the Secretary of State's control of the Commissariat. On establishment of the fourth Secretary of State, it had been intended at once to transfer the Commissariat to the Secretary for War, as Sir Charles Trevelyan noted in July. W. E. Gladstone rather acidly agreed a month later: "The only structural alteration as a result of the creation of the new War Ministry was the removal of the Commissariat from Treasury control, and this was decided upon in the interests not of military efficiency but of financial economy and administrative regularity". The Duke of Newcastle later held that he could not assume control of the Commissariat through lack of office accommodation. Yet as early as 30 June a Treasury Minute approved use of Pembroke House in Whitehall Gardens by the new War Department, and Sir Charles Trevelyan claimed that after 17 July the Secretary of War "was kept informed of the proceedings of the Commissariat and any wishes he expressed were immediately complied with". Trevelyan's statement, however, formed part of an attempt to exonerate the Treasury from responsibility for Commissariat blunders in the Crimea.[55]

Nevertheless, for whatever reason, the Duke of Newcastle had not taken formal charge of the Commissariat by November, and this was interpreted as a sign that the transfer remained in doubt. When in that month, possibly because a second permanent Under Secretary of State had been appointed, Newcastle prepared to assume control, Gladstone attempted to influence the matter. He argued that only supply duties of the Commissariat should be subject to the control of the Secretary for War and that all money business must stay with the Treasury. Newcastle demurred, holding that this would be only a half measure, guaranteed to cause added confusion. Although Gladstone concurred in the Minute, which officially transferred the Commissariat to the Secretary for War, he still believed that Newcastle had accepted special Treasury control of finance and that the War Department would defer to this. So an important administrative reform, carried out six months after originally intended, when finally completed left at least one Cabinet Minister unaware of its actual meaning.[56]

During December 1854 and January 1855 activity in another sphere resulted in assembly of a board under the control of the Secretary for War. Failing to survive the fall of Lord Aberdeen's ministry, it nevertheless suggested that a supervisory board in army administration, so long resisted, might work. Lord Hardinge's disclosure, that meetings concerning national defence took place at the Home Office in 1852 and 1853, showed that policy consultation between civilian ministers and military officers did occur. But neither a permanent organisation nor regular meetings existed for this purpose. Independently, the Clerk of the Ordnance said that "during a part" of 1854 weekly meetings were held at the War Department, which "the Secretary at War, the C-in-C, Sir Hew Ross, as representing the military portion of the Ordnance, and I as representing the civil portion of the Ordnance used to attend". Replying to a question concerning "the medium of communication between the Board (of Ordnance) and the Minister for War", Monsell implied that these meetings occurred under the direction of the Secretary of State for War — possibly, if the Duke of Newcastle did not acquire adequate office acommodation quickly, late in the year.[57]

Early in December 1854 Lord Palmerston and Sidney Herbert suggested that heads of department should meet for discussion at Newcastle's office. Herbert certainly intended to include the First Lord of the Admiralty, but Sir James Graham refused as this would have been contrary to the "central superintendence and authority of the First Lord". This was close to schemes proposed by Lord John Russell and Lord Grey in the past, though there is no written evidence that either supported Palmerston or Herbert in drawing up its outline. Towards the end of December, a Draft Order in Council was submitted to the Queen, declaring: "For the better despatch of the business to be transacted by the Military Departments under the said Secretay of State, namely the Horse Guards, the Ordnance Office and the War Office, it is advisable that the relation of the respective officers of those Departments with the Secretary of State should be more closely defined". It then laid down the members of a board to advise the Secretary of State, who was clearly placed in a superior position: "It is recommended to your Majesty that a Board should be constructed to which Board Your Majesty's Secretary of State would summon the C-in-C, the Master-General of the Ordnance and the Secretary at War to meet periodically at such intervals as shall seem to be necessary". Each member would produce a report of his department's business, the Secretary of State for War would "preside" and he alone determine the agenda of each meeting. The military Under Secretary of State for the War Department was to act as Secretary to the Board and take the minutes: only the Secretary of State could appoint a substitute, if any member were to be absent through "illness or other cause".[58]

Meetings of the Board took place on 3, 10 and 20 January 1855. The C-in-C missed the first, but the Secretary at War and Lieutenant-General of the Ordnance (vice the Master-General, Raglan) attended all three meetings, with Newcastle in the Chair and General Harding acting as Secretary. At each meeting, departmental reports were received, instructions issued to various authorities (including the Admiralty and Medical Board) and sub-committees set up to look into certain questions in depth. Hence the Board, copies of whose minutes were sent to the Queen, Lord Aberdeen and Lord John Russell (in his capacity as Lord President of the Council), did have an executive function.[59] Towards the end of the month, when the Government's survival was in doubt and another assault on army administration by Lord Grey predicted, efforts were made to regularise this *ad hoc* body. On 20 January Aberdeen informed the Queen about Cabinet approval for establishment of a formal board "under the presidency of the Secretary of State for War and including the C-in-C, Master-General and Secretary at War". He added that "in truth it would be a sort of extension of those military meetings which now unofficially take place". A day later he confirmed the Cabinet's determination to give the meetings "an official and compulsory character . . . speedily", and proposed to achieve this by first a Minute, then an Order in Council. Significantly, he hoped that another outburst from Lord Grey would thus be evaded.[60]

In fact, Grey did not provide the main stumbling block to success for, seizing on Cabinet support for the board, Lord John Russell swiftly advanced his own alternative scheme. If such a board were officially established parallel to the Board of Ordnance, two boards would exist, causing "complication, disorder and delay". Lord John supported the aim of consolidation and simplicity, but argued that there were only two ways of achieving it: "(To) give the Secretary of State the entire direction of all existing offices and Boards connected with the Army", or to create a board "with the Secretary of State at the Head, abolishing the Board of Ordnance and controlling the whole civil management of our military force". He favoured the latter, which would include the Secretary at War, Master-General, C-in-C, the officers of the Board of Ordnance and a Commissary-General subordinate to the Secretary for War. This was very close to the arrangement suggested by the Duke of Richmond's Royal Commission in 1833, differed from the board he himself had supported in December and gave rise once more to the suspicion that, having evidently agreed in the Cabinet to formalise Newcastle's existing board, he was seeking personal capital out of his colleagues' discomfort.[61]

To complicate matters further, Queen Victoria tried to bargain her approval of the draft Order in Council for other measures which she considered necessary. In return for her signature, although admitting that they were ill-defined, she sought an assurance that the C-in-C's powers would remain unchanged and also transfer of the Militia to the Secretary for War, without which "our Army system will still remain very incomplete". The next day Russell resigned from the Government, ostensibly because John Roebuck had given notice of a motion which "involves a censure of the War Department with which some of my colleagues are connected". This precipitated a major political crisis, and Palmerston thought that the resignation was really an attempt to force Lord John's ideas of administrative reform through the Cabinet.

Undeterred and in spite of the Government's precarious state, Newcastle pressed for formalisation of his own board, insisting that only in this way could "unity of action" be achieved.[62] Amid feverish activity, primarily concerned with the fate of the Coalition, Newcastle claimed that "the only official document" defining the duties of the Secretary of State for War was the Treasury Minute of 22 December 1854 giving him control of the Commissariat, and on 26 January Roebuck put forward his motion. Virtually at the ministry's last gasp, Grey launched his expected attack on the unsatisfactory development of the Secretary of State's office, establishment of which he thought "a crude and ill-digested" measure. To combat obvious deficiencies in its operation, he proposed a board under the presidency of the Secretary of State for War. Grey's sense of timing once again proved awry and his speech contained more irrelevancies. The very next day Aberdeen's government fell, leaving Grey with another bitter taste of failure.[63]

When Palmerston formed his Cabinet, he selected the whig Panmure as Secretary for War. This may have been partly to secure Lord John Russell's support, but Panmure's known sympathy for the principle of administrative consolidation undoubtedly contributed towards the appointment. Before taking office, Panmure claimed to have demanded unspecified "powers to amalgamate the War Office". But the Deputy Secretary at War, Benjamin Hawes, doubted whether the "various duties" of the several administrative departments could be consolidated without confusion, and he preferred that each should retain its control with the Secretary of State acting in a supervisory capacity. Possibly Hawes' analysis, based on departmental experience, influenced Panmure once in office, although he continued to advise amalgamation of responsibility. Commenting on a memorandum by Prince Albert, he maintained that "the lamentable results which have attended our present expedition ... (are) solely to be attributed to the want of proper control by a single Minister over every Department of the Army". In the Lords, more positively, he looked forward to bringing all the civil administration of the Army "under the control of one Minister", with discipline remaining the duty of the C-in-C.[64] His appointment certainly prompted expressions of support for reform. Lord Ellenborough believed it "indispensably necessary" that Panmure should take control of the entire military forces connected with the Crimean expedition — the Army, Ordnance and Royal Navy — to enable "a comprehensive view of the whole of our operations both by sea and land". And in Parliament William Williams favoured consolidation for economic reasons, arguing that if the Secretary of State for War had "entire charge" of the war effort expense would be cut by "one half".[65]

Not all reform supporters need have been disappointed during the ensuing months, for Panmure did not restrict his activity to words, though the new Secretary of State for War could not please them all.

Moreover, he had to contend with a deluge of contradictory advice and niggling criticism — quite distinct from that connected with conduct of the War. Closer co-operation between the re-constituted Transport Board and the Secretary of State to deal with sea transport in time of war was agreed, and by mid February plans for the break-up of the Ordnance Department had been drawn up, although their final version did not go to the Queen until 10 May. By the end of that month the Secretary of State for War had assumed control of the eight subdivisions of the Ordnance Department and then ruled a sprawling organisation comprising the War Department, War Office, Commissariat and Ordnance with office establishments together totalling 351 clerks. Immediate Parliamentary reactions to the announcement of the Ordnance changes showed how violently opinion remained divided over army administration. Lord Ellenborough insisted that the Secretary of State would now be "overburdened with business", Lord Hardwicke felt that, not only was a civilian Minister of War an "anomaly" but that the Horse Guards and the Transport Board should be brought fully under his control "to make the scheme complete". Lord Panmure agreed with Hardwicke that further alterations might be required in the structure of the Commissariat and also felt that the Medical Department needed attention. It was in an attempt to define the Secretary of State for War's enlarged responsibilities that Panmure received his supplementary patent in May 1855 giving control over Army and Ordnance administration "excepting always so far as relates to and concerns the military command and administration of our Army and Land Forces, as likewise to the appointments to the promotions in the same", which remained within the province of the C-in-C.[66] Early in July Panmure, in a memorandum to the Queen, reviewed his duties, which he believed to include deciding on the location and character of military works "in consultation with the C-in-C and Inspector-General of Fortifications", oversight of the nature and issue of arms, clothing and equipment, control of military lands and pensions and responsibility for all supply depots and corps not directly under the C-in-C (like those specially raised for service in the Crimea), which submitted their regular returns to him. Yet thirteen months after appearance of the fourth Secretary of State, Augustus Stafford complained that Parliament could only indirectly derive information about his powers from statements by individuals like the Duke of Newcastle and Sidney Herbert. He was not mollified by an exhaustive attempt by William Monsell, during a debate on the Ordnance Estimates in August 1855, to demonstrate how effective the reorganised system of administration had proved: "The military departments had failed under the old system, owing to the want of real responsibility in those who managed them. It was almost impossible, till within the last few months, to discover who was responsible for anything", but now "a central control" had been established through the War Department. Stafford retorted by listing areas of continuing uncertainty and blurred responsibility.[67]

There were, too, disturbing indications that much remained to be done and that measures already introduced had not been carefully thought out. Taking refuge in the fact that regimental responsibility for clothing would continue in part until 1857, the War Department admitted that no worthwhile assessment of the advantage of new over old arrangements could be ventured, but hoped that government contracting would ultimately prove cheaper. Towards the end of 1855 Queen Victoria pointed out that she had received no quarterly reports from the War Department since its reorganisation, and was "convinced that the impossibility to report is caused by present confusion". Sharply, she added: "The necessity for drawing up a report showing system and order is the surest way to produce it". Possibly to enable him to deal quickly with accusations of disorganisation, in the new year Sir Benjamin Hawes produced a memorandum for Panmure on the establishment and organisation of the War Department. In little over a month, however, Lord Derby made further, pointed observations in Parliament. There was still no satisfactory delineation between the Horse Guards and War Department, he maintained, and the situation of the Militia caused "confusion and inconvenience": nominally directed by the Home Office, once embodied it came under the Secretary of State for War, but the exact duties of the two government departments had never been explained. Derby then started a prolonged attack on the incomplete and unclear nature of the Secretary of State for War's responsibility. The following day Colonel Dunne criticised the extravagance of a department guilty of so much inefficiency: "Great changes had recently been made in the War Department, and he was afraid that no person in the department could exactly state what were the duties of the new offices which had been created". Not all of these charges could be ascribed to rhetoric. Then, and later, William Monsell agreed that the clothing reorganisation had only just been planned and was by no means yet effective.[68]

Two years after the Crimean War ended, Sir Charles Trevelyan complained that "the War Office* establishment has not been reduced to order and is under no real control", referrring also to "the waste of power and money from the overgrown and unorganised bulk of 400–500 clerks" and "the eccentricities of this mammoth establishment". But Trevelyan's remarks were not altogether free from bias; and it would have been remarkable, if not miraculous, had such a collection of independent offices, each with its traditions and customs, been swiftly moulded into an integral whole. For during the course of a national conflict, the Secretary of State for War had first been created then

* After mid 1855 War Office and War Department were used synonymously in official documents.

acquired responsibility for the Commissariat, War Office, Ordnance Department and Militia, plus a number of manufacturing establishments. It is hardly surprising that some measures were incomplete: for instance until Edward Cardwell's reforms, Lieutenants of Counties retained certain control over reserve forces.[69]

Undeniably, however, important measures of consolidation had been achieved and the basis laid for a more rational system of military administration. Within weeks of the end of the War, additional steps had been taken in the War Department to sift the clerical establishment, despite Sir Charles Trevelyan's later strictures. However physically it continued to expand, so that by 1906 it occupied 300 rooms in nineteen buildings throughout the West End of London. Fifty years afterwards, General Sir Robert Biddulph dismissed changes in the War Department during the Crimean period as a "crude and hasty reconstruction". Measures, rooted in papers and discussions, committees and commissions, of the previous three decades and which re-shaped the administration of the Victorian Army, deserve a more balanced epitaph.[70]

Conclusion

The Significance of Change

It was advisable to let the Crimean War and its horrors sink into oblivion . . . The public conscience was laid to rest, and a reaction set in. (W. H. Russell, 1895).[1]

The structure of army administration which emerged from the Crimean War seemed much simpler than that of March 1854. Duplication of responsibility for military finance and supply had been largely erased, the Board of Ordnance and (effectively) the post of Secretary at War discontinued. Curious anomalies, such as Treasury control of the Commissariat, had been resolved, the Ordnance Corps brought under the Horse Guards and a separate Secretary of State for War appointed. Certain areas of dispute did remain. But the C-in-C now commanded all regular, royal troops and the Secretary for War, having assumed political direction of the Commissariat, Ordnance Department, reserve and line troops together with the legal and financial duties of the War Office, was undoubtedly the minister normally in control of the Army. Instead of the whole mass of independent and disparate authorities, one officer and one minister, the former constitutionally subordinate to the latter, could be identified. In practice, the system was neither so neat nor so satisfactory; yet, undoubtedly, important strides had been made towards a more rational organisation of military administration.*

Only days after the official declaration of war, Lord Grey re-emphasised that failure to achieve military administrative reform to date stemmed from lack of support for positive measures, such as those proposed by his royal commission in 1837. The despatch of troops to the Mediterranean drew attention to the Army, which had received scant political and public appreciation during the long peace. Until a national emergency developed, those anxious to avoid reform and those indifferent to it were sufficiently numerous to deny worthwhile action. Threat of war allowed reformers to rally support in a patriotic cause, and those less enthusiastic, but astute, politicians sensed that the time had come for change. This situation was not original. William Williams withdrew his Parliamentary motion for a reduction in the military establishment, when tension mounted over the disputed Canadian border with Oregon. Significantly, as soon as the matter was settled, he pressed his point again. Nine years later, Williams argued that the

* See illustrations at front and back of this book.

relaxation of political vigilance at a time of military peril could have wide administrative implications: he claimed that the Government took advantage of the Crimean situation to introduce unnecessary and expensive changes.[2]

One feature of administrative adjustments carried out during the Crimean War was the lack of impact made by senior military officers. Without their acquiescence, it is doubtful whether re-organisation could have been carried through at this time. Wellington may not have exerted quite the influence ascribed to him in his declining years, but he certainly made his views known. Both Richmond and Grey acknowledged this. To some extent, perhaps, the patriotism of the Crimean generals decreed that they should concentrate on the business of fighting. So the case against administrative reform went virtually by default: no soldier fought for the *status quo* so hard as Sidney Herbert defended his office. Lord Seaton was primarily concerned with getting reinforcements to the east,[3] Raglan and Sir John Burgoyne were both in the Crimea during the critical period and Sir Hew Ross at the Ordnance constituted a lightweight influence. Significantly, after Lord Hardinge's resignation from the Horse Guards in July 1856, the puzzled search for his successor revealed a paucity of military talent. During the Peninsular campaign, as responsible ministers, Lord Castlereagh and Lord Wellesley had enjoyed considerable political standing in London on the Army's behalf. By contrast, in the Crimean War nobody of their stature spoke out consistently; so the absence of a powerful military voice was crucial. Hardinge should have been more active. Possibly, once having failed to carry his point in private, he was reluctant to reveal disagreement with politicians in public, but good generals are made of sterner stuff. It may be that Hardinge's physical decline began some time before his final collapse at Aldershot, which could explain his susceptibility to political pressure. Palmerston, however, had long expressed doubts about Hardinge's powers of judgement, Granville considered him easily bullied by the Duke of Newcastle, Sidney Herbert and Prince Albert, and Clarendon later implied that he had proved weak when called to advise the Cabinet.[4]

Lack of a forceful military voice determined that by 1856 much tighter political control had been achieved over the Army, and outstanding problems of civil-military relations, as Colonel Knox noted, had moved decisively in favour of the politicians. Future attempts to discover a special relationship between Crown and Army or describe a semi-independent role for the C-in-C were doomed to failure. Wellington held his post at the Horse Guards by letters patent: the Duke of Cambridge received a letter of service from the Secretary for War. And at a lower level, a number of military officers fulfilling staff duties had also been brought more closely under civilian control.[5]

As the War lengthened, enthusiasm at home waned: by the summer of

1855 Londoners were more interested in Lord Grovesnor's bill to prevent Sunday trading. The subsequent Allied capture of most of Sevastopol in September discouraged support for further military action. If events at the front had not actually prompted reform, they did not hinder Palmerston's later efforts towards it. Now even that beneficial assistance had been lost. Furthermore once peace had been signed, age-old reasons for inertia reappeared, tinged with an uncomfortable feeling that the Crimean venture had not been a fair test of the Army's capabilities. Commenting that a book on conditions before Sevastopol, published in May 1855, had appeared "rather late", a reviewer wrote with depressing accuracy: "The incident which robs London of reason to-day is forgotten a week hence; and the sufferings of the army in the Crimea are, for the purposes of excitement, a thing of the past". The corollary to disinterest was retrenchment and reluctance to finance further change. In a narrow sense, Queen Victoria, the Duke of Cambridge and *The United Service Gazette* all saw the main threat to military efficiency as a reduced peacetime establishment, so Palmerston argued: "The numerical amount of a peace establishment is not so important a matter as its organisation and accompanying arrangements". The Cabinet severely pruned Hardinge's draft numbers, as Panmure pointed out, in the interests of "Economy"; and, for the Secretary of State, the aim was "to keep John Bull in good humour". In February 1857 Palmerston told Panmure that, due to Parliamentary pressure, the Army Estimates must be reduced by £350,000.[6]

Florence Nightingale's fear in April 1856, "in six months all these sufferings will be forgotten", was realised. But, because the sufferings had very little effect on the administrative climate, this in itself was not decisive. A more relevant trend involved the mounting barrage of excuses, which contrived to obscure or explain away basic military weakness. Problems had been caused by unpredictable, extraordinary weather, especially that dreadful November hurricane which wrecked so many supply ships, and the failure of Turkish contractors to honour their promises.[7] Commissary-General Filder's claim that the Commissariat, like all other departments, had really coped rather well with a totally foreign set of circumstances began to gain credibility with the passage of time; and Lord Granville sought to discredit the Duke of Newcastle's report from the Crimea, which he visited after leaving office, on the grounds of personal bias. Somerset Calthorpe proved that French medical arrangements had in reality been worse than the more maligned British. Lord Raglan, unable to defend himself, became a convenient scapegoat: after all individuals, not the system, had been to blame.[8] By the end of 1856 public interest had so declined that a mass of unsold prints by Roger Fenton were consigned to the auction room. Before another year had passed, the Indian Mutiny concentrated the national gaze on another continent and another army.

Post-war apathy might not have been significant, if administrative changes had proved satisfactory. They had not; and amid declining interest and increasing demands for economy, further measures became necessary. Creation of a separate Secretary of State for War had in some respects accentuated, rather than muted, disagreement between the War Department and the Horse Guards. Differences over respective duties were heightened by the appointment of the Queen's cousin, the Duke of Cambridge, as C-in-C (for by birth, if not position, he had unrestricted access to the sovereign) and by physical separation of the Horse Guards in Whitehall from the bulk of the new War Department's offices in Pall Mall. Major-General Peel believed that the Horse Guards and War Department should be housed in one building, and Lord Granville cryptically observed: "I have long been of the opinion that the Horse Guards and the War Office are incompatible institutions". More mildly, E. B. de Fonblanque wrote: "The relative positions of the Minister of War and the C-in-C are not, perhaps, as clearly defined as is desirable for the efficient working of these two important departments". In an effort to resolve the central question of political responsibility, the Queen agreed with Sir George Cornewall Lewis's contention that the C-in-C was "subject to our general control over the Government of the Army and the responsibility of the Secretary of State for the exercise of our Royal Prerogative". This statement may have indicated that constitutionally the C-in-C did not hold an independent post, but there was room for contrary interpretations of its precise meaning.[9]

Meanwhile, further adjustments within the framework of the Crimean War reorganisation took place. In 1857 the posts of Clerk of the Ordnance and Deputy Secretary at War were abolished, to be replaced by an Assistant Under Secretary of State and a Secretary for Military Correspondence. So, for all practical purposes, remaining vestiges of the independent Ordnance Department and War Office vanished. The War Department was then divided into thirteen departments, each under a Director in turn responsible to an Under Secretary of State. A year later the whole Department concentrated in Pall Mall, leaving the Horse Guards utterly isolated in Whitehall. Early in 1859 the C-in-C assumed the military duties of the Inspector-General of Fortifications, although that officer officially remained as adviser to the Secretary of State, and the post of Director-General of Artillery disappeared.[10]

These further changes, aimed at smoother operation of the revised system, could not rectify basic problems. De Fonblanque argued that lack of powerful central direction over all the civil departments remained "the great defect of our administrative system", and J. R. Godley, Assistant Under Secretary of State for War, declared: "In a great war it (the War Office) would almost certainly break down". Exasperated at delays on medical projects, Florence Nightingale described the War Office as "a very slow office, and one in which the minister's intentions can be entirely negatived by all his subordinate departments and those of each of the sub-departments by every other". Her view was jaundiced by frustration, but certainly the Secretary of State for War experienced considerable difficulty in dealing with the vast areas of responsibility which he had acquired. To critics of the changes, this had not been unforeseen.[11] C. M. Clode, reflecting in 1869 on the Secretary of State's enhanced power, cited Lord Bacon in support of his thesis that concentration of too much power in one minister's hands made neither for efficiency nor constitutional sense. Moreover, demonstrably there were still a considerable number of unsatisfactory aspects of military administration. In the twelve years following the Crimean War seventeen royal commissions, eighteen select committees, nineteen internal War Office committees and thirty-five committees of military officers dealt in some manner with the subject. Edward Cardwell discovered that there was still much to do, but Sir James Graham's disparaging remark to him about army administration, "there is only one word to describe it and that word is *chaos*", was less than just.[12] Sir John Burgoyne's assertion, that more necessary adjustments were forsworn purely on financial grounds, was also too sweeping. Undoubtedly these constituted an important barrier, but once peace came gnarled pre-war arguments reappeared. Bismarck and Napoleon III were needed to goad the national conscience into military reform once more.

Nonetheless, Crimean War experiences did reinforce oft-repeated cries for military supply services. Several quasi-military "corps" were raised by successive Secretaries of State during the conflict— Medical Staff Corps, Land Transport Corps, Mounted Staff Corps, Army Works Corps and Civil Engineering Corps. Only the former two survived the War to be fully militarised and reorganised respectively as The Army Hospital Corps and The Military Train. Making use of able-bodied soldiers and ultimately commanded by the Horse Guards, they became part of the Army. As an extension of this principle, after 1858 all commissariat officers were recruited from serving subalterns or, in an emergency, the half-pay list. None of this involved the essence of administration, the exercise of power, which in a democratic society centres on politicians not generals. Events during the War re-illustrated that, short of a military disaster affecting the very foundations of the state, battlefield experiences have only a marginal effect upon administration. Moreover, there was more than a grain of truth in Sir Charles Trevelyan's appraisal: "That which has to be extemporised under the pressure of an emergency is generally both badly and wastefully done".[13] Without an emergency, however, nothing at all might have been achieved; and, in a sense, peace reawakened traditional prejudices, which precluded completion of the task until continental sabres began to rattle in earnest a decade hence. The Crimean War basically underlined the fact that 'administration' concerns power, which in the United Kingdom is the province of politicians. The most important manoeuvres, the relevant victories and defeats in the field of army administration occurred not on the Heights of Sevastopol, but in the Palace of Westminster.

Notes

INTRODUCTION

1. Lord Clarendon, Foreign Secretary in Lord Aberdeen's coalition government, argued: "It is the battle of civilisation against barbarism, for the independence of Europe", 31 March 1854, Hansard (all references to the Third Series), cxxxii, c. 150. During the Second Coalition against Napoleon, for instance, Russian troops had not impressed British observers with their military efficiency.

2. T. J. Thackeray, *The Military Administrative Organisation of France* (1856), p. 1; Wolseley writing in T. H. Ward (ed.), *The Reign of Queen Victoria*, i (1887), pp. 196–7; G. Douglas & G. D. Ramsay, *The Panmure Papers*, i (1908), p. 43; A. Forbes, *A History of the Army Ordnance Services*, i (1929), p. 273; A. Symons, *Higher Army Administration 1836–1918*, an unpublished typescript dated 1939 in the Ministry of Defence library, p. 27; O. Anderson, *A Liberal State at War* (1967), p. 67; W. S. Hamer, *The British Army Civil-Military Relations 1885–1905* (Oxford, 1970), p. 5; W. H. Anderson, *Outline of the British Army up to 1914* (1920), p. 29.

3. Cf. 13 November 1854, Florence Nightingale to Sidney Herbert, quoted in I. B. O'Malley, *Florence Nightingale 1820–1856* (1931), p. 267: "The vermin might, if they had but 'unity of purpose' carry off the four miles of beds on their backs and march with them into the War Office and Horse Guards". The Morning State of 2 December 1854 listed 35,069 men in the Expeditionary Force and ninety-five horses with the Mounted Staff Corps: on 16 December the respective figures were "little more than 16,000" under arms and fifty-nine horses, Newcastle Papers, NeC 9925b and 9933a.

4. Clarendon quoted in O. Anderson, op. cit., p. 54; Knox, 7 February 1855, Hansard, cxxxvi, c. 1322; 10 February 1855, Memo. by Palmerston, quoted in B. Connell, *Regina versus Palmerston 1837–1865* (1962), p. 166 et seq.; February 1855, Memo. by Panmure, Dalhousie Muniments (all references to GD 45), 8/178; W. H. Russell, *The Great War with Russia* (1895), p. vi.

5. 29 October 1847, Dr. H. Marshall to Fox Maule, Secretary at War, Dalhousie Muniments, 8/31, quoting C. Audouin, *Histoire de l'Administration de la Guerre*, iv, p. 144: "The various means, employed to raise soldiers, organise, arm, equip, pay and put them in motion — to subsist them in health and sickness — to command them in the field of battle — to profit by their success — to remedy their failure — to reward and to punish them — and to preserve an account of their fortunate and unfortunate operations"; Thackeray, op. cit., p. 7; E. B. de Fonblanque, *Treatise on the Administration and Organisation of the British Army, with special reference to finance and supply* (1858), p. 1.

6. Cf. the Duke of Wellington's comment: "If I had rice and bullocks I had men, if I had men I knew I could beat the enemy", quoted in A. Griffiths, *Wellington: his comrades and contemporaries* (1897), p. 16. Many military historians treat 'administration' and 'supply' as virtually synonymous.

7. 30 August 1848, Hansard, ci, c. 710.

8. A. Vagts, *A History of Militarism* (1959), pp. 61–2, 137–8; Thackeray, op. cit., p. 7.

9. Vagts, op. cit., pp. 64 & 168; G. A. Craig, *The Politics of the Prussian Army 1640–1945* (1968), pp. xv & 26 et seq.; P. Paret, "Clausewitz and the Nineteenth Century", in M. E. Howard (ed.), *The Theory and Practice of War* (1965), p. 26. Paradoxically, subsequent military victory may lead to a conservative reaction and destruction of some administrative reforms, as Prussia discovered immediately post 1815. Daun's work by Craig, "Command and Staff Problems in the Austrian Army 1740–1866", in Howard, *Theory and Practice of War*, op. cit., p. 47 et seq.

10. For a survey of Prussian military administration during these years, see Craig, op. cit., p. 3 et seq.; J. S. Curtiss, *The Russian Army Under Nicholas I 1825–1855* (Durham N. C., 1965), pp. 17 & 96 et seq.

11. S. E. Finer, *The Life and Times of Sir Edwin Chadwick* (1952), pp. 301 & 333 et seq.; undated (probably 1 April 1856), Florence Nightingale to Sidney Herbert, quoted in O'Malley, op. cit., p. 382, complaining of having 130 typhus patients with no wine for their treatment; 13

August 1855, Hawley to his father, S. G. P. Ward (ed.), *The Hawley Letters* (Society for Army Historical Research, 1970), p. 68. For a fuller consideration of medical treatment in the mid nineteenth century, see N. Cantlie, *A History of the Army Medical Department* (Edinburgh & London, 1974), particularly vol. i.

12. W. L. Burn, *The Age of Equipoise* (1964), p. 288; J. Ridley, *Lord Palmerston, 1784–1865* (1970), p. 107: in 1830 dispatches from Paris or Brussels to London took a minimum two days, from Madrid or St. Petersburg ten days, Constantinople or Washington a month.

13. Cobden in 1836 quoted in J. Morley, *The Life of Richard Cobden* (1878), p. 47. Walter Bagehot, writing in 1858, drew attention to the immense social changes which had occurred in dramatic, if rather optimistic, terms: "The world of the 'Six Acts', of the frequent executions, of the Draconic criminal law, is so far removed from us that we cannot comprehend its ever having existed", quoted in Burn, op. cit., p. 57. By 1861 town dwellers in England and Wales numbered 10,960,998, exceeding the population in rural areas by 1,855,772, ibid., p. 309.

14. Cobden's speech at Birmingham in 1845 quoted in J. Bright and J. E. T. Rogers (ed.), *Cobden's Speeches on Questions of Public Policy* (1878), p. 172; Bright's letter of April 1848 quoted in G. M. Trevelyan, *The Life of John Bright* (1913), p. 183; *The Times*, 9 February 1854.

15. Two legal rulings in 1832, quoted in W. C. Costin & J. S. Watson, *The Law and Working of the Constitution, Documents 1660–1914*, ii (1952), in the Case of the Bristol Rioters and Rex versus Pinney, pp. 259 & 262 respectively, emphasised that "the law acknowledges no distinction between the soldier and the private citizen . . . (all being) bound to prevent the perpetration of outrage, to put down riot and tumult, and to preserve the lives and property of the people". Mr. Justice Littledale in the latter case implied that an officer should in these circumstances act in his status as a citizen, without awaiting formal direction from a magistrate.

16. D. Le Marchant, *Memoirs of the late Major-General Le Marchant* (1841), p. 62: the Duke of York made this point to J. G. Le Marchant, when the RMC plan was submitted to him, ibid., p. 65.

17. Cf. 7 March 1833, Wellington to Lord Hill, App. I to P(arliamentary) P(apers), 1833, vii, p. 274; Napier quoted in J. Luvaas, *The Education of an Army: British Military Thought 1815–1940* (1965), p. 37; J. F. Burgoyne, *Army Reform* (1857), p. 28; 6 December 1853, Brown to Lord Hardinge, Brown Papers, MS 1848/177; 5 January 1854, letter by Brown, ibid., MS 2854.

18. Ellenborough, 7 April 1854, Hansard, cxxxii, c. 658. Once war had been declared, urging development of a permanent centre at Aldershot, Prince Albert wrote: "You can now ask parliament for anything you want. Strike while the iron is hot!", quoted in J. Walters, *Aldershot Review* (1970), p. 20.

19. 7 December 1854, Aberdeen to Queen Victoria, Aberdeen Papers, British Museum Additional Manuscripts (hereafter Add. MS) 43050, noting that Russell "did not deny" Aberdeen's assessment of his conduct.

20. Cf. the Secretary for War's exasperated query to the Horse Guards about responsibility for defective entrenching tools, PRO WO 6/76, and the notorious incident when iron beds arrived at Scutari but their legs went to Balaclava in another ship, noted by Sidney Herbert to Lord Lansdowne, 8 January 1855, (Sidney) Herbert Papers, Miscellaneous Political Correspondence 1834–61 file.

CHAPTER I

1. House of Lords, 7 April 1854, Hansard, cxxxii, c. 611.

2. Final report of the Select Committee on Army and Ordnance Expenditure, 21 July 1851, P.P., 1851, vii, p. 790; *The United Service Gazette*, 22 April 1854, letter dated 10 April; C. M. Clode, *The Military Forces of the Crown*, ii (1869), p. 390; Wolseley writing in T. H. Ward, op. cit., p. 196.

3. H. Gordon, *The War Office* (1935), p. 77; A. Briggs, *Victorian People* (1954), p. 70; C. Hibbert, *The Destruction of Lord Raglan* (1961), p. 7; E. L. Woodward, *The Age of Reform 1815–1870* (Oxford, 1962), p. 269; *St James' Chronicle*, 26 April 1794. Gordon, for instance, claims: "Administration was so scattered as to be almost incapable of united action", Briggs: "There was no system at all, merely a division of responsibility" and Woodward: "The division of responsibility was incredible".

4. Lord Grey (5 June 1854, Grey to Henry Drummond, Grey Papers), Sir John Pakington (17 July 1854, Hansard, cxxxv, c. 329) and William Monsell, Clerk of the Ordnance (2 August 1855, Hansard, cxxxix, c. 1662) thought five, but Benjamin Hawes, Deputy Secretary at War (Memo. dated 8 February 1855, Dalhousie Muniments, 8/316) listed the following eight: War Department, War Office, Ordnance, C-in-C, Army Medical Board, Admiralty for sea

transport, Treasury for all extraordinary expenditure, Home Office for the Militia.

5. Symons, op. cit., p. 5 (fourteen); J. S. Omond, *Parliament and the Army 1642-1904* (1933), p. 73 (thirteen); Clode, op. cit., ii, p. 769 (eleven); W. B. Pemberton, *Battles of the Crimean War* (Pan edition, 1962), p. 20 (nine); Hibbert, op. cit., p. 7 (seven); Gordon, op. cit., p. 32 and Anon., *Military Administration 1855-1870* (1870), p. 24 (both six). Clode lists: two Secretaries of State ("War and the Colonies" and "Home"), the C-in-C, Ordnance Office (sub-divided into six), Treasury, Secretary at War, Army Medical Department, Audit Office, Commissioners of Chelsea Hospital, Board of General Officers and Paymaster-General; Symons lists: Secretary at War, C-in-C, Master-General of the Ordnance, Treasury, Judge Advocate General, Home Secretary, Secretary of State for War and the Colonies, Controllers of Military Accounts, Board of General Officers, Army Medical Board, the Commissaries of Barracks, Commissary-General of Musters, Paymaster-General and Commissioners of Chelsea Hospital.

6. 4 November 1841, Melbourne to Queen Victoria, A. Benson & Viscount Esher (ed.), *The Letters of Queen Victoria 1837-1861*, i (1908), p. 358.

7. Fox quoted in Constitutionalist, *Army Administration in Three Centuries* (1901), p. 16; Palmerston quoted in Clode, op. cit., i, preface v; Macaulay quoted in Vagts, op. cit., p. 169.

8. W. Bagehot, *The English Constitution* (Fontana ed., 1968), p. 205: see also Richard Crossman's introduction, especially p. 14.

9. 12 January 1812, Lord Granville to his father, quoted by Grey, 7 April 1854, Hansard, cxxxii, c. 636.

10. The Bill of Rights, 1689 (1 Will. and Mary, sess. 2, c. 2), stated: "The raising or keeping a standing army within this kingdom in time of peace, unless it be with consent of parliament, is against the law".

11. Burke quoted on the title page of Clode, op. cit., i; complaint of unnamed M.P., dated 6 March 1815, and Speaker's action, P.P., 1814-15, xiii, p. 3; Russell, 26 February 1816, Hansard, xxxii, c. 843. In December 1821 Joseph Hume opposed a large standing army as a danger to civil liberty, Anon., *Observations upon the Peace Establishments of the Army* (1822), p. 7.

12. An officer, *Observations on the Army* (1825), p. 4: "The establishment of a standing army has ever been viewed by the people with a jealous eye, as hostile to the spirit of the British Constitution"; Crawford's unsuccessful amendment to the Army Estimates, 4 March 1844, Hansard, lxxiii, c. 538; Wellington, 11 August 1846, ibid., lxxxviii, c. 602; F. Head, *The Defenceless State of Great Britain* (1850), p. 238: "I have inherited a good old English hatred to a standing army; the thing I tell ye is unconstitutional; and besides this, I cannot and will not afford it"; Memo. by Panmure, February 1855, Dalhousie Muniments, 8/178.

13. Clode, op. cit., i, p. 5 and ii, p. 316.

14. G. J. Hay, *The Constitutional Force* (1906), for a full discussion; also the transcript of Corelli Barnett's lecture, "The British Armed Forces in Transition" R(oyal) U(nited) S(ervice) I(nstitution) Journal, June 1970, Peter Paret's article, "Nationalism and the Sense of Obligation", *Military Affairs*, February 1970, and Vagts, op. cit., p. 49.

15. Clode, op. cit., ii, pp. 260-1; the Secretary at War introduced "a Bill to regulate the Stations of Soldiers during Parliamentary Elections" on 26 March 1847, P.P., iv, p. 355; Lord Stanmore, *Sidney Herbert, Lord Herbert of Lea*, i (1906), pp. 79-80.

16. Wellington quoted in M. E. Howard, *Studies in War and Peace* (1970), p. 62; Newcastle, 7 April 1854, Hansard, cxxxii, c. 651.

17. T. H. Ward, op. cit., pp. 4 & 27; Clode, op. cit., i, p. 136. Between 1777 and 1781 Sir William Howe's two successive Quartermaster-Generals amassed a combined profit of £417,592 through the hiring of transport. In 1785 a naval commission of inquiry was set up "to inquire into the Fees, Gratuities, Perquisites and Emoluments ... received ... in Publick Offices ... and to examine into any abuses". Three years later it reported that receipt of fees and gifts for services rendered was widespread, and steps were taken to curb these practices, B. Pool, *Navy Board Contracts 1660-1832* (1966), pp. 113-14.

18. 4 May 1848, William Shaw to Fox Maule, Dalhousie Muniments, 8/41, concerning military contractors; November 1841, Wellington to Lady Wilton, quoted in the Duke of Wellington (ed.), *Wellington with His Friends*, Letters of the First Duke of Wellington (1965), p. 174 on forged Treasury bills: a month later Edward Beaumont Smith was transported for life; John Sadleir M.P. committed suicide and William Roupell M.P. was sentenced to penal servitude for life, Burn, op. cit., p. 32.

19. Clode, op. cit., ii, p. 222; P.P., 1837, xxxiv, Pt. I, p. 16; Memo. by Trevelyan, 13 October 1855, P(ublic) R(ecord) O(ffice) W(ar) O(ffice) 43/103/159744.

20. See Illustration within front boards of this book.

21. Memo. by Prince Albert, 11 July 1850, quoted in F. Eyck, *The Prince Consort: a political biography* (1959), p. 139. For an example of pressure from the Queen, see 3 July 1854, Queen Victoria to Newcastle, Benson & Esher, op. cit., iii, p. 37, asking about "the effective state" of national defences, and advice from her, 2 October 1855, Queen Victoria to Panmure, Douglas & Ramsay, op. cit., i, p. 418: her objection to the proposed appointment of Sir William Codrington to command in the Crimea was not heeded.

22. 4 July 1854, Queen Victoria to the Earl of Clarendon, Benson & Esher, op. cit., iii, p. 37, complaining that Clarendon did not act "by the unanimous desire of the Cabinet", as he claimed, but "under the authority of the Queen"; need for Secretary of State's counter-signature, P.P., 1860, vii, p. 6.

23. P.P., 1837, xxxiv, Pt. I, pp. 5–6; 28 February, 1 & 10 March 1854, for example, Clarendon to Raglan, R(aglan) M(ilitary) P(apers) 6807/290, forwarding information on Russian troop movements gleaned by British ambassadors abroad; 21 March 1854, Secretary of State for War and the Colonies to Foreign Secretary, PRO WO 6/75, asking Clarendon to get Turkish "unskilled labour" through the ambassador in Constantinople.

24. Militia Act, 1802 (42 Geo III, c. 90) and Militia Act, 1852 (15 & 16 Vict., c. 50) quoted in Costin & Watson, op. cit., ii, pp. 29 & 100; H. B. Thomson, *The Military Forces and Institutions of Great Britain and Ireland* (1855), p. 308; War Office, *Warrants and Regulations concerning Finance* (1841), sections 11, 43–5, 49–51; PRO WO 47/2746/1342; A. Walshe & J. H. Stocqueler (ed.), *Standing Orders* (1855), p. 66. For instance, after Wellington's death, the Home Secretary approved General Orders before publication, PRO WO 43/95/152444.

25. P.P., 1837, xxxix, Pt. I, p. 5; 28 November 1854, Newcastle to Mr. Engleheart, Newcastle Papers, NeC 9683b; 20 April 1854, Prince Albert sent to Newcastle his ideas on British strategy in Turkey, ibid., NeC 9689.

26. Clode, op. cit., ii, p. 181 et seq. On 3 February 1854 clerks in the C-in-C's office petitioned Lord Hardinge concerning rates of pay and he referred the matter to the Treasury, which gave a ruling on 28 June, PRO WO 43/78/103000; 2 July 1854, Raglan to Trevelyan, RMP 6807/290, asked for Interpreters to be exempt from Income Tax. Other examples of Treasury action in pre-war years are found in PRO WO 46/87/216, PRO WO 47/2745/6922, 6925, 6926, PRO WO 47/2746/2731, PRO WO 47/2747/5403, PRO WO 59/73/3085, PRO WO 59/75/1857, 3008, PRO WO 43/91/120, 121, PRO WO 43/90/117714.

27. Until 1855 the artillery and engineers (collectively known as the Ordnance Corps) were virtually a separate army under the Master-General of the Ordnance. The minimum annual number of troops voted between 1835 and 1851 under the C-in-C was 81,271 and the Master-General 8,297, the maximum 113,847 and 14,200 respectively, although the numbers actually serving frequently fell short of those voted, P.P., 1852, xxx, p. 2: at the death of William IV (1837) troops under the C-in-C were 9,619 below establishment, T. H. Ward, op. cit., p. 156.

28. Wood before the Select Committee on Official Salaries, P.P., 1850, xv, q. 46; entry in Gladstone's diary, dated 24 July 1846, records a conversation with Sir Robert Peel eleven days earlier: "He spoke of the immense multiplication of details in public business . . . he said the mass of public business increased so fast that he could not tell what it was to end in", quoted in Costin & Watson, op. cit., ii, p. 393.

29. Palmerston, 17 July 1854, Hansard, cxxxv, c. 329; see, for instance, Hibbert, op. cit., p. 7: "The complication, the muddle, the duplication, the mutual jealousies, the labyrinthine processes of supply and control, were astounding".

30. Cf. 25 November 1852, Grey to his brother Charles, Grey Papers: "The fault of our present system . . . (is that) authority is so divided, and is exercised in so inconvenient a manner that it practically renders it impossible that the administration of this vitally important business should be really vigorous and consistent", and his speech in the Lords, 7 April 1854, Hansard, cxxxii, c. 606 et seq.; cf. 28 April 1854, Monsell to Raglan, RMP 6807/289, and 2 August 1855, Hansard, cxxxix, c. 1662, introducing the Ordnance Estimates: "At the commencement of the present war the administration of the army was divided into five separate departments . . . and there was no union among them or central control over them". As Lord Howick, Grey had chaired the Royal Commission on the Civil Administration of the Army, whose report in 1837 had not been implemented.

31. 16 February 1834, Burgoyne to Sir John Bisset, Secretary to the Duke of Richmond's Royal Commission, P.P., 1837, xxxiv, Pt. I, p. 182. In a memo. dated February 1855, Lord Panmure used similar words: "The chimerical dread therefore of a standing army is absurd", Dalhousie Muniments, 8/178.

32. Over 500 letters, most of them of a routine nature, passed between the Adjutant-General and the Military Secretary, both at the Horse Guards, in one two-month period, PRO WO 3/326; Howick's Commission recorded: "For years the C-in-C and the Secretary at War have been writing letters which were waste paper", P.P., 1837, xxxiv, Pt. I, p. 12.

33. Pool, op. cit., pp. 113–14; M. Lewis, *The Navy of Britain* (1949), pp. 347, 373 & 375; Sir John Jervis, Earl of St. Vincent, wrote in 1797: "The Civil Branch of the Navy is rotten to the core" and, when he became First Lord of the Admiralty four years later, proceeded to attack corruption, Pool, op. cit., pp. 117–18; cf. P. B. Maxwell, *Whom Shall We Hang?* (1855). The Administrative Reform Association of 1855 was motivated by the drive for efficiency: "The whole system of Government Office is such as in any business would lead to inevitable ruin", quoted in Burn, op. cit., p. 143

34. Edwin Chadwick discovered that 276 towns in England and Wales had no sanitary authority in 1847 and another ninety-two corporations lacked powers concerning drainage, sewage, cleansing and paving, Finer, *Chadwick*, op. cit., pp. 302 & 355; Burn, op. cit., p. 138 et seq.

35. Lewis, op. cit., p. 380. Finer's comment, that "it is impossible to overstate the primitiveness of sanitary science in 1847", op. cit., p. 298, is interesting in this context. See, too, Anon., *Military Administration 1855–1870*, op. cit., p. 5: "No one who has read the blue books on army reform (alas! too numerous), but must have been struck with the strong bias in favour of his own department or corps, which each witness displays".

36. Memo. by Palmerston, 23 November 1836, Grey Papers.

CHAPTER II

1. Two Mounted Sentries, *The Horse Guards — a satire upon the Duke of Wellington* (1850), frontispiece.

2. 16 November 1830–14 September 1852.

3. Census returns show a rapid expansion of population, particularly in the towns, in the early nineteenth century. During the first thirty years Liverpool grew from 82,000 to 202,000, Leeds from 53,000 to 123,000 and London doubled its size to about two million people. The whole population of England and Wales rose from 8,872,980 to 17,929,609 in the first half of the century.

4. W. H. Anderson, op. cit., p. 26; Luvaas, op. cit., p. 3.

5. G. M. Young, *Portrait of an Age* (1936), p. 27; Ridley, op. cit., pp. 276 & 409; Finer, *Chadwick*, op. cit , pp. 160 & 181; C. Petrie, *The Victorians* (1960), p. 221.

6. Many of the military bills concerned minor or routine matters, for instance: "For dissolving the St. George's Fund or Troopers' Fund in the Royal Regt. of Horse Guards and distributing the fund", P.P., 1833, iv, p. 583, and "For consolidating and amending the Laws relating to the Payment of Army Prize Money", P.P., 1831–2, 1, p. 189. Select committees included one on Army and Navy Appointments, P.P., 1833, vii, p. 1, and that on Army and Ordnance Expenditure chaired by Lord Seymour, which produced 4 reports (the first virtually a notice of intent): P.P., 1849, ix, p. 1; P.P., 1849, ix, p. 5; P.P., 1850, x, p. 1; P.P., 1851, vii, p. 735.

7. In the period 27 June–5 September 1844, Hansard, lxxvi, fifty-three divisions occurred in the Commons and all or part of thirteen days' business was devoted to Poor Law Relief. No matter of army administration was considered in either House during these weeks. When Sidney Herbert was at the War Office in 1845–6 the Cabinet was preoccupied with the Corn Laws, Stanmore, op. cit., p. 39 et seq.

8. Major-General J. G. Le Marchant had been instrumental in establishing the Junior and Senior Departments of the RMC, aimed respectively at training officer cadets and staff officers. During the last five years of the Peninsular War only one officer on the staff of the Quartermaster-General had not passed through the Senior Department. However, the number of students declined and the final examination became rudimentary, Le Marchant, op. cit., p. 44 et seq.; R. H. Thoumine, *Scientific Soldier: A Life of General Le Marchant, 1766–1812* (1968), p. 41 et seq.; A. R. Godwin-Austen, *The Staff and the Staff College* (1927), pp. 62 & 75–6.

9. Craig, op. cit., p. 39 et seq.; Woodward, op. cit., pp. 18–19 & 618 et seq. notes that the existing professions (church, law and medicine) improved their standards and other bodies, such as the Institution of Civil Engineers, became established. Sir John Hackett, *The Profession of Arms* (1962), p. 33, notes: "In the nineteenth century true professionalism emerges. Before 1800 there was virtually no such thing as a professional officer corps anywhere. After 1900 no world power of any significance was without one."

10. F. G. Guggisberg, *The Shop: the Story of the RMA* (1902), pp. 46 & 72: between 1825 and 1849 twenty-five per cent of the cadets failed to gain commissions and between 1841 and 1854 ninety-eight were removed from the RMA for unsatisfactory progress; "Instructions issued by the Commander-in-Chief respecting Examinations to be required on the Admission and Promotion of Officers in the Army", P.P., 1849, xxii, p. 109 and 1850, xxxv, p. 101.

11. Appalled by poor swordsmanship and incompetent staff work in Flanders 1793–5, Le Marchant aimed to make officers more efficient by writing: "Treatise on the Sword Exercise, An Elucidation of several parts of His Majesty's Regulations for the formation and movements of Cavalry" and "Instructions for the formation and discipline of Provisional Cavalry". See, for instance, S. P. Huntington, *The Soldier and the State* (Cambridge, Massachusetts, 1967), S. E. Finer, *The Man on Horseback: the Role of the Military in Politics* (1967) and Hackett, op. cit., on the military profession.

12. Wellington quoted in A. Brett-James (ed.), *Wellington at War. A Selection of his wartime letters* (1961), p. xxxix and 21 August 1827 quoted in Wellington, *Wellington with his Friends*, op. cit., p. 76; 20 January 1854, Hardinge to Brown, Brown Papers, MS 1849/4, referring to a previous, undated conversation; 14 March 1854, Cathcart to Brown, ibid., MS 1849/41; 23 September 1852, Raglan to his son Richard, R(aglan) P(rivate) P(apers) 124/3/184.

13. 21 August 1827, Wellington to Charles Arbuthnot, quoted in Wellington, *Wellington with his Friends*, op. cit., p. 76, referring to his refusal to support George Canning's government: "I stated repeatedly ... that I should support the Government whenever their measures were calculated to promote the Honour and Integrity of the Country" and 11 August 1843, Wellington to Thomas Raikes quoted in H. Raikes (ed.), *Private Correspondence of Thomas Raikes with the Duke of Wellington* (1861), p. 347: "My object was to maintain in Spain the means of power, and the preservation of the ancient organisation, of the powers of the State, so as that the country must be governed, notwithstanding the existence of a democratical constitution of Government"; 24 March 1855, Raglan to Queen Victoria, RMP 6807/280, expressing his consistent view which distinguished between the Crown's and Parliament's control of the Army.

14. 17 September 1855, Prince Albert to Clarendon, Douglas & Ramsay, op. cit., i, p. 390: "The soldier is disliked, the officer almost seeks to excuse himself for being an officer", and Wolseley in 1887 believed that public opinion after 1815 thought military preparations "wrong on moral grounds", T. H. Ward, op. cit., p. 156; cf. Gladstone, quoted in Vagts, op. cit., p. 158 and 6 March 1854, Hansard, cxxxi, c. 357 et seq.; Cobden in an undated letter to Herbert, Herbert Papers, Miscellaneous Papers; Bright, 31 March 1854, Hansard, cxxxii, c. 267.

15. Positive attempts were made to improve this: in the period 1841–52 flogging was debated three times in the Lords, eight in the Commons; and three divisions were forced. It may also be significant that, despite economy in other votes, the Army Estimates included £11,000 for Divine Service, 1842–3 (P.P., 1842, xxvii, p. 137) and £16,800, 1848–9 (P.P., 1847–8, xli, p. 81).

16. Between 1848 and 1853 British exports of corn doubled: war would cut off access to valuable markets and raw materials. A Peace Society developed in the 1840s, which reached its zenith with a series of International Congresses, and, though never influential in policy making, received considerable press coverage.

17. R. W. Proctor, writing in 1856, noted the feeling that the Army denied working men their rights, Burn, op. cit., p. 71: Sir Henry (later Lord) Hardinge, however, argued that the standing army was a defender of their rights by permitting free speech, Clode, op. cit., i, p. 339.

18. 15 August 1837, Russell to Queen Victoria, Benson & Esher, op. cit., 1, p. 90, noted need to use the military at elections to curb unrest; at Bradford the cavalry fired on a mob intent on preventing operation of the new Poor Law, Finer, *Chadwick*, op. cit., p. 129; during Chartist riots in Preston troops killed "three or four persons", 15 August 1842, Sir James Graham to Queen Victoria, Benson & Esher, op. cit., i, p. 423.

19. 27 February 1843, Hansard, lxvi, c. 1352 & c. 1356, Crawford and Williams: in the same debate Williams unsuccessfully divided the House. In May 1852 Major-General Thomas was alleged to have put pressure on a pensioner in Enniskillen concerning his vote, 28 May 1852, Hansard, cxxi, c. 1332 et seq.: see also Chapter VI below; proposals to arm out-pensioners with staves and put them under half-pay officers "whenever it would be necessary to employ them in the preservation of the public peace" (7 August 1843, Hansard, lxxi, c. 359) caused a political uproar: on eight days between 7 and 21 August the Commons debated the matter

and divided on six occasions. Similar objections were raised on 11 March 1846, Hansard, lxxxiv, c. 973 and noted in a memo. by Lt.-Col. (later Colonel) Tulloch to the Secretary at War, 29 April 1848, Dalhousie Muniments 8/44.

20. Wolseley, writing in T. H. Ward, op. cit., p. 175, dismissed "dreams of universal peace, of general disarmament, and of international courts of arbitration" as "a fool's paradise", but recognised that, in a conducive atmosphere, "the poorest babbler of philosophic commonplace can easily pooh-pooh the most accomplished expert on war subjects".

21. The Army's strength was so pared after Waterloo that four regiments, which returned to England in 1829 after twenty-four years abroad, went overseas again within five years: to raise expeditions to Portugal in 1826 and Canada in 1837-8 troops had to be withdrawn from Gibraltar and Mediterranean garrisons drastically reduced. On colonial reliefs, see the final report of Lord Seymour's Committee, P.P., 1851, vii, p. 753; 17 January 1849, Wellington to Maule, Dalhousie Muniments, 8/20: Maule (by then Panmure), in a memo. of February 1855, claimed that ministers often courted popularity by reducing military expenditure, ibid., 8/178.

22. Report dated 12 July 1849, P.P., ix, p. 5 et seq.: between 1830 and 1847 expenditure on Ordnance services rose from £1,959,140 to £2,897,867. Drawing attention to expansion of British colonial possessions, new systems of defence, improved living conditions for soldiers etc., the report concluded that "several expenses now provided for in the Ordnance Estimates were formerly defrayed by other departments ... a mere comparison therefore of the sums expended by the Ordnance in different years would lead to erroneous conclusions". The Army Estimates between 1849–50 and 1852–3 dropped from £6,262,161 to £6,010,372, although the number of men voted rose from 131,521 to 132,434, P.P., 1852, xxx, p. 5.

23. Final report the Seymour Committee, P.P., 1851, vii, pp. 742, 756 & 790; Report of the Select Committee on Small Arms, P.P., 1854, xviii, p. 1 et seq. One important impulse for Poor Law reform was the cost of relief, which ran at £8 million in 1818 and remained £7 million fourteen years later although the price of bread had dropped by one-third, Finer, Chadwick, op. cit., p. 42.

24. With so many different social, economic and philosophical interests, the radicals could offer no coherent party, though Melbourne's conclusion was too harsh: "The Radicals have neither ability, honesty nor numbers. They have no leaders of any character", Melbourne to Queen Victoria, 7 May 1839, Benson & Esher, op. cit., i, p. 155.

25. Hume became involved, for instance, in controversy over the size of the peacetime army, public health, poor relief, ecclesiastical canonries, abolition of the post of Lord Lieutenant of Ireland, entrance fees for cathedrals, reduction of building grants for Buckingham Palace, flogging and military barracks; and on numerous occasions he divided the House. Russell dubbed him the "Inquisitor-General", quoted in W. B. Pemberton, Lord Palmerston (1954), p. 21, and The United Service Gazette, 16 April 1853, referred to "the eternal Joseph".

26. 27 April 1855, Layard to Granville, Granville Papers, PRO 30/29/18; Disraeli quoted in J. Morley, The Life of William Ewart Gladstone, i (1905), p. 352. The United Service Gazette, 16 April 1853, referred to Cobden as a "demagogue" and Queen Victoria noted: "His main reputation Mr. Cobden gained as a successful agitator", 14 October 1847, Queen Victoria to Russell, Benson & Esher, op. cit., ii, p. 131.

27. Debate on the Ordnance Estimates, 8 April 1850, Hansard, cx, c. 21 et seq.; debate on the Army Estimates, 19 March 1852, Hansard, cxix, c. 130 et seq.; 25 May 1846, Hansard, lxxxvi, c. 1204. Short debates on the Army Estimates, 4 March 1844 and 11 March 1850, ended at 12.15 am and 1 am respectively; on the Ordnance Estimates, 31 July 1848, 16 March 1849 and 12 July 1849, "shortly before 1 am", 12.45 am and 1 am respectively.

28. Confidential Memo. by Maule, January 1850, Douglas & Ramsay, op. cit., i, p. 29; Two Mounted Sentries, op. cit.; 16 February 1852, Russell to Prince Albert, Benson & Esher, op. cit., ii, p. 365; The United Service Gazette, 25 September 1852, 3 June & 8 July 1854; Manchester Guardian, 15 February 1854; Illustrated London News, 10 June 1854.

29. O. Wheeler, The War Office Past and Present to 1914 (1914), p. 129; Gleig quoted in W. Verner, The Military Life of George, Duke of Cambridge (1905), i, p. 35; Griffiths, Wellington, op. cit., p. 218; Hamley, op. cit., p. 107; J. B. Conacher, The Aberdeen Coalition 1852–1854 (Cambridge, 1968), p. 385; Hamer, op. cit., p. 4.

30. G. R. Gleig, History of the Life of Arthur, Duke of Wellington, iv (1860), p. 102 et seq.; Godwin-Austen, op. cit., pp. 80-3: "By God! If there is a mutiny in the Army — and in all probability we shall have one — you'll see that these new-fangled schoolmasters will be at the bottom of it", quoted, ibid., p. 82; 7 March 1833, Wellington to Lord Hill, P.P., 1833, vii, App. I,

concerning purchase; 8 December 1845, Wellington to Fitzroy Somerset, Stanmore, op. cit., p. 74 concerning N.C.O.s' pensions.

31. Concerning Kabul, 19 January 1843, Wellington to Lady Wilton, quoted in Wellington, *Wellington with his Friends*, op. cit., p. 186; about Marmont, Gleig, op. cit., p. 104; Hanoverian Militia, 15 June 1852, Hansard, cxxii, c. 728; *The United Service Gazette*, 8 July 1854. The reference to Torres Vedras concerned Wellington's withdrawal to prepared, defensive lines outside Lisbon in 1810, from which his troops successfully repelled repeated French attacks.

32. Ridley, op. cit., p. 150; C. Petrie, *Wellington: A Re-assessment* (1956), p. 253: 15 November–9 December 1834 Wellington awaited Peel's return from Italy.

33. 6 January 1832, Wellington to the Bishop of Exeter, quoted in Petrie, *Wellington*, op. cit., p. 249, and 11 September 1849, Wellington to Miss Burdett-Coutts, quoted in Wellington, *Wellington with his Friends*, op. cit., p. 279, admitting poor health; Greville quoted in M. Wellesley, *Wellington in Civil Life: Through the Eyes of Those Who Knew Him* (1939), p. 270; strokes, ibid., pp. 274, 287, 290 & 302: in November 1839 the Cabinet actually discussed funeral arrangements.

34. On the Bedchamber Crisis, 8 May 1839, Queen Victoria to Melbourne, Benson & Esher, op. cit., i, p. 157; Wellington's correspondence, Wellesley, op. cit., p. 347, and H. Maxwell, *The Life of Wellington*, ii (1907), pp. 281–2; concerning the Horse Guards, see, for instance, 31 March 1850, Somerset to Brown, Brown Papers, MS 1848, showing his staff at pains to settle a disciplinary matter without disturbing Wellington: the correspondence connected with Brown's later resignation as Adjutant-General revealed that under Wellington he had exercised more power than Hardinge was prepared to allow.

35. 26 February 1852, Memo. by Queen Victoria, Benson & Esher, op. cit., ii, p. 374.

36. A Ci-devant Cavalry Officer, *Army Reform: a practical method of reducing the Army Estimates a Million without diminution of its numerical force* (1833): the author claimed that "the C-in-C and his numerous co-adjutators . . . (were) rejetons of Tory growth". To assist him Richmond (the Postmaster-General) had four other commissioners: Lord John Russell (Paymaster of the Forces), Edward Ellice (Secretary at War), Sir James Kempt (Master-General of the Ordnance) and Major-General Sir Robert Dundas. They were all "appointed to inquire into the practicability and expediency of Consolidating the different departments connected with the civil administration of the Army". The draft report was dated 29 March 1834.

37. Richmond's draft report held that the new Board would cost £10,800 per year and allow the following offices to be abolished: Master-General of the Ordnance, Secretary to the Master-General, Secretary at War, Deputy Secretary at War, Paymaster-General, two Comptrollers of Army Accounts, Secretary to the Comptrollers, Surveyor-General of the Ordnance, Clerk of the Ordnance, Treasurer of the Ordnance, Secretary of the Ordnance, Agent for Commissariat Supplies, Deputy Agent for Commissariat Supplies (together drawing annual salaries of £21,080); Symons, op. cit., p. 5.

38. P.P., 1837, xxxiv, Pt. I, App. p. 105 et seq.; Richmond before the Commission, ibid., pp. 30–1; Richmond's resignation, ibid., p. 8: Richmond and three other Cabinet ministers resigned on 27 May over a proposal to use Irish Church revenue for secular purposes; 16 February 1834, Burgoyne to Sir John Bisset, Secretary to the Commissioners, ibid., p. 182; Grey's Whig government was replaced by Melbourne's First Ministry in July 1834, which in turn gave way to Peel's Tory government in December.

39. P.P., 1837, xxxiv, Pt. I, pp. 8–16: report dated 27 February 1837.

40. 31 December 1837, Melbourne to Queen Victoria, Benson & Esher, op. cit., i, p. 100. The five ministers were Howick, Russell, T. Spring Rice, Palmerston and Hobhouse: a sixth commissioner was Lord Strafford.

41. Russell, 2 March 1854, Hansard, cxxxi, c. 259; 25 March 1837, Memo. by Wellington to Somerset, Herbert Papers, Cabinet & Other Memoranda 1837–1861 file; 4 January 1838, Wellington to Melbourne, enclosed in 8 January 1838, Melbourne to Howick, Grey Papers; Wellington quoted in P.P., 1859 (Sess. 2), ix, p. 8.

42. 18 October 1836, Howick to Russell, Russell Papers, PRO 30/33/2B; (undated) 1836, Howick to Russell, ibid., concerning the King's objections; 3 March 1837, Glenelg to Howick, Grey Papers; 3 January & 8 January 1838, Melbourne to Howick, ibid., noting Hill's objections; 31 December 1837, Melbourne to Queen Victoria, Benson & Esher, op. cit., i, p. 100, noting the reaction of the King of the Belgians; 24 September 1836, L. Sulivan, Deputy Secretary at War, to Howick, Grey Papers.

43. 10 April 1837, Memo. by Donkin, Grey Papers, 25 February 1837, Howick to Vivian, ibid.; 2

March 1837, Vivian to Howick, ibid.; 15, 18, 22 & 25 November 1837, Howick to Vivian, ibid.; 18 & 19 November 1837, Vivian to Howick, ibid.

44. 18 October 1836, Howick to Russell, Russell Papers, PRO 30/22/2B; 30 October 1836, Strafford to Howick, Grey Papers; 8 December 1836, Hobhouse to Russell, Russell Papers, PRO 30/22/2B; 22 December 1836 & 30 January 1837, Palmerston to Howick, Grey Papers.

45. 13 November 1837, Palmerston to Howick, Grey Papers.

46. 17 & 25 November 1837, Russell to Howick, Grey Papers; 30 December 1837, Melbourne to Queen Victoria, Benson & Esher, op. cit., i, p. 99; 9 January 1838, Russell to Melbourne, Grey Papers; 18 January 1838, Howick to Melbourne, ibid.; 22 January 1838, Russell to Melbourne, 28 January 1838, Howick to Melbourne, ibid.; 27 August 1839, Russell to Howick, ibid.

47. 29 November 1836, Memo. by Howick and 8 December 1836, Hobhouse to Russell, Russell Papers, PRO 30/22/2D; 15 August 1837, Russell to Queen Victoria, Benson & Esher, op. cit., i, p. 90; 31 December 1837, Melbourne to Queen Victoria, ibid., i, p. 100.

48. 14 & 18 October 1836, Howick to Russell, Russell Papers, PRO 30/22/2B; 27 December 1837, Melbourne to Queen Victoria, Benson & Esher, op. cit., i, p. 98; Howick to Sidney Herbert, quoted in Stanmore, op. cit., p. 60; 20 November 1838, Melbourne to Queen Victoria, Benson & Esher, op. cit., i, p. 132: "Lord Melbourne fears, from what he hears of the language of Lord Howick and Mr. Monson, that much difficulty will be found in making arrangements and deciding upon questions"; 10 February 1839, Melbourne to Queen Victoria, p. 147; 10 May 1839, Extract from Queen Victoria's Journal, ibid., p. 170; 26 August 1839, Queen Victoria to Melbourne, ibid., p. 185: "Lord Melbourne may rely on the Queen's secrecy concerning Howick . . . Normanby hinted at his wish to get rid of Howick"; 27 August 1893, Russell to Howick, Grey Papers, noting that he had resigned.

49. Herbert quoted in Stanmore, op. cit., p. 59. With war imminent and the weakness of an unreformed administrative system already apparent, Russell's condemnation of Wellington may be seen as an attempt to justify personal lack of action. See also Panmure's Memo. on Military Organisation, February 1855, Douglas & Ramsay, op. cit., i, p. 48: "Had the report of the Commissioners of 1837 been followed out, this (chaos in the Crimea) would not have occurred".

50. Two Mounted Sentries, op. cit., p. 25; William Williams, 26 March 1852, Hansard, cxx, c. 178; Maule's memo., Douglas & Ramsay, op. cit., i, pp. 29–30.

51. 6 April 1850, Prince Albert to Wellington, quoted in 22 January 1854, Memo. by Prince Albert, Aberdeen Papers, Add. MS 43048. Before the Select Committee on Army and Navy Appointments seventeen years earlier, Sir Henry Parnell stated that he planned to unite the offices of Adjutant-General and Quartermaster-General, but remained at the War Office only ten months, P.P., 1833, vii, q. 2766–8.

52. P.P., 1851, vii, p. 791.

CHAPTER III

1. Anon., *Military Administration 1855-1870: a Sketch* (1870), p. 36.

2. *The United Service Gazette*, 18 September 1852; G. C. Moore Smith, *The Life of John Colborne, Field-Marshal Lord Seaton* (1903), pp. 349–50.

3. Memo. by Prince Albert, 17 September 1852, Benson & Esher, op. cit., ii, p. 393, and *The United Service Gazette*, 18 September 1852, emphasised the youth of Cambridge; Joseph Hume, drawing attention to Burgoyne's inability to hold the highest command in the Army, pointed out that as an artillery officer Napoleon would have suffered from the same disability if British, 2 March 1854, Hansard, cxxxi, c. 229.

4. Although Somerset was generally considered a strong candidate and appeared, for instance, in *The United Service Gazette*'s short list of five "freely mentioned in society" on 18 September 1852, Prince Albert's memo. of 17 September suggested that the Prime Minister, Lord Derby, considered only Cambridge and Hardinge as alternative successors to Wellington.

5. L. Strachey & R. Fulford (ed.), *The Greville Memoirs 1814–1860*, iv, (1938) p. 365; e.g. 8 July 1846, Queen Victoria to Hardinge, thanking him for his "interesting communications", Benson & Esher, op. cit., ii, p. 88; 22 September 1852, Prince Albert to Derby, ibid., p. 396, concerning payment of fees.

6. Somerset had been Secretary to the Embassy in Paris immediately after Napoleon's capitulation and assisted Wellington on diplomatic missions to Verona and St. Petersburg;

but almost continuously since 1819 had been in desk appointments, successively as Secretary to the Ordnance and Military Secretary to the C-in-C. Hardinge had been attached to Prussian troops during the occupation of France after Waterloo, then Clerk of the Ordnance and later twice Chief Secretary for Ireland and twice Secretary at War. Between 1844 and 1847 he had acted as Governor General of India and been acclaimed for his military competence in the First Sikh War. On his return to Britain he served on the staff in Ireland and in February 1852 succeeded the Marquess of Anglesey as Master-General of the Ordnance.

7. Memo. by Prince Albert, 17 September 1852, Benson & Esher, op. cit., ii, p. 392.
8. Hardinge's work at the War Office, PRO WO 43/OS 1161, 6251, 22830, 23882 & PRO WO 46/270/439; J. H. Stocqueler, *A Personal History of the Horse Guards* (1873), p. 209; Wheeler, op. cit., p. 135, and R. Biddulph, *Lord Cardwell at the War Office* (1904), p. 48; most authorities agree that he found only fifty serviceable field guns in Britain in 1852, but estimates of the number that he added vary from 100 to 300. At the Great Exhibition, Hardinge told Edward Cardwell that he had unsuccessfully been pressing Wellington to arm the infantry with the Minié rifled musket, Biddulph, op. cit., p. 47.
9. *The United Service Gazette*, 18 & 25 September 1852.
10. Cf. 19 September 1853, Cobden to Mr. McLaren, quoted in Morley, *Cobden*, op. cit., p. 303; 6 November 1853, Sir George Cathcart to Sir George Brown, Brown Papers, MS 1848, concerning riots in Wigan and Blackburn.
11. Aberdeen, 27 December 1852, Hansard, cxxiii, c. 1721; *The Times*, 28 March 1853; Russell, 10 February 1853, Hansard, cxxiv, c. 18; 14 January 1853, Granville to Prince Albert, Granville Papers, PRO 30/29/18, noting that it was "difficult in the present state of religious feeling to adopt any great National Plan ... (in) respect to the extension of education". 4 April 1853, Hansard, cxxv, c. 522, Russell introduced his education bill; first reading without debate, 7 April 1853, ibid., c. 722; 9 July 1853, Gladstone to Russell, Russell Papers, PRO 30/22/11A, suggests the Cabinet was divided: Milner Gibson and Sir Robert Inglis had summarised the objections on 4 April 1853, Hansard, cxxv, c. 552 & 559 resp.
12. Queen's Speech, 31 January 1854, Hansard, cxxx, c. 3–5; *The Times*, 25 January 1854; 28 February 1853, Hansard, cxxiv, c. 772; Seymour, 17 February 1854, Hansard cxxx, c. 816; Hume, 2 March 1854, Hansard, cxxxi, c. 223; Select Committees on the Ordnance and Commissariat abroad (P.P., 1852–3, lix, p. 539), Recruiting (P.P., 1852–3, lix, p. 395), Ordnance Establishment (P.P., 1852–3, lviii, p. 223), the Provision of Small Arms (P.P, 1854, xviii, p. 1).
13. *The United Service Gazette*, 1 January 1853, commented on Herbert's "liberality of principle, strong commonsense, purity of character and official aptitude" and drew particular attention to his months at the War Office between February 1845 and July 1846, when he "introduced more beneficial measures than any other secretary in five times the number of years".
14. At various times during the 1840s Wellington, Burgoyne, Palmerston and Sir William Napier had emphasised the vulnerability of south coast and Channel Island defences. The revolution in 1848, the coup d'état three years later in France, apparent anti-British pamphlets with military connotations by the Prince de Joinville and Captain Maurice and the development of steam vessels, which would facilitate amphibious landings, added weight to their arguments.
15. 30 August 1852, PRO WO 46/89/371, Hardinge's memo. on coastal defences; Queen Victoria quoted in Connell, op. cit., p. 154; Channel Island defences, PRO WO 46/42; Burgoyne, as Inspector-General of Fortifications, to Secretary of State for War and the Colonies, 14 & 16 December 1852, PRO WO 44/510; cf. 25 November 1852, 18 December 1852, 3 February 1853 & 22 April 1853, Board of Ordnance out letters, PRO WO 46/43.
16. J. Fergusson, *The Perils of Portsmouth* (1851); *The United Service Gazette*, 8 January 1853; 10 January 1853, Palmerston to Aberdeen, Palmerston Letterbooks, Add. MS 48578; 12 January 1853, Memo. by Burgoyne on coastal defences, Palmerston Papers under "National Defences"; 31 January 1853, Palmerston to his brother William, quoted in E. Ashley, *The Life of Henry John Temple, Viscount Palmerston*, ii, (1876), p. 6; Stanmore, op. cit., p. 180; Hume, 28 February 1853, Hansard, cxxiv, c. 754.
17. 29 May 1853, Seaton to Capt. W. C. Yonge, Moore Smith, op. cit., p. 350, reporting a disagreement with Burgoyne the previous day; cf. 17, 23 & 25 June 1853, PRO WO 46/43; Graham's tour, Conacher, op. cit., p. 175; land purchase, December 1853 and April 1854, PRO WO 44/286; *The United Service Gazette*, 17 December 1853; 10 April 1854, Burgoyne to Palmerston, Palmerston Papers.
18. 31 October 1852, entry in Grey's Journal, Grey Papers; Board of Ordnance out letters, PRO

WO 46/43; cf: *The United Service Magazine*, January 1853 'England on the Defensive' and February 1853 'The Political State of Europe': in the latter, Fergusson's pamphlet was also reviewed; 16 November 1852, Grey to his brother Charles, Grey Papers.

19. Malmesbury, 6 December 1852, Hansard, cxxiii, c. 970; Sir Frederick Smith, ibid., c. 1019; 27 January 1853, Cobden's speech at Manchester, quoted in Bright & Rogers, op. cit., p. 525; Cobden condemned, *The United Service Gazette*, 5 February 1853; 5 February 1853, Palmerston to Herbert, quoted in Stanmore, op. cit., p. 178; *The United Service Gazette*, 12 February 1853; 14 February 1853, Hansard, cxxiv, c. 85, Cobden quoting a letter signed "Peer of the Realm"; Disraeli, 18 February 1853, ibid., c. 246.

20. *The United Service Magazine*, June 1853; 24 February 1854, Queen Victoria to Aberdeen, Aberdeen Papers, Add. MS 43048.

21. August 1853 survey, PRO WO 46/43/106; 26 September 1853, "Memorandum on the Advantages of Aldershot for a proposed Permanent Encampment", PRO WO 33/1; 24 September 1853, Hardinge to Palmerston, Palmerston Papers under "Hardinge"; 2 October 1853, Palmerston to Aberdeen, Aberdeen Papers, Add. MS 43069. The extra cost of annual hiring was illustrated by the large number of claims paid out after the 1853 manoeuvres on Chobham Common: e.g. £20 to John Argent of Egham and £92 to Rev. John Monsell, PRO WO 58/41/164.

22. Treasury Committee report, 12 April 1852, P.P., 1853, xxx, p. xiii, found that recommendations in Seymour's first interim report of 1849 had been followed and, similarly the Commissariat Minutes show that duplication of Commissariat and Ordnance resources in the colonies had been reduced as finally recommended by Seymour in July 1851, Minutes of 9 November 1852 & 8 April 1853, PRO WO 59/72/21233 & 59/73/6910 respectively; Report of the Treasury Committee of Inquiry, 17 December 1853, p. 1, A Papers 1/53; Ordnance Minutes, 19 January 1854 & 7 February 1854, PRO WO 47/2748; Monsell, 27 February 1854, Hansard, cxxx, c. 1393.

23. Herbert, 28 February 1853, Hansard, cxxiv, c. 670 & 674; 9 February 1853, Board of Ordnance out letter concerning Hythe, PRO WO 46/43/32.

24. *The United Service Magazine*, August 1853; Brown's memo., 18 August 1853, quoted in *The United Service Gazette*, 27 August 1853; Hardinge, 7 April 1854, Hansard, cxxxii, c. 657.

25. Cynical observers declared that "the march of the troops on to Chobham Common could be compared with nothing we know on earth" and that military manoeuvres resembled "a scene partaking of Greenwich Fair and Derby Day", *The United Service Magazine*, June 1853; commenting on the camp, *The United Service Gazette*, 30 July 1853, complained: "They (the British troops) are the worst appointed of any nation except the Spanish or Portuguese"; Seaton's approval of the Commissariat, 30 August 1853, PRO WO 58/41/21; 22 August 1853, Adjutant-General to Commissary-General Sir Randolph Routh, PRO WO 3/321/11; a paper dated 12 January 1854, Herbert Papers, Miscellaneous Papers, revealed that the total cost of the Chobham Camp was £56,887 15s. 2d.

26. 7 April 1854, Hansard, cxxxii, c. 655.

27. 23 October 1852, Queen Victoria to the Earl of Derby, Benson & Esher, op. cit., ii, p. 396; 9 January 1853, Hardinge to Palmerston, Palmerston Papers under "Hardinge"; 10 January 1853, Palmerston to Aberdeen and Aberdeen to Palmerston, Aberdeen Papers, Add. MS 43069; Hardinge, 7 April 1854, Hansard, cxxxii, c. 655; 4 November 1856, Panmure to Queen Victoria, Douglas & Ramsay, op. cit., p. 316; 9 April 1860, Defence Committee Minute, Palmerston Papers under "National Defence".

28. Hume, 28 February 1853, Hansard, cxxiv, c. 743; William Williams on the RMA, 1 March 1854, Hansard, cxxxi, c. 142; 10 December 1852, Deputy Secretary at War to the Treasury, protesting about the Treasury decision, Herbert Papers, Miscellaneous Papers; 6 December 1852, Hansard, cxxiii, c. 1018–19, Hume queried an Ordnance demand for £400,000 to develop large guns and dismissed Martello Towers as "monuments of folly"; 7 December 1852, ibid., c. 1088, Pechell objected to a further £14,000 arguing that, with repairable pieces, 23,963 guns already existed in "all parts of England"; Report of the Treasury Committee on Naval, Ordnance and Commissariat Establishments and Expenditure in the Colonies, 12 April 1852, P.P., 1952, xxx, p. xiv.

29. P.P, 1851, vii, p. 762.

30. Hardinge's agreement in the Ordnance out letter of 10 November 1852, PRO WO 46/43/6; Anglesey's rejection, 20 May 1850, PRO WO 43/92/120486; Hardinge's agreement to the Commission of Inquiry, 18 March 1852, ibid.; 12 December 1852, Raglan to Hardinge, PRO WO 46/88/148.

31. 4 December 1852, Treasury to Secretary at War, undated (early 1853) Memo. by Hardinge and the Royal Warrant, 14 February 1853, PRO WO 43/92/120486. Some saving of staff did occur, e.g. enforced retirement of Mr. J. Stewart, noted 18 April 1853, PRO WO 90/34.

32. 28 February 1853, Hansard, cxxiv, c. 743–4.

33. On 30 November 1853 4,000 Turks were killed by a Russian naval squadron, which penetrated Sinope harbour and used explosive shells at sea for the first time. British public opinion was inflamed at this "massacre". On 4 January 1854 British naval vessels entered the Black Sea to ensure that Russian warships returned to port: war was declared on 28 March 1854.

34. Grey, 31 January 1854, Hansard, cxxx, c. 62; *The Times*, 8 February 1854; Seymour, 17 February 1854, Hansard, cxxx, c. 816.

35. Ibid., c. 817.

36. 2 March 1854, Hansard, cxxxi, c. 223 et seq.

37. Stanmore, op. cit., pp. 1, 2, 14, 175 et seq.: Herbert had taken an ordinary degree at Oxford due to his health and was never thereafter strong; *The United Service Gazette*, 1 January 1853.

38. 23 January 1853, Airey to Brown, 24 January 1853, Raglan to Brown, 24 January 1853, 6 December 1853 & 11 December 1853, Brown to Hardinge, Brown Papers, MS 1848; 15 February 1854, Memo, by Brown, ibid., MS 1849; *The United Service Gazette*, concluded: "Reform stank in his nostrils. He abhorred the idea of improvement" and Lord Panmure later observed: "I never knew a man who so cordially hated all change, whether good or bad", 25 May 1855, Panmure to Raglan, Douglas & Ramsay, op. cit., i, p. 120; *The United Service Gazette*, 31 December 1853.

39. *The United Service Gazette*, 18 December 1852; *The United Service Magazine*, January 1853; Pechell, 28 February 1853, Hansard, cxxiv, c. 755.

CHAPTER IV

1. Trevelyan quoted in J. Fortescue, *History of the British Army*, xiii (1930), p. 34.

2. Instead of relying on civilian contractors to supply waggons and horses, in 1794 a military Corps of Waggoners of five companies was raised to accompany the Duke of York's expedition to Flanders. The corps proved so ill-disciplined and unsatisfactory, that by August 1795 it had been disbanded and the officers retired on half pay. A less ambitious experiment, commenced in 1799, did survive in truncated form till 1823.

3. R. C. Jarvis, 'Army Transport and the English Constitution', *Journal of Transport History*, November 1955; H. Le Mesurier, *A System for the British Commissariat on Foreign Service* (1796), p. 1 et seq.

4. Wellington, referring to the army officer's distaste for commissaries, quoted in Forbes, op. cit., i, p. 184: "The prejudice of society against a commissary almost prevent him from receiving the common respect due to the character of a gentleman"; Lt. Richards in the Crimea, quoted in Hibbert, op. cit., p. 113; Trevelyan, P.P., 1854–5, ix, Pt. II, q. 14021; 3 June 1854, Seaton to his son, quoted in Moore-Smith, op. cit., p. 352; G. R. Emerson, *Sebastopol, the Story of its Fall* (1855), p. 42; Estcourt to Henry Addington, Estcourt Papers, D1571/32/17.

5. Treasury Minute, 22 December 1854, PRO WO 43/103/159744, noted its origin; Treasury, rather than military, responsibility for the Commissariat appointments to the Crimean expedition was emphasised by such documents as one of 14 June 1854, PRO WO 28/49: "By authority of the Lords Commissioners of the Treasury the following appointments have been made in the Commissariat Department . . ."; the Seymour Committee, P.P., 1851, vii, p. 782, noted: "The Commissariat is wholly under the management of the Treasury, by which department the Annual Estimate of its expenditure is prepared, its patronage administered and all its operations directed and controlled".

6. 22 August 1854, Trevelyan to Gladstone, Newcastle Papers, NeC 10545; de Fonblanque, op. cit., p. 49 et seq. The Commissariat Estimates, spread over fourteen different votes, averaged approximately £400,000 in the years immediately prior to the Crimean War: see, for instance, P.P., 1846, xxvi, p. 99 et seq. An example of military reliance on commissariat efficiency was shown in the Crimea, when in November 1854 the Quartermaster-General's Department ordered material for huts, which could only be conveyed to the front by the Commissariat, P.P., 1856, xxi, p. 15.

7. The Duke of Newcastle, in explaining why a particular commissariat clerk could not be promoted for a further year, underlined this to Lord Raglan, 13 January 1855, Newcastle Papers, NeC 10003.

8. Seymour's final report, P.P., 1851, vii, p. 780; War Office, *Commissariat Regulations and Instructions* (1853); Report of the Treasury Committee of Inquiry upon the Ordnance Office (appendix on the transfer of Commissariat business in the United Kingdom to the Ordnance), A Papers 1/53. Symons claims, without corroborative evidence, that even after 1834 the Commissariat provided forage in Ireland, op. cit., p. 11. The table of ranks was laid down on 19 March 1810 and noted in all Army Lists before 1852.

9. In the Crimea, for example, civilians working on construction of the rail link from Balaclava to the Sevastopol Heights were paid by the Commissary-General, 6 December 1854, Newcastle to Raglan, RMP 6807/280/166; during one five-month period in 1854 the Commissariat reimbursed £73,031 17s. 5d. to Agents-General for Crown colonies, PRO WO 58/41.

10. Even when no dispute had arisen the commissary-general must refer to London on a host of matters. For instance, in Bulgaria a Board, which included Commissary-General Filder, agreed on the issue of sugar and coffee, but its decision required ratification by the Treasury, General Order, 28 June 1854, PRO WO 28/48.

11. *The Army List* (1852); Clode, op. cit., ii, p. 193 et seq.; Le Mesurier, op. cit.; de Fonblanque, op. cit., pp. 61–2; H. B. Thomson, op. cit., p. 55. The theory of "waggons of the country" — securing transport in the theatre of operations — had been discredited in campaigns such as Helder (1799), yet the Duke of Newcastle was content to rely upon its effectiveness for Lord Raglan's force, 11 May 1854, Hansard, cxxxiii, c. 140. Wellington on several occasions complained about the absence of promised local supplies: cf. 24 July 1809 to J. H. Frere, British envoy to the Spanish junta, quoted in Brett-James, *Wellington at War*, op. cit., p. 157. To ensure fresh meat supplies, six steamers were attached to the Commissariat in the Crimea, Trevelyan before the Sevastopol Select Committee, P.P., 1854–5, ix, Pt. II, q. 13844.

12. Forbes, op. cit., i, pp. 182–4; Commissariat Minute, 17 February 1854, "attached" Filder to the Expeditionary Force, PRO WO 59/75/3294; 20 February 1854, Trevelyan to Raglan, informing him of Filder's appointment, RMP 6807/290; Wrottesley, P.P., 1854–5, ix, Pt. I, q. 1824; Evans, ibid., q. 679. S. G. P. Ward, *Wellington's Headquarters* (Oxford, 1957), p. 47, notes that in 1809 the Treasury appointed John Murray as Wellington's Commissary-General despite his objections.

13. Treasury Minute, 14 March 1854, quoting Commissariat Regulations, gave Filder specific instructions concerning diet, A Papers 4/54.

14. Financial burdens alone increased enormously during the Crimean campaign. The Estimates for 1854–5, when only colonial stations were involved, totalled £600,000, those for the following year £2,351,199. £600,000 of the new figure was allocated to the United Kingdom and £1,200,000 to the Crimea, of which £238,250 went on land transport, 12 March 1855, Hansard, cxxxvii, c. 438 et seq.

15. R. D. Barbor, 'The Administration of the English and French Armies in the Crimea', *RUSI Journal*, July 1913, later claimed that there were 114 commissariat officers, all outside England.

16. 13 February 1854, Trevelyan to Raglan, Newcastle Papers, NeC 10498; 16 January 1855, Trevelyan to Newcastle, ibid., NeC 10557; Filder insisted that he was sixty-four not seventy as critics claimed, 2 January 1855, Filder to Newcstle, ibid., NeC 10555. Filder, for instance, served as a commissary with the Light Division during the last four years of the Peninsular War, and a strong point in favour of his successor, Sir George MacLean, was his recent active service in South Africa.

17. Newcastle, 7 April 1854, Hansard, cxxxii, c. 647; original numbers, Treasury Minute, 31 March 1854, P.P., 1854–5, ix, Pt. II, p. 375; Filder's complaints, 15 April and 14 September 1854, Filder to Trevelyan, ibid.; Trevelyan's evidence, ibid., q. 13427, 13428, 13458 & 13470; Filder's letter of defence, 27 February 1856, P.P., 1856, xl, p. 337 et seq. By late June 1854 Trevelyan claimed that Filder had "upwards of sixty efficient officers and clerks" with more on the way, 1 July 1854, Trevelyan to Newcastle, Newcastle Papers, NeC 10540a, including a memo. by Filder, dated 20 June 1854, ibid., NeC 10840c; for continuing problems, see for instance Commissariat out letter to Sir Richard Mayne, Metropolitan Police Commissioner, 5 September 1855, noting the "urgent need" for fifteen more storekeepers for the Crimea, PRO WO 58/42/153.

18. Newcastle on supply arrangements, 27 April 1854, Hansard, cxxxii, c. 910; 11 May 1855, Memo. on the Commissariat by S. Petrie, Dalhousie Muniments, 8/234; 20 May 1854, Smith to Trevelyan, Newcastle Papers, NeC 10532; 14 July 1854, Brown to Raglan, Brown Papers, MS 1849/179; Seymour, 12 March 1855, Hansard, cxxxvii, c. 451; 20 June 1854, Memo. by

Filder, Newcastle Papers, NeC 10840c; 31 March 1855, Raglan to Panmure, RMP 6807/286/230, concerning the need for animals.

19. Newcastle, 27 April 1854, Hansard, cxxxii, c. 913; Horsford before the Sevastopol Select Committee, P.P., 1854–5, ix, Pt. II, c. 13386; McNeill and Tulloch, First Report, P.P., 1856, xx, p. 26.

20. Lucan, P. P., 1854–5, ix, Pt. I, q. 6690; McNeill and Tulloch, First Report, P.P, 1856, xx, p. 26; Journal entry, 9 July 1854, referred to "young and inexperienced" commissaries, S. J. G. Calthorpe, *Letters from Headquarters*, i (1856), p. 89; Evans, P.P., 1854–5, ix, Pt. I, q. 874–6.

21. 4 June 1854, Raglan to Herbert, Herbert Papers, Crimea & China file 1854–61; G. Brown, *Memoranda and Observations on the Crimean War 1854–5* (1879), pp. 19–20; 27 February 1856, letter by Filder replying to McNeill and Tulloch's strictures, P.P, 1856, xl, p. 337; Colonel Horsford said that the Commissariat had not provided fuel during the South African campaigns, P.P, 1854–5, ix, Pt. II, q. 13369: Trevelyan stated that troops normally provided their own but the Crimea constituted "very exceptional circumstances", ibid., q. 14027; 13 January 1855, Newcastle to Raglan, Newcastle Papers, NeC 9955a.

22. Indexing, *Commissariat Regulations*, op. cit., p. 98, para. 215; water, ibid., p. 87, paras. 173–6; undated (February 1855), Memo. by Panmure, Douglas & Ramsay, op. cit., i, p. 45; greatcoat episode, Hibbert, op. cit., p. 215; see also 14 December 1854, Memo. by Raglan, RMP 6807/280, concerning the issue of potatoes to a regiment: "The person who delivered the application is informed that the Commissary-General cannot issue less than two tons. I hope this is not true." Only under "extraordinary circumstances" could bread be issued without forms, P.P., 1854–5, ix, Pt. II, q. 13540–5.

23. Cambridge, P.P, 1854–5, ix, Pt. I, q. 3841–2; Evans, ibid., q. 464.

24. 13 April 1855, Panmure to Raglan, RMP 6807/283/75, noting that the line to Kadikoi had been completed on 17 March, but that the Commissariat was still reluctant to use it; Filder's instructions, Treasury Minute, 17 February 1854, enclosed in a letter from Trevelyan to Filder, 20 February 1854, RMP 6807/290; 17 April 1855, Raglan to Panmure, RMP 6807/286/256; 9 February 1855, Newcastle to Raglan and 11 May 1855, Panmure to Raglan, RMP 6807/283; *The Daily News*, 10 July 1854.

25. Report from the Select Committee on Army and Ordnance Expenditure (Army), P.P., 1851, vii, p. 735 et seq.; Report of the Treasury Committee on Naval, Ordnance and Commissariat Establishments and Expenditure in the Colonies, P.P, 1852, xxx, p. xiv et seq.

26. Paulet and Trevelyan, P.P, 1851, vii, pp. 784 & 781 resp.; Commissariat Minute, 23 April 1853, PRO WO 58/62/253. During the Crimean War John Ricardo held that "most respectable houses" would not compete for a contract, knowing that the Treasury would accept the lowest tender. Hence "a very inferior article" was procured and supply problems caused at the front, 12 March 1855, Hansard, cxxxvii, c. 452.

27. Don quoted in de Fonblanque, op. cit., p. 51; 16 May 1850, Memo. by Trevelyan, P.P, 1854–5, Pt. II, p. 362; P.P, 1851, vii, p. 788; Layard questioning Evans, P.P., 1854–5, ix, Pt. I, q. 678–80; de Fonblanque, op. cit., p. 329; 24 July 1854, Raglan to Newcastle, RMP 6807/282.

28. Even before facilities in northern Spain were opened up in the wake of Wellington's advance, English ports were only 800 miles from Lisbon: the Crimea lay 3,000 miles away, for which the development of faster, steam-powered vessels could not fully compensate. De Lacy Evans and Raglan both emphasised that friendly territory represented a distinct advantage and previous French bad faith in not honouring payment a welcome bonus for Wellington: Evans, P.P., 1854–5, ix, Pt. II, q. 672; 20 January 1855, Raglan to Queen Victoria, Benson & Esher, op. cit., iii, p. 69.

29. 8 August 1809, Wellington to his brother William, 11 August 1809 to General Don Gregorio Cuesta and 12 August 1809 to John Villiers, quoted in Brett-James, *Wellington at War*, op. cit., pp. 159 & 161; 8 August 1808, Wellington to Castlereagh, quoted in E. Longford, *Wellington: The Years of Sword* (1969) p. 148.

30. Burgoyne quoted in de Fonblanque, op. cit., p. 63; 1 May 1854, Trevelyan to Newcastle, Newcastle Papers, NeC 10517a; concerning Chobham, 22 August 1853, Adjutant-General to Commissary-General Sir Randolph Routh, PRO WO 3/319/11, 30 August 1853, Lord Seaton, commander of the forces at Chobham, to Routh, PRO WO 58/41/21; Newcastle, 7 April 1854, Hansard, cxxxii, c. 647, 8 May 1854, Filder to Raglan, RMP 6807/293.

31. 10 April 1854, Burgoyne to Raglan, quoted in Wrottesley, op. cit., ii, p. 37; 30 May 1854, Raglan to Lord Cowley, British Ambassador at Paris, RMP 6807/293. *The United Service Gazette* of 29 April 1854, for instance, complained that at Gallipoli "there is not such a thing as

a pound of butter in the whole country and meat is very scarce"; but few British troops stayed there long.

32. 24 July 1854, Raglan to Newcastle, RMP 6807/282; 27 July 1854, Raglan to William Monsell, Clerk of the Ordnance, ibid., 6807/289; rice shortage, 13 July 1854, Light Division Assistant Commissary-General to Sir George Brown, Brown Papers MS 1849/175; 24 July 1854, Airey to Raglan, RMP 6807/292.

33. F. Robinson, *Diary of the Crimean War* (1856), p. 224; D. A. Reid, *Memories of the Crimean War* (1911), p. 12; 6 January 1855, Newcastle to Raglan, RMP 6807/281/202; 12 January 1855, Queen Victoria to Newcastle, Benson & Esher, op. cit., iii, 168; cf. the attack of William Beresford, 22 February 1855, Hansard, cxxxvi, c. 1731.

34. For a full discussion of the transfer see Chapter VI below concerning the Secretary of State for War.

35. 17 February 1856, Panmure to Queen Victoria, Douglas and Ramsay, op. cit., ii, p. 107, claimed that "the public accounts from the Army confirmed too fearfully by the casualties that were occurring" caused the McNeill and Tulloch investigation; instructions to McNeill and Tulloch, P.P, 1856, xl, p. 375 and P.P., 1856, xx, p. 2; Palmerston and Warner, 22 February 1855, Hansard, cxxxvi, c. 1732; two reports, P.P., 1856, xx, p. 5 et seq. and p. 27 et seq.

36. Royal Warrant of 25 February 1856 to establish the Board of General Officers, P.P., 1856, xl. p. 375; Report of the Board of General Officers, P.P., xxi, p. 31.

37. 13 February 1855, Palmerston to Panmure, 15 February 1855, Panmure to Raglan, Douglas & Ramsay, op. cit., i, pp. 63 & 65, 22 February 1855, Palmerston to Raglan, quoted in Ashley, op. cit., ii, p. 81.

38. On 29 January 1855 the House of Commons approved Roebuck's resolution "that a Select Committee be appointed to inquire into the condition of our army before Sevastopol, and into the condition of those Departments of the Government whose duty it has been to minister to the wants of the army", Hansard, cxxxvi, c. 979; the Committee issued five reports, which were not completed and presented until 17 July 1855, P.P., 1854–5, ix, Parts I, II and III.

39. For example, Frederick Peel, Under Secretary of State for War, stated that the suggestion by McNeill and Tulloch that a special officer be appointed to supervise the issue of supplies would not be followed, 7 February 1856, Hansard, cxl, c. 383; and the Duke of Cambridge's suggestion, supported by the Sevastopol Select Commitee, that the Commissariat should become completely military and under the Horse Guards similarly bore no immediate fruit, P.P., 1854–5, ix, Pt. I, q. 4073.

40. 5 March 1855, Report on the Civil Departments of the French Army by Major-General W. Knollys, George Maclean Commissary-General, R. M. Laffan Captain RE, PRO WO 33/1/193.

41. Thackeray, op. cit., especially i, pp. 11, 19, 31–6, and ii, p. 21 et seq.; 4 August 1854, Report by M. Vico, prepared on Lord Raglan's orders, Newcastle Papers, NeC 10645.

42. 15 April 1854, Brown to Newcastle, Newcastle Papers, NeC 10320; 14 December 1854 & 17 January 1855, Burgoyne to Colonel Matson, Assistant Adjutant-General of the Royal Engineers at the Ordnance Office, G. Wrottesley, *The Life and Correspondence of Sir John Burgoyne*, ii (1873), pp. 154 & 192.

43. Entry of 20 November 1854, 'Anonymous Contemporary Notes from the Crimea', J(ournal of the) S(ociety for) A(rmy) H(istorical) R(esearch), xlvi (1968), p. 119; 22 December 1854, Clifford to Mr. Pearce, Fitzherbert, op. cit., p. 132; Trevelyan, P.P., 1854–5, ix, Pt. II, q. 13448 & 14019; Calthorpe, op, cit., ii, p. 455 et seq.; 11 January 1855, Commissariat Minute to Maclean, PRO WO 58/41/358.

44. 6 January 1855, Raglan to Newcastle, RMP 6807/282; 8 February 1855, Burgoyne to Matson, Wrottesley, op. cit., ii, p. 219; 12 March 1855, Lt. Col. McMurdo to Ellenborough, Ellenborough Papers, PRO 30/12/18: he alleged that the Commissariat was "chaotic", 5,000 soldiers (equivalent to one-third of available "effective bayonets") were attached to it, or acting as batmen, and clerks and divisional commissaries were not subject to supervision by an inspecting officer.

45. Burgoyne quoted in Pemberton, *Battles of the Crimean War*, op. cit., p. 29; McNeill and Tulloch, First Report, P.P., 1856, xx, p. 10; Estcourt's comment on Newcastle's despatch of 6 January 1855, Estcourt Papers, D 1571/32/18.

46. Entry in Journal, 5 May 1854, Calthorpe, op. cit., i, p. 24; 13 May 1854, Cambridge to Queen Victoria, Benson & Esher, op. cit., iii, p. 28; Brown's board, General Orders of 22 & 25 June 1854, A. Gordon (ed.), *General Orders issued to the Army in the East* (1856): details of its

proceedings are not traceable; 2 December 1854 & 5 January 1855, Clifford to Mr. Pearce, C. Fitzherbert (ed.), *Henry Clifford V.C.: his letters and sketches from the Crimea* (1956), pp. 133 & 139; Turks, General Order, 2 June 1854, A. Gordon, op. cit.; French, 6 December 1854, Mrs. Duberly's Diary, quoted in K. Chesney, *Crimean War Reader* (1960), p. 143; 24 June 1854, Raglan to Newcastle, RMP 6807/282; e.g. General Orders of 9 May & 6 July 1854, A. Gordon, op. cit., noting transport problems.

47. 15 January 1855, Confidential Memo. by Burgoyne, RMP 6807/288; 8 December 1854 & 23 January 1855, Estcourt to Herbert, Herbert Papers, Miscellaneous Papers; 20 January 1855, Lucan to Raglan, RMP 6807/292; 8 January 1855, Herbert to Lord Lansdowne, Herbert Papers, Misc. Political Correspondence 1834 61 file; 9 January 1855, Newcastle to Palmerston, Palmerston Papers under "Hardinge"; 10 February 1855, Memo. by Palmerston on Cabinet decision to form a Land Transport Corps, Palmerston Papers under "Cabinet Papers"; 12 February 1855, Panmure to Palmerston, Douglas & Ramsay, op. cit., i, pp. 53–4.

48. 16 June 1855, Estcourt to Henry Addington, Estcourt Papers, D 1571/33 noting that the Corps was "forming itself by degrees". For a fuller discussion of the formation of the Corps, see J. Sweetman, 'Military Transport in the Crimean War, 1854–1856', *(The) E(nglish) H(istorical) R(eview)*, January 1973.

49. Frederick Peel on details of the reorganisation, 3 March 1856, Hansard, cxl, c. 1745; undated Cabinet Memo. concerning the peace establishment, Dalhousie Muniments, 8/404; War Dept. to Military Secretary at the Horse Guards, 15 August 1856, P.P., 1857 (Sess I), ix, p. 163, including details of a Royal Warrant of the previous day; see T. J. Edwards, 'Precedence of Administrative Departments of Corps', *RUSI Journal*, August 1956, pp. 427–37, for details of post-war development.

50. 24 March 1855, Beatty to Messrs. Peto, Dalhousie Muniments, 8/202; 12 March 1855, McMurdo to Ellenborough, Ellenborough Papers, PRO 30/12/18; Lucan before the Sevastopol Select Committee, P.P., 1845–5, ix. Pt. I, q. 6692: "My representations to Mr. Commissary-General Filder were never attended to at any time whatever".

51. Statement of Filder about supplies (Newcastle Papers, NeC 9960c) enclosed in the despatch of 20 January 1855, Raglan to Newcastle, ibid., NeC 9960b; 1 January 1855, Newcastle to Raglan, to which Filder added his comments on 18 January, RMP 6807/281/192; McNeill and Tulloch, First Report, P.P., 1856, xx, Pt. I, p. 25 (judgement on Filder).

52. Ball and North, 19 February 1855, Hansard, cxxxvi, c. 1594 et seq.; Trevelyan before the Sevastopol Select Committee, P.P., 1854–5, ix, Pt. II, q. 13495 et seq.; McNeill and Tulloch, First Report, P.P., 1856, xx, pp. 12 & 13; 9 February 1855, Panmure to Raglan, RMP 6807/283; 5 March 1855, Herbert to Raglan, Herbert Papers, Crimea & China 1854–61 file; McNeill and Tulloch, First Report, P.P., 1856, xx, p. 25; 10 June 1855, Palmerston to Panmure, Douglas & Ramsay, op. cit., i, p. 232.

53. 27 February 1856, Filder to the War Dept., a letter he wished to be placed before Parliament, P.P., 1856, xl, p. 337 et seq.; Filder's evidence, P.P., 1856, xxi, p. 392 et seq.; judgement on Filder, ibid., p. 31.

54. Dunne, 12 March 1855, Hansard, cxxxvii, c. 449 et seq.; 30 January 1855, Raglan to Newcastle, RMP 6807/282/164; 24 March 1855, Raglan to Panmure, RMP 6807/286/216 and 219; Filder applied to the Treasury for a floating bakery on 28 November 1854, RMP 6807/281/164.

55. P.P. 1857, ix, p. 85 et seq.; 13 September 1854, Filder to Trevelyan, Herbert Papers, Miscellaneous Papers.

56. Royal Warrant, 28 October 1858, P.P., 1859, xv, p. 187; Lord Louvaine, for instance, 12 March 1855, Hansard, cxxxvii, c. 453, thought to have supply services in civilian hands "not the best" arrangement.

57. Panmure, 18 May 1855, Hansard, cxxxviii, c. 761; auditing transfer, 15 January 1856, Panmure to the Lords of the Treasury, P.P., 1856, xl, p. 23; cf. 12 March 1855, Hansard, cxxvii, c. 453, Louvaine drew attention with approval to India, where the Commissariat recruited "large numbers" of officers from the army.

58. Williams, 8 February 1855, Hansard, cxxxvi, c. 1378.

59. Newcastle, 7 April 1854, ibid., cxxxii, c. 645; 4 June 1855, Panmure to Raglan, RMP 6807/287.

60. Wheeler, op. cit., p. 143; Cabinet Confidential Memo. on the Ordnance, 1 May 1855, A Papers, 27/55. In 1846 the Master-General's annual salary was £3,000, Marquis of Anglesey (ed.), *One Leg: Life and Letters of the First Marquis of Anglesey* (1961), p. 320; 31 December 1826, Anglesey to the King, quoted in ibid., p. 165; 13 April 1827, Canning's offer to Anglesey, ibid.,

p. 169; 23 September 1852, Fitzroy Somerset to his son, Richard, RPP 124/3/184; Newcastle before the Sevastopol Select Committee, P.P., 1854–5, ix, Pt. II, q. 14746; 27 February 1852, Memo. by Prince Albert on Hardinge's appointment, Benson & Esher, op. cit., ii, p. 376; Russell, 17 July 1854, Hansard, cxxxv, c. 323.

61. The Master-General did not sit in the Fox-North (April 1783) or Addington (February 1801) Cabinets, but both were unusually small and he was a member of the Government: perhaps for a similar reason he left the Cabinet in June 1798, when Earl Camden entered as Minister Without Portfolio. When Wellington joined the Cabinet as Master-General in January 1819 his predecessor, the Earl of Mulgrave, already had Cabinet status. Wellington argued that inclusion of the Master-General was "the best constitutional means of bringing an officer of experience and ability into the Cabinet", quoted in Gleig, op. cit., iv, p. 110.

62. 24 February 1852, Derby to Hardinge, quoted in Viscount Charles Hardinge, *Viscount Hardinge* (1891), p. 180; see also 23 February 1852, Derby to Hardinge, and Hardinge to Derby, ibid., pp. 179 & 180. All important Ordnance posts were subject to political approval: 4 December 1853, Aberdeen to Russell, noted the Prime Minister's rejection of Lord Raglan's suggestion that Raglan's own son be appointed Secretary to the Master-General, and 5 December 1853, Aberdeen to Russell, agreed that Captain Boyle should fill the post, Aberdeen Papers, Add. MS 43067.

63. The Master-General did not himself need to be an Ordnance officer and once the post ceased to command Cabinet status, it may have been viewed as something of a veteran's sinecure. "The Master-General, who in his military character as C-in-C over the Artillery and Engineers, has in his Civil capacity the entire control over the whole Ordnance Department", Report of the Parliamentary Select Committee on Finances, 19 July 1797, quoted by Lord Panmure in his Cabinet Confidential Memo., 4 May 1855, Dalhousie Muniments, 8/230.

64. The Corps of Royal Sappers and Miners derived from the Corps of Soldier-Artificers founded at Gibraltar in 1772 and the Corps of Military Artificers raised in the United Kingdom fifteen years later. The Corps of Royal Engineers, originally composed of warrant officers but since 1757 an all-commissioned body, commanded the Sappers and Miners and formally absorbed them in 1856. Marching companies of cadets had been attached to the Royal Artillery since 1722, but a Royal Warrant of 30 April 1741 established the RMA Woolwich, with the Master-General as its Governor. In the decade before 1850, the Ordnance Corps averaged just under 9,000 officers and men, compared with 30,770 in 1813. Expectation of hostilities led to a strength of 18,197 in 1853 and 19,266 a year later, Memo. by Panmure, 22 July 1855, Herbert Papers, Miscellaneous Papers.

65. H. B. Thomson, op. cit., p. 80; Ordnance Department, *Orders and Regulations of the Corps of Royal Engineers* (1851); Anon., *The Royal Artillery* (1855), pp. 33–4; Report of the Treasury Committee of Inquiry upon the Ordnance Office, 17 December 1853, PRO WO 44/523; C. H. Roads, *The British Soldier's Firearm 1850–1864* (1964), p. 27; de Fonblanque, op. cit., p. 192; Guggisberg, op. cit., p. 69.

66. A French cartridge design was considered by an Ordnance Select Committee in 1852, PRO WO 46/88/1, six months later it examined plans for a breech-loading gun, PRO WO 46/87/306, and Lord Dundonald's revived scheme for using sulphur fumes against coastal fortifications was similarly dealt with, C. Lloyd, *Lord Cochrane* (1947), p. 110. Worried by the advent of steam vessels, Lord Hardinge set up his special Ordnance committee to look into the efficiency of British coastal batteries, 30 August 1852, PRO WO 46/89/371. When the Master-General (Lord Raglan) was in the Crimea, the C-in-C needed to ask the Lieutenant-General (Sir Hew Ross) if Ordnance N.C.O.s might transfer to the Land Transport Corps, 20 February 1855, Assistant Adjutant-General to Lieutenant-General of the Ordnance, PRO WO 3/324/221.

67. Report of the Treasury Committee of Inquiry, 17 December 1853, PRO WO 44/523; "The Master-General attends the board only on special and very rare occasions, but all its proceedings in the form of minutes are regularly submitted to him for his approval, and are subject to his control. His authority is supreme in all matters, and he is considered responsible for the manner in which the department is generally conducted", P.P., 1837, xxxiv, Pt. I, p. 7. This reinforced the view of the 1797 Select Committee on Finances, quoted by Panmure in his memo. of 4 May 1855, Dalhousie Muniments, 8/230: "He (the Master-General) can alone do any act which can otherwise, if he does not interfere, be done by the Board".

68. The post of Lieutenant-General was "discontinued" on 3 January 1831, that of Clerk of Deliveries abolished on 28 March 1831 and the Treasurer's office ended on 1 November 1836. The Seymour Committee on Army and Ordnance Expenditure, reporting on 12 July 1849,

noted: "The number of the Board being now reduced to three, the signature of one of the three, with the counter-signature of one of the Secretary and Chief Clerk, is sufficient on orders of payment", Memo. of Panmure, 4 May 1855, Dalhousie Muniments, 8/230.

69. Report of the Treasury Committee of Inquiry, 17 December 1853, PRO WO 44/523; Board of Ordnance Minute, 17 January 1854, PRO WO 47/2748; Cabinet Confidential Memo., 4 May 1855, Dalhousie Muniments, 8/230; Monsell, 2 August 1855, Hansard, cxxxix, c. 1662. In his memo. Panmure noted that after 1850 the Surveyor-General had "no peculiar duties . . . (and had) not been generally employed in the business of the Board and department".

70. George Stacey, a principal clerk in the Storekeeper's branch of the Ordnance, told Viscount Ebrington's 1833 Parliamentary Select Committee on Army and Ordnance Appointments, that the Ordnance supplied "about 27,000" greatcoats annually, P.P., 1833, vii, q. 1188; before the same committee the Clerk of the Ordnance, Lt. Col. Maberly, noted that clothing had been supplied to "the veteran companies in Newfoundland, the African Corps, the Mounted Cape Corps, the Ceylon Riflemen, the Maltese Fencibles and, lately, the Jersey Militia, and almost universally to the Militia, when called on to do so by the Secretary at War", ibid., q. 965.

71. Report of the Treasury Committee, 17 December, 1853, PRO WO 44/523; Confidential Cabinet Memo., 4 May 1855, Dalhousie Muniments, 8/230; Howick Commission, P.P., 1837, xxxiv, Pt. I, p. 7. There were curious anomalies: Lord Grey revealed that the Ordnance provided the cavalry with their carbines and all infantry and cavalry swords, except those for infantry serjeants, 7 April, Hansard, cxxxii, c. 609.

72. Memo. by Panmure, 4 May 1855, Dalhousie Muniments, 8/230; Roads, op. cit., especially Chap. I; 31 January 1853, 2 February 1853 and 4 April 1853, Board Minutes referring to Ordnance land and vessels, PRO WO 47/276; Crimean supplies, 2 September 1854, Newcastle to Raglan, PRO WO 6/69/94, 7 February 1854, Deputy Adjutant-General to the Secretary to the Board of Ordnance, PRO WO 3/322/89; William Monsell, 5 March 1855, Hansard, cxxxvii, c. 111 et seq.: between November 1854 and January 1855 the Ordnance sent out about 2,000 tons of warm clothing.

73. 8 December 1846, Anglesey to Grey, Secretary of State for War and the Colonies, Grey Papers, concerning colonial fortifications; 19 October 1852, Adjutant-General to the Secretary to the Board of Ordnance, PRO WO 3/318/288; 29 May 1846, Hansard, lxxxvi, c. 1430, Ordnance Estimates; Burgoyne's service 1849–51, Finer, *Chadwick*, op. cit., pp. 364, 369, 371 & 441; concerning Public Health Act duties, PRO WO 44/514.

74. Treasury Minutes, 24 July 1822 & 10 April 1834, respectively gave responsibility for barracks and troops in them, App I to the Treasury Report, 17 December 1853, PRO WO 44/523; Seymour Report, P.P., 1849, ix, p. 9, 41 & 44; Minutes of 22 March 1854, PRO WO 47/2748; Staff in 1820 and 1828, P.P., 1837, xxxiv, p. 109; between 1845 and 1850 the London establishment dropped by fourteen officers, PRO WO 44/523, p. 6.

75. Complaints about muskets, 23 & 25 April 1853, Adjutant-General to the Board of Ordnance, PRO WO 3/319/410 & 416; 23 April 1853, PRO WO 58/62/253, minute about bread; 4 May 1848, Shaw to Maule, Dalhousie Muniments, 8/41; Lt. Col. Maberly before Ebrington's Select Committee, P.P., 1833, vii, q. 985; *Commissariat Regulations and Instructions*, op. cit., App. I, p. 189; Report of the Treasury Committee, 17 December 1853, PRO WO 44/523.

76. Select Committee Report, P.P., 1851, vii, p. 799; Monsell, Report of 1853 Treasury Committee, PRO WO 44/523; Grey in *The Naval and Military Gazette*, 14 February 1854; 28 March 1854, Drew to Grey, Grey Papers.

77. Lysons, quoted in Moore Smith, op, cit., p. 292n; see Howick's correspondence at the time of his Royal Commission, 25 February 1838, Howick to Sir Hussey Vivian, and 28 January 1838, Howick to Melbourne, Grey Papers; 26 October 1848, Grey to Queen Victoria, Benson & Esher, op. cit., ii, p. 201; 10 April 1837, Memo. by Donkin, Grey Papers; 20, 24 & 27 September 1841, Hansard, lix, c. 619, 803–4 & 823; Cabinet Confidential Memo. by Panmure, January 1850, Douglas & Ramsay, op. cit., i, p. 29; Newcastle, 7 April 1854, Hansard, cxxxii, c. 645.

78. Hardinge and Peel, 20 & 24 September 1841, Hansard, cix, c. 619 & 806; Evidence of J. Pearse, P.P., 1833, vii, q. 549–53; 19 January 1854, Board of Ordnance Minute on clerks' examination, PRO WO 47/2748; Report of the Treasury Committee, 17 December 1853, noted that it had been "anticipated" by a similar Board commission, PRO WO 44/523; Monsell, 27 February 1854, Hansard, cxxx, c. 1393 et seq.; 28 April 1854, Monsell to Raglan, RMP 6807/289. Virtually on the eve of war, Raglan pointed out that the Ordnance had given

"general satisfaction" in supplying contracted provisions in the United Kingdom, 7 February 1854, Raglan to Gladstone, Gladstone Papers, Add. MS 44377.

79. 12 November 1854, Burgoyne to Colonel Matson, Wrottesley, op. cit., ii, p. 122; Hastings, Comptroller of Stores and Principal Storekeeper, before the Sevastopol Select Committee, P.P., 1854–5, ix, Pt. III, q. 18506–7; Newcastle, quoted in J. H. Stocqueler, *A Familiar History of the British Army* (1871), p. 259; Dunne, 5 May 1854, Hansard, cxxxii, c. 1389.

80. Entrenching tools, *The Times*, 10 June 1854, *The United Service Gazette*, 19 August 1854, George Hadfield, 6 July 1854, Hansard, cxxxiv, c. 1267–8; rusty weapons noted 9 & 17 January 1855, Hawley to his father, S. G. P. Ward (ed.), *The Hawley Letters* (Society for Army Historical Research, 1970), pp. 21 & 22; 23 January 1855, Raglan to Newcastle, RMP 6807/282, complaining about boots; poor tents, Serjeant Gowing and Capt. Ross-Lewin, quoted in Hibbert, op. cit., p. 155; Muntz, 5 March 1855, Hansard, cxxxvii, c. 125; Board difficulties, 7 May 1854, Monsell to Raglan, RMP 6807/289.

81. Muntz on Monsell, Monsell himself and Newdegate, 5 March 1855, Hansard, cxxxvii, c. 125, 111 & 136 respectively; Dunne, 19 June 1855, Hansard, cxxxviii, c. 2251; Williams, 8 February 1855, Hansard, cxxxvi, c. 1377–8; Peel, 17 July 1855, Hansard, cxxxix, c. 970; 16 March 1854, Russell to Aberdeen, Aberdeen Papers, Add, MS 43067; quoting Maule; 19 March 1854, Aberdeen to Russell, ibid.

82. 5 March, Hansard, cxxxvii, c. 124 et seq.; de Fonblanque, op. cit., p. 206n, alleged that of 100,000 barrels of gunpowder used at Sevastopol, 32,000 were manufactured in the USA or Belgium; 27 April 1855, Palmerston to Ross, Palmerston Letterbooks, Add. MS 45879. Roads, op. cit., p. 86, notes that by December 1854 forty regiments in the Crimea were relying on Belgian manufacturers, who on 31 October had undertaken to produce 20,000 1853 pattern Miniés by 31 May 1855.

83. Forbes, op. cit., i, p. 263; Grey, 29 January 1855, Hansard, cxxxvi, c. 1073.

84. 5 December 1854, Raglan to Newcastle, PRO WO 6/70, 4 January 1855, Newcastle to Raglan, ibid.; 12 April 1855, Panmure to Raglan, RMP 6807/283/72; 27 February 1855, Raglan to Panmure, RMP 6807/286/181, enclosing a duplicate of a requisition dated 25 November 1854 in case the original had gone astray.

85. 19 March 1854, Aberdeen to Russell, Aberdeen Papers, Add. MS 43067; 2 & 25 April, Aberdeen to Russell, and 11 August 1854, Russell to Aberdeen, ibid., Add. MS 43068; 12 April 1854, Monsell to Raglan, RMP 6807/289, concerning Paget's appointment; Russell, 17 July 1854, Hansard, cxxxv, c. 325.

86. 16 March 1854, Russell to Aberdeen, Aberdeen Papers, Add. MS 43067, quoting Maule's views; 10 April, Newcastle to Burgoyne, 11 April 1854, Burgoyne to Newcastle, Wrottesley, op. cit., ii, pp. 42–3; 29 April 1854, Aberdeen to Palmerston, Aberdeen Papers, Add. MS 43069, noting Ross's appointment; Gladstone, 2 August 1854, Hansard, cxxxv, c. 1181. In fact Ross was promoted full general over Burgoyne, 14 December 1854, Burgoyne to Matson, Wrottesley, op. cit., ii, p. 156.

87. Hardinge, 7 April 1854, Hansard, cxxxii, c. 656; 31 May 1854, Memo. by Russell, Aberdeen Papers, Add. MS 43068; 21 & 30 June 1854, Monsell to Newcastle, Newcastle Papers, NeC 10331 & 10332.

88. Herbert and Dunne, 17 July 1854, Hansard, cxxxv, c. 335–6 & 341; 14 August 1854, Gladstone to Trevelyan, Newcastle Papers, NeC 10544; Marx quoted by Chesney, op. cit., p. 182.

89. 8 & 16 January, 6 February, Newcastle to Ross, 9 January, Ross to Newcastle, 16 January 1855, Memo. by Director-General of Artillery, P.P., 1854–5, xxxii p. 703 et seq.; 15 January 1855, Monsell to Newcastle, Newcastle Papers NeC 10342; 22 January 1855, Memo, by Russell, Aberdeen Papers, Add. MS 43068; Grey, 29 January 1855, Hansard, cxxvi, c. 1085.

90. 10 February 1855, Memo. by Palmerston on that day's Cabinet, Palmerston Papers, under "Cabinet Papers"; 15 February 1855, Gladstone to Panmure, Dalhousie Muniments, 8/8/6; Panmure, 16 February 1855, Hansard, cxxxvi, c. 1412; Panmure's Cabinet Confidential Memo., dated 17 February but not circulated until 3 May, ibid., 8/3/16; 23 February 1855, Ross to Raglan, RMP 6807/289; Palmerston, 5 March 1855, Hansard, cxxxvii, c. 147; Monsell, 9 March 1855, Hansard, cxxxvii, c. 378.

91. 16 April 1855, Solicitor to the Treasurer to Trevelyan, Dalhousie Muniments, 8/128; 1 May 1855, Memo. by Trevelyan, Palmerston Papers; Cabinet confidential memos., 1, 2 & 3 May 1855, A Papers, 27-9/55; Cabinet Confidential Memo., 4 May 1855, Dalhousie Muniments, 8/230; Palmerston, 11 May 1855, Hansard, cxxxviii, c. 426.

92. 18 May 1855, Hansard, cxxxviii, c. 736 et seq. The Clerk of the Ordnance became "the chief

of the civil staff of the War Department, and the executive officer of the Minister of War, directing all the ordinary business of the subordinate departments", Order in Council, 6 June 1855, P.P., 1854–5, xxxii, p. 677.

93. 23 May 1855, Panmure to Ross, RMP 6807/289; Panmure to Ross and Panmure to Hastings, prepared on 25 May but sent on 28 May 1855, Dalhousie Muniments, 8/316; 21 May 1855, Ross to Raglan, RMP 6807/289 concerning patronage; *The United Service Gazette*, 25 May 1855; 25 May 1855, Panmure to Raglan, Douglas & Ramsay, op. cit., i, p. 210.

94. Clerks' transfer, P.P., 1845–5, xxxii, p. 675; 31 May 1855, Panmure to the Lords of the Treasury, Dalhousie Muniments, 8/279; papers produced by the Under Secretary of State, Frederick Peel, in August 1855 claimed that total Ordnance salaries were reduced from £71,369 to £66,144 per year; P.P., 1854–5, xxxii, p. 671 et seq.; Monsell noting 1 June preparation, 15 June 1855, Hansard, cxxxviii, c. 2033; 2 June 1855, Panmure's submission that the powers of the Board of Ordnance were now "vested in me", Dalhousie Muniments, 8/252; 6 June 1855, Order in Council, P.P., 1854–5, xxxii, p. 677.

95. Concerning Crimean handover, General Order, 12 July 1855, A. Gordon, op. cit.; Monsell, 2 August 1855, Hansard, cxxxix, c. 1665; 18 & 19 Vict. c. 117, 14 August 1855, P.P., 1860, vii, p. 5.

96. 21 May 1855, Raglan to Panmure, 4 June 1855, Panmure to Raglan, RMP 6807/287; see, for example, 23 February & 20 April 1855, Ross to Raglan, RMP 6807/289, giving information about possible changes; 5 June 1855, Raglan to his son Richard, RPP 124/7/240. Panmure may have deemed it unnecessary to consult Raglan closely before announcing his plans, as he appears to have informed his deputy Ross, at least in part. However, it is conceivable that Panmure relied upon Raglan's devotion to duty, equivocal temper and personal friendship to accept a decision of the Crown: A. W. Kinglake, *The Invasion of the Crimea*, viii (Edinburgh & London, 1887), p. 312, n. 1 to Chapter X, claims that this was the only time that Panmure and Raglan disagreed.

97. 23 February 1855, Ross to Raglan, RMP 6807/289; Fortescue, *History of the British Army*, op. cit., xiii, p. 171; Hardinge, 29 January 1855, Hansard, cxxxvi, c. 1109; 7 June 1855, Hardinge to Raglan, RMP 6807/289; 15 June & 23 July 1855, Hardinge to Airey, Airey Papers, G/IV/A/433 & 437. Hardinge certainly determined to make the new organisation work, for he quickly proposed that Ross be made Adjutant-General of Artillery at the Horse Guards, 1 June 1855, Hardinge to Airey, ibid., G/IV/A/430. As early as mid April, he accepted that he was to control the Ordnance Corps, 20 April 1855, Ross to Raglan, RMP 6807/289.

98. 29 May 1855, Hastings to Ross, ibid.; Newdegate on Hastings, 5 March 1855, Hansard, cxxxvii, c. 136; 15 February 1855, Gladstone to Panmure, Dalhousie Muniments, 8/186, noting Monsell's threat to resign.

99. War Department establishment, November 1855, PRO WO 43/103/159744; 15 January 1856, Panmure to the Lords Commissioners of the Treasury, noting the report of a Committee of Inquiry under Hawes dated 3 January 1856, Dalhousie Muniments, 8/316; undated (probably February 1856), Memo. by Hawes to Panmure on further reorganisation which would have saved £3,775 per annum, ibid.

100. 19 November 1856, Queen Victoria to Panmure, Douglas & Ramsay, op. cit., i, p. 495; 4 April 1856, Panmure to Codrington, ibid., ii, p. 180, noting Canadian deficiencies; 17 July 1856, Hardinge to Panmure, ibid., p. 302.

101. July 1854 (no date), Ross to Raglan, RMP 6807/289; Panmure, 18 May 1855, Hansard, cxxxviii, c. 736 et seq.

CHAPTER V

1. 18 March 1831, Hill, the C-in-C, to W. W. Wynn, Secretary at War, PRO WO 43/45/27513; 8 October 1831, Hill to his nephew, quoted in E. Sidney, *Lord Hill* (1845), p. 352.

2. The Horse Guards building was erected in Charles II's reign, but did not come into regular use as Army Headquarters until 1795, S. G. P. Ward, *Wellington's Headquarters*, op. cit., p. 17.

3. Clode, op. cit., ii, p. 335; Omond, op. cit., pp. 66–7; Symons, op. cit., pp. 2–3. The standing Board of General Officers was created in 1714 to deal with financial disputes and problems of regimental precedence within the Army and to exercise responsibility for its clothing: after 1793, only the latter function remained to it.

4. Patent issued to Wellington (to which that of Hardinge was identical), Herbert Papers,

Miscellaneous Papers; 16 September 1852, Memo. on the duties of the C-in-C, counter-signed by the Secretary at War and Quartermaster-General, PRO WO 43/95/15244; C-in-C's clerks, Ridley, op. cit., p. 36, return on the estimates for the C-in-C's office, P.P., 1821, xv, p. 85 & PRO WO 43/78/103000; the C-in-C's own office staff in 1812 comprised: C-in-C, four ADCs, 1 Chaplain, 1 Military Secretary, 1 Private Secretary, 1 Assistant Military Secretary, 1 Principal Clerk, 3 Established Clerks, 4 Junior Clerks, 4 Temporary Clerks, 1 Office Keeper, 1 Store Keeper, 3 Messengers, 3 Women Servants & 1 Coal Porter; Crawford, 27 February 1843, Hansard, lxvi, c. 1352: the Army Estimates of 1845–6 & 1846–7 for the C-in-C's office were £16,465 8s. 7d. and £16,732 13s. 1d. respectively, of which roughly £750 was spent on postage, P.P., xxvi, p. 68.

5. Memo. of 16 September 1852, acknowledged by the Secretary at War, PRO WO 43/95/152444; C-in-C out-letter, 12 April 1853, noting that the Inspecting Field Officer at York would inspect the Lincolnshire Militia at their annual camp, PRO WO 3/114/424; 1 April 1853, concerning the inspection of Yeoman cavalry, PRO WO 3/114/411; 10 October 1853, order for the inspection of Chelsea out-pensioners in Ayr district, PRO WO 3/115/231; 26 April 1853, note that NCOs of twenty years service could volunteer as Militia staff, PRO WO 3/114/458; 8 November 1852, Prince Albert to Hardinge, Benson & Esher, op.cit., ii, p. 398; *The United Service Gazette*, 25 September 1852; Clode, op. cit., ii, p. 406.

6. 6 August 1853, Hardinge's personal inspection of Aldershot Heath, PRO WO 46/43/106; 9 February 1853, Memo. by Hardinge on Hythe, PRO WO 46/43/32; 20 March 1854, Deputy Adjutant-General's Memo. on Hythe, PRO WO 3/322/216.

7. Clode, op. cit., ii, p. 359; 12 February 1844, Hansard, lxxii, c. 514, the Secretary at War noted the C-in-C's action about the Brighton affray; concerning Devonport and charges, C-in-C out-letter, 2 November 1852, PRO WO 3/114/87; concerning Cardigan, 25 August 1852, Brown to Lt. Gen. Blakeney, Brown Papers, MS 1848/61; 20 January 1854, Hardinge to Brown, ibid., MS 1849/4; uniforms and weapons, for example, ibid., MS 1848.

8. Duke of York, Stocqueler, *British Army*, op. cit., p. 214; Hardinge, 10 February 1854, Newcastle to Queen Victoria, Newcastle Papers, NeC 9785; examples of Wellington's complaints 1810–15, quoted in Brett-James, *Wellington at War*, op. cit., pp. xxxiii, 198 & 306; concerning Schoedde & Paulet, 22 December 1854, Raglan to Major-General York, 23 & 30 December 1854, Raglan to Hardinge, RMP 6807/289; 17 February 1854, Estcourt to his brother Tom, Estcourt Papers, D1571/33.

9. 12 February 1855, Burgoyne to Matson, Wrottesley, op. cit., ii, p. 221: "Lord Hardinge has no control or power over Lord Raglan"; 26 November 1855, Panmure to Codrington, Douglas & Ramsay, op. cit., i, p. 505; 13 July 1854, Hardinge to Raglan, RMP 6807/289; February 1854, Lady Raglan to Priscilla, Lady Westmorland, RPP, Miscellaneous Papers, noted Raglan's interviews; 7 March 1854, de Ros to Raglan, RMP 6807/292; 25 April 1853, Adjutant-General to C-in-C Bengal, PRO WO 3/114/456.

10. 16 March 1817, Memo. by Palmerston on the Military Secretary's pay, PRO WO 43/95/151483; Clode, op. cit., ii, p. 343; Torrens quoted in R. Glover, *Peninsular Preparation* (Cambridge, 1963), p. 44; 18 May 1854, Hardinge to Airey, Airey Papers, G/IV/A/373. Applications for commissions, promotions and appointments went through the Military Secretary, and his influence on their success or failure cannot accurately be gauged: cf. 21 October 1843, Gladstone to Fitzroy Somerset, Gladstone Papers, Add. MS 44527, applying for "a staff or any other suitable military appointment" for Lt. Col. Fraser.

11. Brown originally submitted his resignation on 24 January 1853, because he had not gained Hardinge's "confidence", withdrew it after pleas from Airey and Raglan and finally resigned on 11 December 1853, Brown Papers, MS 1848.

12. Cf. 25 May 1850, Memo. by the Adjutant-General, announcing his decision to proceed with the court-martial of Captain Douglas, ibid.; 23 February 1854, Deputy Adjutant-General's memo. concerning the passage of an officer to Mauritius, PRO WO 3/322/125; 23 February 1854, Deputy Adjutant-General to Commandant at Chatham, concerning the transfer of Pte. Witchell to the 98th Regiment, PRO WO 3/322/126; in 1811 the Adjutant-General ordered commanding officers to organise regimental schools in every batallion or corps, A. C. T. White, *The Story of Army Education, 1643–1963* (1963), p. 21; Estcourt's comments on the Duke of Newcastle's despatch, dated 6 January 1855, Estcourt Papers, D1571/32/18; 9 November 1854, Hardinge to Airey, Airey Papers, G/IV/A/394.

13. Cf. 26 November 1852, Adjutant-General to the Inspector-General of Cavalry, acknowledging his "confidential reports and returns", PRO WO 3/114/141; 6 November 1853, Adjutant-General to Sir George Cathcart, acknowledging information about the state of forces in

northern England, Brown Papers, MS 1848/164; 16 January 1854, Deputy Adjutant-General noted report from Lt. Gen. Wood, commanding in the West Indies, PRO WO 3/322/7; Clode, op. cit., ii, p. 335 et seq.

14. 14 March 1854, Cathcart to Brown, Brown Papers, MS 1849/41; Macdonald before Lord Ebrington's Select Committee, P.P., 1833, vii, q. 2299 & 2301; Calvert's work, S. G. P. Ward, *Wellington's Headquarters*, op. cit., pp. 18–19; P.P., 1836, xxxviii, p. 108, returns of officers in Adjutant-General's department; P.P., 1846, xxvi, p. 68, 1845-6 estimate for the Adjutant-General's department totalled £12,838 7s. 4d.; 27 February 1843, Hansard, lxvi, c. 1352, Sharman Crawford complained that a £12,000 expense for the Adjutant-General's department was "enormous" and unjustified.

15. P.P., 1836, xxxviii, p. 108, returns of the Quartermaster-General's department; 27 February 1843, Hansard, lxvi, c. 1352, Sharman Crawford noted that the Adjutant-General's department estimate was for £12,000 and the Quartermaster-General's £6,000.

16. Clode, op. cit., ii, p. 342; Board of General Officers Inquiry into the McNeill & Tulloch reports, P.P., 1856, xxi, p. 12; Omond, op. cit., p. 66. Cf. 9 November 1854, Hardinge to Airey, Airey Papers, G/IV/A/394: "We have ordered out a full proportion of QMG (sic) stores such as cooking kettles etc".

17. Undated (February 1854), Lady Raglan to Priscilla, Lady Westmorland, RPP, Miscellaneous Papers; Godwin-Austen, op. cit., p. 62 et seq.; 3 June 1854, Seaton to his son, quoted in Moore-Smith, op. cit., p. 352; 25 February 1855, Sir James Freeth to Airey, Airey Papers, G/IV/A/418. Eventually, in November 1855, a Chief of Staff was appointed in the Crimea to co-ordinate the activities of the Adjutant-General and Quartermaster-General, with the Military Secretary retaining responsibility for the expeditionary commander's military correspondence.

18. 1 February 1828, Wellington to Hill, 20 November 1830, Sir Herbert Taylor to Hill, 9 August 1842, Hill to Peel, quoted in Sidney, op. cit., pp. 336, 343 & 372; 10 August, Peel to Queen Victoria, 12 August 1842, Wellington to Queen Victoria, Benson & Esher, op. cit., i, pp. 420 & 421; 12 December 1845, Wellington to Queen Victoria, ibid., ii, p. 55.

19. Concerning Hill in 1837, Clode, op. cit., ii, p. 347: during this particular controversy Lord John Russell argued that the Tories had always sent a political sympathiser to the Horse Guards, refusing to appoint either Lord Anglesey or Lord Strafford, 13 September 1837, Russell to Melbourne, Russell Papers, PRO 30/22/2D; 12 December 1845, Wellington to Queen Victoria, Benson & Esher, op. cit., ii, p. 55; 11 January, 2 February, 23 March & 23 July 1855, Hardinge to Airey, Airey Papers, G/IV/A/410, 412, 423 & 437; 8 October 1831, Hill to his nephew, quoted in Sidney, op. cit., p. 352; Wellington, quoted in M. E. Howard, *Wellingtonian Studies* (Aldershot, 1959), p. 85.

20. 29 June 1854, Queen Victoria to Aberdeen, Aberdeen Papers, Add. MS 43048, noted that the Prince Consort had no legal position; 17 February 1852, Memo. by Prince Albert, Benson & Esher, op. cit., ii, p. 392: he noted that Derby considered Cambridge as an alternative, "but perceived that his rank as Major-General and youth would hardly entitle him to such an advancement".

21. Queen Victoria quoted in Benson & Esher, op. cit., i, p. 8; George Monck's commission of 3 August 1660 designated him "Captain-General and C-in-C of all Forces", R. E. Scouller, *The Armies of Queen Anne* (1966), p. 54; 16 August 1811, Memo. by Palmerston, Herbert Papers, Miscellaneous Papers.

22. George IV's remark, noted 9 May 1827, Duke of Rutland to Lady Shelley, and quoted in Anglesey, op. cit., p. 169; 21 May 1827, King to Wellington, ibid., p. 172; William IV to Hill, 1830: "I hope you will long continue to command my army", quoted in Sidney, op. cit., p. 343; 2 April 1854, Prince Albert to Aberdeen, Aberdeen Papers, Add. MS 43049, reporting a conversation with Lord Grey the previous day; cf., too, 9 April 1855, Queen Victoria to Raglan, RMP 6807/280, describing control of the Army as "one of the Queen's dearest prerogatives".

23. 24 April 1841, Melbourne to Queen Victoria, Benson & Esher, op. cit., i, p. 262, about possible political action to remove Lord Cardigan from command of his regiment over the notorious Easter flogging incident: "Nothing is more to be apprehended and deprecated than such an interference of the House of Commons with the interior discipline and government of the Army". One of Prince Albert's reasons for rejecting nomination as Wellington's successor at the Horse Guards was the fear that, after he left the post, closer political control would be exercised over the Army than at present, Memo. dated 6 April 1850, attached to another of 22 January 1854, Aberdeen Papers, Add. MS 43048.

24. 24 & 25 April 1841, Melbourne to Queen Victoria, Benson & Esher, op. cit., i, pp. 262 & 263; 26 March 1847, Hansard, xc, c. 489, Russell on the Short-Service Bill.

25. Wellington quoted in Constitutionalist, op. cit., p. 12; 27 February 1843, Hansard, lxvi, c. 1347–9; 4 July 1843, Hansard, lxx, c. 611–15.

26. 21 August 1827, Wellington to Charles Arbuthnot, quoted in Wellington, *Wellington with his Friends*, op. cit., p. 76; cf. 15 January 1855, Raglan to Newcastle, RMP 6807/282, which concluded "that I no longer enjoy your confidence", but added: "My duty however to the Queen will induce me to persevere in doing my best to carry on the service to the utmost of my ability".

27. 2 March 1854, Hansard, cxxxi, c. 228, Joseph Hume stated that the Secretary at War "(was) required to answer all questions in Parliament connected with the administration of the Army and could offer such suggestions as he might think fit to the C-in-C"; Omond, op. cit., p. 69; 29 May 1812, Prince Regent's Minute in Council, Herbert Papers, Miscellaneous Papers.

28. There was no C-in-C 5–22 January and again from 5 May to 27 August 1827. 19 January 1827, PRO WO 43/95/152444, King's comment appended to the draft G.O; 5–22 January, several relevant letters passed between the Adjutant-General, Henry Torrens, who resented the Secretary at War's claims, Palmerston and the King; 4 May, Palmerston to the Lords of the Treasury, 5 May 1827, Treasury approval for his arrangements, PRO WO 43/17/1469.

29. 18 March, Hill to Wynn, & 30 March 1831, Wynn to Hill, PRO WO 43/45/27513; 31 August & 13 September, Hill to Hobhouse, 11 September 1832, Hobhouse to Hill, PRO WO 43/28/11626.

30. 20 September 1852, Beresford to Derby, PRO WO 43/95/152444; Memos. of Brown & Airey, plus Brown's note, all dated 16 September 1852, ibid.

31. In 1825 the Horse Guards resisted a War Office suggestion concerning the provision of military savings banks: in 1823 & 1826 an argument erupted as to whether an officer should apply to the Secretary at War or the C-in-C for travelling expenses, Ridley, op. cit., pp. 58 & 82.

32. 2 March 1837, Vivian to Howick, Grey Papers; letter to the editor, dated 10 April 1854, *The United Service Gazette*, 22 April 1854.

33. 29 November 1854, Hardinge to Airey, Airey Papers, G/IV/A/390; concerning Airey, 18 September 1854, Newcastle Papers, NeC 9973; on Jones, 2 January 1855, Newcastle to Raglan, PRO WO 6/70/195; Raglan's promotion, 18 November 1854, Prince Albert to Newcastle, Newcastle Papers, NeC 9696 & 6 December 1854, Queen Victoria to Newcastle, ibid., NeC 9752; 15 June 1854, Raglan to Hardinge, RMP 6807/289; Palmerston, 16 February 1855, Hansard, cxxxiv, c. 1405.

34. 5 April 1854, Hardinge to Raglan, A Papers, 14/55; 22 July 1854, Hardinge to Airey, Airey Papers, G/IV/A/382; concerning Lucan, 2 March 1855, Hardinge to Raglan, RMP 6807/289; 11 July 1855, Memo. on Medical Officers' servants, PRO WO 3/325/310; 4 May 1855, Memo. by Adjutant-General on transmission of weekly states, PRO WO 3/325/36; 22 November 1855, Queen Victoria to Hardinge, Benson & Esher, op. cit., iii, p. 153.

35. On Lucan's staff, 22 March 1854, Deputy Assistant Adjutant-General to the Military Secretary, PRO WO 3/322/221; 17 September 1854, Burgoyne to Colonel Sandham, noting his letter to Hardinge, Wrottesley, op. cit., ii, p. 87; 19 October 1854, Hardinge to Burgoyne, ibid., p. 108: Burgoyne never held the post of Commanding Royal Engineer in the Crimea, as he informed Sandham: "I have no position in the Army, and am merely (here) as an amateur"; 9 May 1854, Hardinge to Raglan, RMP 6807/289, appointing Raglan Colonel of the Blues; 5 May 1855, Military Secretary to Brown, Brown Papers, MS 1850/86, noting that Hardinge had recommended him as Colonel of the 7th Royal Fusiliers; 6 & 29 December 1854, Newcastle to Queen Victoria, Newcastle Papers, NeC 9786, concerning the Order of the Bath.

36. 10 February 1854, Newcastle to Queen Victoria, Newcastle Papers NeC 9785, about Hardinge's organisation of the Expeditionary Force; on Malta, 29 January 1855, Memo. by Hardinge, ibid., NeC 10092b; 15 November 1854, Memo. by Hardinge on cavalry drafts to the Crimea, ibid., NeC 10087b.

37. Concerning Raglan, 10 February 1854, Newcastle to Queen Victoria, Newcastle Papers, NeC 9785; on Cambridge, undated (February 1854), Hardinge to Newcastle, ibid., NeC 10059d; on Brown, 12 February 1854, Hardinge to Newcastle, ibid., NeC 10061.

38. Entry in Cambridge's diary, 11 February 1854, quoted in E. Sheppard (ed.), *George, Duke of Cambridge*, i (1906), p. 114; 19 July 1854, Newcastle to Queen Victoria, Newcastle Papers, NeC 9785, concerning Cathcart; 9 July 1855, Panmure to Queen Victoria, Douglas &

Ramsay, op. cit., i, p. 282, noted discussion with Hardinge on Simpson's successor; 20 October 1855, Panmure to Codrington, ibid., p. 453, informing him of consultations with Hardinge concerning two corps; for details of Newcastle's board see Chapter VI below; Wrottesley, op. cit., ii, p. 286, states that after his return from the Crimea, Sir John Burgoyne attended two Councils of War at Windsor with the Emperor of France, his Minister of War, the Prince Consort, Lord Hardinge and "the War Committee of the Cabinet"; 1 December 1854, Aberdeen to Queen Victoria, Add. MS 43050, noted that Hardinge attended a Cabinet meeting on 30 November, proposing with Newcastle and Sidney Herbert establishment of an army of reserves at Malta; entry in Lord Granville's diary, 4 January 1856: "Clarendon, Lyons and Hardinge attended the War Committee this morning besides the usual members", E. Fitzmaurice; *The Life of Granville George Leveson Gower, Second Earl Granville K.G. 1815–1891*, i (1905), p. 137.

39. 23 March 1855, Hardinge to Airey, Airey Papers, G/IV/A/423; 27 July 1854, Raglan to Newcastle, Newcastle Papers, NeC 9801, concerning sickness reports; 15 December 1854, Newcastle to Raglan, ibid., NeC 9994, on Bentick.

40. 8 December 1854, Hardinge to Airey, Airey Papers, G/IV/A/399; Hardinge, 29 January 1855, Hansard, cxxxvi, c. 1108; 8 July 1854, Hardinge to Airey, Airey Papers, G/IV/A/381.

41. Panmure, 21 February 1856, Hansard, cxl, c. 1034; cf. *The United Service Gazette*, 7 April 1855: "The Minister of War should be a Soldier of experience with the rank of Marshal . . . he should be actually C-in-C of the Army"; Palmerston, 6 March 1855, Hansard, cxxxvii, c. 190; Hardwicke, 3 May 1855, Hansard, cxxxviii, c. 13; P.P., 1854–5, ix, Pt. II, q. 14724; Panmure's supplementary patent, quoted in Biddulph, op. cit., p. 235: see also Chapter VI below.

42. 7 June 1855, Hardinge to Raglan, RMP 6807/289; 18 June 1855, Panmure to Prince Albert, Douglas & Ramsay, op. cit., ii, p. 240; 17 July, Hardinge to Panmure, acknowledged 22 July 1855, Dalhousie Muniments, 8/380; 22 July 1855, Memo. by Panmure, Herbert Papers, Miscellaneous Papers; 18 August, 14 & 24 September 1855, Hardinge to Airey, Airey Papers, G/IV/A/441, 447 & 450.

43. 21 February 1856, Hansard, cxl, c. 1033 et seq.; 22 February 1856, Panmure to Queen Victoria, Douglas & Ramsay, op. cit., ii, p. 118; 22 February 1856, Panmure to Codrington, ibid., p. 122; 21 January 1855, Queen Victoria to Aberdeen, Benson & Esher, op. cit., iii, p. 71: see also Chapter VI below.

44. 22 January 1855, Queen Victoria to Aberdeen, Benson & Esher, op. cit., iii, p. 71; February 1855, Queen Victoria, quoted in Connell, op. cit., p. 171; 15 June, Queen Victoria to Panmure, 17 June 1855, Prince Consort to Panmure, Douglas & Ramsay, op. cit., i, pp. 237 & 239; 17 September 1855, Prince Albert to Clarendon, ibid., p. 390 et seq.; 15 February 1856, Panmure to Codrington, Douglas & Ramsay, op. cit., ii, p. 105; 18 February 1856, Palmerston to Panmure, ibid., p. 111; July 1856, Queen Victoria, quoted in Connell, op. cit., p. 205.

45. 19 February 1855, Hansard, cxxxvi, c. 1568, Colonel Knox called for the C-in-C to be in the Cabinet; 13 June 1854, Hardinge to Airey, Airey Papers, G/IV/A/377, concerning Court procedure; 8 July 1854, Hardinge to Airey, ibid., G/IV/A/381.

46. 7 April 1854, Hansard, cxxxii, c. 606 et seq.

47. 5 June, Grey to Drummond, 7 & 9 June 1854, Wood to Grey, Grey Papers.

48. Grey, 29 January 1855, Hansard, cxxxvi, c. 1086 et seq.; 25 January 1855, Gladstone to Aberdeen, Aberdeen Papers, Add. MS 44089; April 1855, Memo. on Military Organisation, by Cambridge, quoted in Verner, op. cit., i, p. 105.

49. 18 May 1855, Hansard, cxxxviii, c. 736 et seq.

50. 15 June 1855, Queen Victoria to Panmure, Douglas and Ramsay, op. cit., i, p. 237; 17 June 1855, Prince Albert to Panmure, ibid., p. 239.

51. 18 June 1855, Panmure to Prince Albert, ibid., p. 240; 22 July 1855, 'Memo. as to the Conduct of Military Affairs in the War Department, submitted by Lord Panmure to the Queen and approved by Her Majesty', Herbert Papers, Miscellaneous Papers; 23 May 1855, Panmure to Hardinge, P.P., 1860, vii, p. 5, informing him that he should "forthwith" assume command of the Ordnance troops. See also Chapter VI below for further discussion of the Secretary of State's position.

52. 23 October 1857, Queen Victoria on Cambridge's reaction, quoted in G. St. Aubyn, *The Royal George — The Life of the Duke of Cambridge* (1963), p. 109; 30 October 1857, Queen Victoria to Cambridge, Verner, op. cit., i, p. 170.

53. Hardinge, 21 February 1856, Hansard, cxl, c. 1044; 18 July 1856, Cambridge's letter of

service, P.P., 1860, vii, p. 6: the Duke did not officially become "C-in-C" until 1887; Cambridge before the Select Committee on Military Organisation, ibid., q. 3889, and Graham, q. 4103.

CHAPTER VI

1. 16 August 1811, Memo. by Palmerston, Herbert Papers, Miscellaneous Papers.

2. Wellington's comment of 1836, cited in P.P., 1859 (Sess. 2), ix, p. 8; Hardinge quoted in a memo. by Sir James Graham (probably summer 1832), Herbert Papers, Miscellaneous Papers.

3. Clode, op. cit., ii, p. 222; Fortescue, *History of the British Army*, op. cit., iv, p. 872. A century after the disappearance of the office, W. B. Pemberton, *Lord Palmerston*, op. cit., p. 14, remarked: "Only an obstinately unmilitarily-minded nation could have evolved such an office as that of Secretary at War".

4. H. Gordon, op. cit., pp. 16 & 38; 16 August 1811, Memo. by Palmerston, Herbert Papers, Miscellaneous Papers: the first War Office records were dated 21 January 1669. Olive Anderson, 'The Constitutional Position of the Secretary at War 1642–1855', *JSAHR*, xxxvi (1958), and H. Gordon, op. cit., p. 15, suggest that the Clerk to the Committee of War of the Privy Council during the Civil War fulfilled the later functions of the Secretary at War.

5. War Office circular, 25 September 1826, printed in the *London Gazette* next day: "The Rt. Hon. Lord Viscount Palmerston, His Majesty's Secretary at War, has appointed Lawrence Sulivan Esq. to be His Deputy"; and, similarly, Fox Maule appointed Benjamin Hawes on 31 October 1851, PRO WO 43/95/151483; 16 August 1811, Memo. by Palmerston, Herbert Papers, Miscellaneous Papers.

6. Howick Report, P.P., 1873, xxxiv, Pt. I, p. 6; P.P., 1851, vii, p. 737; 1846–7 Estimates prepared by Sidney Herbert, P.P., 1846, xxvi, pp. 94–5; Sir Henry Hardinge, the Secretary at War, 7 March 1842, Hansard, lxi, c. 157; third reading of the Mutiny Bill, 15 April 1842, Hansard, lxii, c. 519 et seq.; 19 March 1846, Hansard, lxxxiv, c. 1267.

7. Life Guard allowances, 13 June 1845, Hansard, lxxxi, c. 530–1; on a pension to Col. Uniacke's widow, 31 May 1849, Hansard, cv, c. 1013; concerning the Militia Act, Costin & Watson, op. cit., ii, p. 100; Board of Ordnance, noting pensioner authorisation, 29 October & 10 November 1852, PRO WO 47/2745; payment to Artillery officers noted, 14 January 1853, PRO WO 47/2746; military prisons, 21 February 1853, ibid.: this and many other authorised expenses amounted to less than £20; 6 March 1854, Sir John Kirkland to Raglan, noted the Secretary at War's authorisation of payment to Raglan and his staff, RMP 6807/305; 18 November 1854, Col. Matson to Burgoyne, Wrottesley, op. cit., ii, p. 128, that he had approached the Secretary at War about Burgoyne's staff pay.

8. Cap covers, 29 April 1854, Deputy Adjutant-General memo., PRO WO 3/322/329; on C-in-C's clerks, 25 May 1854, Military Secretary to Deputy Secretary at War, and 28 June 1854, Trevelyan to Secretary at War, PRO WO 43/78/103000; pay, Walshe, op. cit., p. 162; on private finance, 5 February 1853, Secretary at War to Mrs. Pentland, PRO WO 4/271/13; pension limitation, P.P., 1851, vii, p. 767, and 28 July 1855, Secretary at War to Mrs. Alexander, PRO WO 4/1038/415.

9. For further details of the Secretary at War's financial responsibilities, see Clode, op. cit., ii, pp. 538–9, H. Gordon, op. cit., p. 235, H. B. Thomson, op. cit., p. 50, and War Office, *Warrants and Regulations*, op. cit., section 1 et seq.; Treasury Report on the War Office, 23 December 1852, Herbert Papers, Miscellaneous Papers; Seymour Committee, P.P., vii, p. 737.

10. War Office, *Warrants and Regulations*, op. cit., sections 26 & 33; P.P., 1837, xxxiv, Pt. I, p. 6; 12 March 1844, Hansard, lxxiii, c. 862, Hardinge answering Thomas Gill; 11 March 1844, ibid., c. 801, concerning Col. Fawcett's widow; 12 January 1853 & 1 September 1854, Secretary at War to the Solicitor to the Treasury, PRO WO 4/271/6 & 257, asking for a ruling on billeting and the sale of alcohol respectively.

11. 16 August 1811, Memo. by Palmerston, Herbert Papers, Miscellaneous Papers; Crawford, 28 May 1852, Hansard, cxxi, c. 1322: "There was nothing which the people of this country were more jealous of, or ought to be more adverse to, than the interference of military officers in influencing votes for Members of Parliament". On 14 June 1852, Hansard, cxxii, c. 597, Beresford, after an investigation, refuted Crawford's charge.

12. Hardinge, 31 July 1843, Hansard, lxxi, c. 8; Maule, 17 May 1847, Hansard, lxxxii, c. 951, and, answering Colonel Reid, 21 June 1850, Hansard, cxii, c. 150; Panmure, 18 May 1855, Hansard, cxxxviii, c. 750.

13. Cf. 16 March 1817, Memo, by Palmerston and other correspondence 1817–18, PRO WO 43/95/151483; wartime establishment, Ridley, op. cit., p. 36; clerical staff, PRO WO 43/ OS 098 & PRO WO 4/725/339; undated (1854), Memo. by Hawes, PRO WO 43/95/151483.

14. Payment of out-pensioners bill, 11 March 1846, Hansard, lxxxiv, c. 973; White, op. cit., p. 33; 1 February 1845, Herbert to his mother, quoted in Stanmore, op. cit., i, p. 33, and his remark on re-appointment, ibid., p. 174; October 1851, Memo, by Lawrence Sulivan, Deputy Secretary at War, PRO WO 43/95/151483; P.P., 1851, vii, p. 752.

15. 2 July 1846, Lord John Russell, Prime Minister, to Maule, Douglas & Ramsay, op. cit., i, p. 27; 23 December 1852, Queen Victoria to Aberdeen, Benson & Esher, op. cit., ii, p. 423.

16. For more details of events in 1810–12, 1827 & 1852, see Chapter V above; on Palmerston in 1827, Ridley, op. cit., p. 92; 17 September 1852, Memo. by Prince Albert, Benson & Esher, op. cit., ii. p. 394; 4 September 1852, Airey to Brown, Brown Papers, MS 1848/65; 17 July 1837, Howick to Lord Glenelg, Grey Papers.

17. For a discussion of the Richmond and Howick commissions, see Chapter II above; 14 July 1848, Queen Victoria to Grey, Benson & Esher, op. cit., ii, p. 185, replying to Grey's memo. of the previous day; 17 September 1852, Memo. by Prince Albert, ibid., p. 394; Herbert, 2 March 1854, Hansard, cxxxi, c. 239.

18. G. MacMunn, *The Crimea in Perspective*, (1935), p. 245: "If there were to be a purgatory for Ministers who let their country down, the unfortunate Mr. Herbert must have had, and may still be having, a remarkably bad time"; on the Ambulance Corps, 6 April 1854, Secretary of State to Secretary at War, PRO WO 6/75; concerning the Purveyor, 14 November 1854, War Office Instructions to the Purveyor-in-Chief in the East, A Papers, 5/54.

19. P.P., 1854–5, ix, Pt. III, q. 19782, Herbert's defence; Whiteside, 7 February 1855, Hansard, cxxxvi, c. 1321; 12 December 1854, Adjutant-General to Military Secretary, PRO WO 3/323, noting the Secretary at War's acceptance of one serjeant and fifty-four men for Scutari; on Purveyor's clerks, 5 January 1855, Newcastle to Lord William Paulet, PRO WO 6/70/201.

20. Grey, 7 April 1854, Hansard, cxxxii, c. 606 et seq.; 24 April 1854, Memo. by Russell, Aberdeen Papers, Add. MS 43068; 5 May 1854, Russell to Aberdeen, ibid.; 31 May 1854, Memo by Russell, ibid.; 5 June 1854, Grey to Henry Drummond, Grey Papers.

21. 5 March 1855, Herbert to Raglan, Herbert Papers, Crimea and China 1854–61 file; 17 June 1854, Hardinge to Airey, Airey Papers, G/IV/A/378.

22. Stuart, 29 June 1854, Hansard, cxxxiv, c. 921; Pakington, 17 July 1854, Hansard, c. 333; Herbert, ibid., especially c. 338 et seq.; 5 June 1854, Russell to Aberdeen, Aberdeen Papers, Add. MS 43068.

23. 17 November 1854, Russell to Aberdeen, Aberdeen Papers, Add. MS 43068. Russell appeared to anticipate this interpretation of his motive, for next day he addressed a kind of postscript, explaining that Newcastle's laudable efforts had been frustrated "as he had not had the (personal) authority requisite for so great a sphere", 18 November 1854, Russell to Aberdeen, ibid.

24. 18 November 1854, Aberdeen to Russell, ibid.; 21 November 1854, Aberdeen to Russell, Newcastle Papers, NeC 10298.

25. 28 November 1854, Russell to Aberdeen, ibid., NeC 10300; 30 November 1854, Aberdeen to Russell, ibid., NeC 10301; 3 December 1854, Russell to Aberdeen, ibid., NeC 10302.

26. 3 December 1854, Palmerston to Russell, Russell Papers, PRO 30/22/11; 7 December 1854, Aberdeen to Queen Victoria, Aberdeen Papers, Add. MS 43050, informing her of the Cabinet decision; 9 December 1854, Memo. by Prince Albert, Benson & Esher, op. cit., iii, p. 58. W. E. Gladstone and John Roebuck later paid tribute to Herbert's conduct of his office during the early part of the War, indirectly confirming the difficulty of shifting him at this time. On 15 October 1855, Gladstone wrote to R. M. Milnes (later Lord Houghton): "I wish some one of the thousand who in prose justly celebrate Miss Nightingale would say a single word for the man of 'routine' who devised and projected her going", quoted in J. W. Reid, *The Life, Letters, and Friendships of Richard Monckton Milnes, First Lord Houghton* (1890), i, p. 521; Roebuck, 17 July 1855, Hansard, cxxxix, c. 964: "No man could have been more intent upon the honour of his country and on performing the duties of his office. He was conscientiously endeavouring to perform his duty, and was always present."

27. 4 February, Palmerston to Herbert, and 7 February 1855, Herbert to Palmerston, Herbert Papers, Correspondence between Lord Palmerston and Lord Herbert of Lea 1853–61 file; entry in Queen Victoria's Journal, with details of Palmerston's visit, 5 February 1855, quoted

in Connell, op. cit., p. 163; 10 February 1855, Memo. by Palmerston to Queen Victoria, ibid., p. 166.

28. *The United Service Gazette*, 10 February 1855; Stafford, 2 August 1855, Hansard, cxxxix, c. 1667.

29. Palmerston even suggested falling in with Russell's plan for the War Department to save the Coalition, 24 January 1855, Palmerston to Aberdeen, Aberdeen Papers, Add. MS 43069.

30. February 1855, Memo. by Panmure, Dalhousie Muniments, 8/178.

31. Between 1762 and 1782, three Secretaries of State had been appointed. 9 July 1794, Dundas to Pitt, quoted in J. H. Rose, *Pitt and the Great War* (1914), p. 271; 1, 4 & 5 November 1834, Melbourne to Queen Victoria, Benson & Esher, op. cit., i, pp. 356, 358 & 359.

32. Glover, op. cit., p. 15; H. B. Thomson, op. cit., p. 47. By 1860 the colonies consisted of 3,319,649 square miles, the increase since 1815 including Gold Coast, Natal, Hong Kong and new settlements in New Zealand and Australia, *The Stateman's Year Book* (1864), p. 273. Defending himself against the charge that he had been inattentive to correspondence with the Colonial Office as lieutenant-governor of Lower Canada, Sir John Colborne noted that in a single eleven-month period he personally wrote seventy-five despatches and drafted 1332 letters, 2 December 1835, Colborne to Lord Glenelg, quoted in Moore Smith, op. cit., p. 263.

33. Examples of reserve responsibility, PRO WO 59/72/15560 & 24007, and out-pensioners, PRO WO 59/75/648; cf. 14 April 1836, Lord Glenelg to Sir John Colborne, offering him command of British forces in Canada, Moore Smith, op. cit., p. 271.

34. Clode, op. cit., ii, p. 330; Stocqueler, *British Army*, op. cit., p. 211; Verner, op. cit., i, p. 102; Omond, op. cit., p. 68.

35. Newcastle, P.P., 1854–5, ix, Pt. II, q. 14729; 29 December 1854, Newcastle to Raglan, Newcastle Papers, NeC 9998: "Complaints come in so thickly and so strongly ... (with) relatives of officers reproaching me for leaving the Army to die away from want of proper care"; 10 April 1854, Newcastle to Raglan, PRO WO 6/69/22; 13 April 1854, Newcastle to Raglan, Newcastle Papers, NeC 9973; Hardinge, Hansard, cxxxii, c. 657; 2 February 1855, Hardinge to Airey, Airey Papers, G/IV/A/412.

36. 10 April 1854, Newcastle to Raglan, PRO WO 6/69/22; 11 April 1854, Brown to Newcastle, Newcastle Papers, NeC 10318a, noting de Redcliffe's request: 21 March 1854, Newcastle to Brown, PRO WO 6/69/4, in issuing instructions to Brown, pointed out that he was "neither under His Excellency's orders, nor dependant on him for instructions as to your proceedings". For example, sickness report, 29 July 1854, Raglan to Newcastle, Newcastle Papers, NeC 9801, and clothing, 15 October 1855, Panmure to Simpson, PRO WO 6/70/225, acknowledging a return of 4 September.

37. 10 April 1854, Newcastle to Raglan (secret), PRO WO 6/74/1: this was received by Raglan in Paris probably on 14 April, see 13 April 1854, Newcastle to Raglan, Newcastle Papers, NeC 9973, warning of its imminent arrival; 22 April & 3 May 1854, Newcastle to Raglan, ibid.; 28 June 1854, Newcastle to Raglan (private), RMP 6807/282; 29 June 1854, Newcastle to Raglan (official), PRO WO 6/74/5.

38. 22 November 1854, Newcastle to Hardinge, Newcastle Papers, NeC 10084b; 12 January 1855, Palmerston to Newcastle, ibid., NeC 10049; 12 November 1855, Newcastle to Raglan, RMP 6807/281/203; 29 January 1855, Newcastle to Raglan, PRO WO 6/74; 26 March, 23 April, 4 May & 8 June 1855, Panmure to Raglan, ibid.

39. Beatson, 16 August, Raglan to Newcastle, 19 October 1854, Newcastle to Raglan, RMP 6807/281/53 & 127; on Airey and Estcourt, 19 March 1855, Panmure to Raglan, ibid., 6807/283/49; 23 March 1855, Panmure to Raglan, PRO WO 6/74; 11 May 1855, Panmure to Raglan, ibid., 6807/283/118; 12 January 1855, Queen Victoria to Newcastle, Benson & Esher, op. cit., iii, p. 68; 11 August 1855, Entry in *Journal*, Pt. I, Newcastle Papers, NeC 10884a; 22 September 1854, Hardinge to Newcastle, ibid., NeC 10072a.

40. Howick Report, P.P., 1837, xxxiv, Pt. I, p. 5; 10 February, Newcastle to Hardinge and 13 February 1854, Newcastle to Queen Victoria, Newcastle Papers, NeC 9785; May 1856, Palmerston to Queen Victoria, quoted in Connell, op. cit., p. 178; 6 December 1854, Newcastle to Delane, Newcastle Papers, NeC 9913a.

41. Cf. *The Times*, 8 February 1854, *The United Service Gazette*, 17 June 1854, 7 & 21 April 1855; 29 March 1854, Newcastle to Lieutenant-General Fergusson, Governor of Malta, PRO WO 6/69/6; 10 February 1854, ibid., Newcastle Papers, NeC 9785; 22 August 1854, Newcastle to Raglan, ibid., NeC 9973.

42. P.P., 1851, vii, p. 790; Herbert, 2 March 1854, Hansard, cxxxi, c. 234 et seq.; *The United Service Gazette*, 18 March 1854, noted Mundy's appointment; 2 April 1854, Aberdeen to Queen

Victoria, Aberdeen Papers, Add. MS 43049; 2 April 1854, Prince Albert to Aberdeen, ibid.; 30 June 1846, Memo, by Prince Albert, Benson & Esher, op. cit., ii, p. 84.

43. 7 April 1854, Hansard, cxxxii, c. 606–39: the small attendance at this debate, noted by Lord Ellenborough (ibid., c. 657), illustrated lack of interest in army administration.

44. Newcastle, ibid., c. 640–54; *The United Service Gazette*, 15 April 1854.

45. 24 April 1854, Memo. by Russell, Aberdeen Papers, Add. MS 43068; 5 May 1854, Russell to Aberdeen, ibid.; *The Times*, 6, 20 & 24 May 1854; Memos. by Sir Charles Wood, Lord Clarendon (both 22 May), W. E. Gladstone & Sidney Herbert (both 23 May), Russell Papers, PRO 30/22/11D.

46. 28 & 30 May 1854, Aberdeen to Queen Victoria, Aberdeen Papers, Add. MS 43049; 30 May, Aberdeen to Russell, ibid., Add. MS 43068; 31 May, Memo. by Russell, and Russell to Aberdeen, ibid.

47. 1 June, Drummond to Grey, 5 June 1854, Grey to Drummond, Grey Papers.

48. 2 June 1854, Aberdeen to Russell, Aberdeen Papers, Add. MS 43068; 8 June 1854, Memo. by Prince Albert, Benson & Esher, op. cit., iii, pp. 33 & 34; 9 June 1854, Hansard, cxxxiii, c. 1302 et seq.

49. 5 June, Grey to Russell, Russell to Aberdeen and Aberdeen to Russell, 7 June, Aberdeen to Russell, 8 June, Russell to Aberdeen, 9 June 1854, Russell to Aberdeen, Aberdeen Papers, Add. MS 43068: for details of other political manoeuvres at this time, see Conacher, op. cit., pp. 406–8. A later suggestion, in an unsigned memo. of 28 November 1854, Newcastle Papers, NeC 9683b, that the new minister was the Colonial Secretary, not the Secretary for War, is wrong as Sir George Grey immediately sat in the Commons.

50. On his office accommodation, Newcastle, 26 January 1855, Hansard, cxxxvi, c. 959; 13 June 1854, Newcastle to Raglan, Newcastle Papers, NeC 9973; *The United Service Gazette*, 17 June 1854; Marx quoted in O. Anderson, op. cit., p. 56.

51. *The United Service Gazette*, 17 June 1854; 25 June 1854, Grey to his brother Charles, Grey Papers; 8 July 1854, Palmerston to Aberdeen and Aberdeen to Palmerston, Aberdeen Papers, Add. MS 43069; Russell, 17 July 1854, Hansard, cxxxv, c. 317 et seq.

52. 6 October, Newcastle to the Lords Commissioners of the Treasury, 8 November, Sir Charles Trevelyan to Newcastle, 14 November, Order in Council, and 23 November 1854, appointment of Roberts, Dalhousie Muniments, 8/161.

53. 23 November, 7 & 15 December, Aberdeen to Queen Victoria (the latter reporting Russell's conversation with Panmure "yesterday"), 25 November, 1 & 7 December 1854, Queen Victoria to Aberdeen, Aberdeen Papers, Add. MS 43050; 18, 21 & 30 November, Aberdeen to Russell, 17, 18, 23, 28 November & 3 December 1854, Russell to Aberdeen, ibid., Add. MS 43068. For further discussion of the implications for the War Office, see consideration of the Secretary at War above.

54. Grey and Newcastle, 18 December 1854, Hansard, cxxxvi, c. 425; Derby and Newcastle, 26 January 1855, ibid., c. 958–9; 28 November 1854, Russell to Aberdeen, Aberdeen Papers, Add. MS 43068.

55. 8 July 1854, Memo. by Trevelyan, Newcastle Papers, NeC 10541a & b; 23 August 1854, Gladstone to Newcastle, Gladstone Papers, Add. MS 44529; Newcastle, 26 January 1855, Hansard, cxxxvi, c. 959; Treasury Minute, Symons, op. cit., p. 61; 2 February 1857, Memo. by Trevelyan, P.P., 1857, ix, p. 109.

56. 30 October 1854, Gladstone to Trevelyan, Gladstone Papers, Add. MS 44529; 17 November 1854, Memo. by Gladstone, ibid., Add. MS 44744; 3 & 6 November 1854, Newcastle to Gladstone, ibid., Add. MS 44262; 22 December 1854, Treasury Minute completing the formal transfer, PRO WO 43/98/15622; 13 January 1855, Gladstone to Trevelyan, Gladstone Papers, Add. MS 44530.

57. Hardinge, 7 April 1854, Hansard, cxxxii, c. 655; Monsell before the Sevastopol Select Committee, P.P., 1854–5, ix, Pt. III, q. 19177.

58. 4 December 1854, Palmerston to Newcastle, Newcastle Papers, NeC 10044 and P.P., 1854–5, ix, Pt. III, q. 20159; 27 December 1854, Graham to Aberdeen, Aberdeen Papers, Add. MS 43191 (Graham's refusal); Draft Order in Council, Newcastle Papers, NeC 10856: the date is missing but as the First Lord of the Admiralty is not included, it is almost certainly between Graham's letter of 27 December 1854 and the first meeting of the Board on 3 January 1855.

59. Minutes of the three meetings, Newcastle Papers, NeC 10857, 10858 and 10859 respectively; e.g. 3 January 1855, the Ordnance Department was directed to buy 500 cart horses and as many baggage horses and mules as possible and the Medical Department was required to ensure that 200 tons of medical stores were despatched "in every fortnightly steamer from

Liverpool", ibid., NeC 10857; despatch of copies of the Minutes noted in General Harding's handwriting on the rough copy of the minutes of 3 January 1855, ibid.; 22 January 1855 Newcastle to Queen Victoria, ibid., NeC 9786 (minutes of third meeting).

60. 20 January 1855, Aberdeen to Queen Victoria, Aberdeen Papers, Add. MS 43050; 21 January 1855, Aberdeen to Prince Albert, ibid.

61. 22 January 1855, Memo. by Russell on the Army Departments, ibid., Add. MS 43068.

62. 22 January 1855, Queen Victoria to Aberdeen, ibid., Add. MS 43050; 23 January 1855, Russell to Aberdeen, Benson & Esher, op. cit., iii, p. 72 (the resignation); concerning Russell, 24 January 1855, Palmerston to Aberdeen, Aberdeen Papers, Add. MS 43069; 26 January 1855, Newcastle to Aberdeen, Herbert Papers, Miscellaneous Papers, and Newcastle in Parliament, Hansard, cxxxvi, c. 993. At this time, too, Sir James Graham proposed that a reorganised Transport Board should be placed under the War Department for the duration of the war, 20 January 1855, Aberdeen to Queen Victoria, Aberdeen Papers, Add. MS 43050.

63. Newcastle, 26 January 1855, Hansard, cxxxvi, c. 959, and Roebuck, ibid., c. 979; Grey, 29 January 1855, ibid., c. 1066 et seq.: 30 January Roebuck's motion was carried by 305 votes to 148, with the result that "instead of the usual cheering there was a murmur of amazement, ending in derisive laughter", *Annual Register*, xcvii, 1855, p. 20.

64. 7 February 1855, Panmure to Russell, Russell Papers, PRO 30/22/12; 8 February 1855, Memo. by Hawes, Dalhousie Muniments, 8/316; February 1855 (no precise date), Memo by Panmure, ibid., 8/178; 16 February 1855, Hansard, cxxxvi, c. 1412

65. 10 February 1855, Ellenborough to Panmure, Ellenborough Papers, PRO 30/12/18; Williams, 19 February 1855, Hansard, cxxxvi, c. 1563.

66. Panmure on Transport Board, 16 February 1855, Hansard, cxxxvi, c. 1411; Ellenborough, Hardwicke and Panmure, 18 May 1855, Hansard, cxxxviii, c. 753, 760 & 761 respectively; 18 May 1855, Panmure's "supplementary patent . . . revocable at pleasure", P.P., 1860, vii, p. 5. For a full discussion of the Ordnance transfer see Chapter IV above. Details of the War Department establishment in November 1855, PRO WO 43/103/159744; the Ordnance subdivisions with their clerical establishments were: Clerk of the Ordnance (14), Store (42), Contracts (12), Army Clothing (7), Accountant-General (55), Inspector-General of Fortifications, Engineer Branch (11), Inspector-General of Fortifications, Barrack Branch (11), Naval Director of Artillery (1).

67. 2 July 1855, Memo. by Panmure concerning the responsibility of the War Department "approved" by Queen Victoria, Dalhousie Muniments, 8/259; Stafford, 31 July 1855, Hansard, cxxxix, c. 1559; Monsell and Stafford, 2 August 1855, ibid., c. 1662 & 1667 respectively.

68. 11 August 1855, War Department Memo. attached to a clothing return, P.P., xl, p. 133; 16 November 1855, Queen Victoria to Panmure, Douglas & Ramsay, op. cit., i, p. 488; 3 January 1856, Hawes to Panmure, in P.P., 1856, cl, p. 22; Derby, 21 February 1856, Hansard, cxl, c. 1023 et seq.; Dunne & Monsell, 21 February 1856, ibid., c. 1250 & 1256 respectively; Monsell, 7 March 1856, ibid., c. 2066: he also answered criticism of incomplete reorganisation of the supply establishments and inefficiency at Enfield.

69. 31 December 1858, Trevelyan to G. A. Hamilton, Financial Secretary to the Treasury, quoted in J. Hart, 'Sir Charles Trevelyan at the Treasury', *E.H.R.*, January 1960, p. 92; 18 November 1859, Florence Nightingale to Sidney Herbert, quoted in Stanmore, op. cit., ii, p. 369. Responsibility for the Militia was transferred from Home Office to War Department in March 1855.

70. 1906 locations, Hamer, op. cit., p. 8; Biddulph, op. cit., preface p. vi.

CONCLUSION

1. W. H. Russell, op cit., p. vii.

2. Grey, 7 April 1854, Hansard, cxxxii, c. 607; Williams, 4 April 1845, Hansard, lxxix, c. 210, 13 July 1846, Hansard, lxxxvii, c. 1097 and 9 March 1855, cxxxvii, c. 366.

3. Cf. 28 November 1854, Sir George Napier to Seaton, praising Seaton's call for reinforcements, and Seaton's reply, quoted in Moore Smith, op. cit., pp. 355–60.

4. 9 June 1847, Palmerston to Lord John Russell, quoted in Ashley, op. cit., p. 23; Granville quoted in O. Anderson, op. cit., p. 36; Clarendon quoted in St. Aubyn, op. cit., p. 109.

5. Knox, 3 March 1856, Hansard, cxl, c. 1746; Cambridge's letter of appointment, 18 July 1856, Herbert Papers, Miscellaneous Papers.

6. *The Spectator*, 2 June 1855; review of 'A Trip to the Trenches in February and March 1855. By an Amateur'; April 1856, Queen Victoria to Palmerston and Palmerston to Queen Victoria, quoted in Connell, op. cit., p. 199; 15 August 1856, Cambridge to Panmure, Verner, op. cit., i, p. 119; *The United Service Gazette*, 2 February 1856; 9 September 1856, Panmure to Queen Victoria, Douglas & Ramsay, op. cit., ii, p. 296; 7 August 1856, Panmure to Cambridge, Verner, op. cit., i, p. 117; 5 February 1857, Douglas & Ramsay, op. cit., ii, p. 347.

7. April 1856, Florence Nightingale quoted in C. Woodham-Smith, *Florence Nightingale* (1964), p. 197; on the weather, cf., Lt. Col. Horsford before the Sevastopol Select Committee, P.P., 1854–5, ix, Pt. II, q. 13370; Benson & Esher, op. cit., iii, p. 56 n.1, claim that thirty British transports were wrecked, of which *The Prince* alone carried a cargo worth £500,000; Trevelyan on the Turks, P.P., 1854–5, ix, Pt. II, q. 13528.

8. 16 January 1855, Filder to the Quartermaster-General, App. VII to the Second Report of McNeill & Tulloch, P.P., 1856, xx, p. 578; 16 September 1855, Granville to Clarendon, Granville Papers, PRO 30/29/18; Calthorpe, op. cit., ii, particularly p. 434 et seq.; cf. 4 February 1856, Lord Grey to his brother Charles: "The chief blame rests with poor Lord Raglan, whose business it was to see that those under him did their duty in their several departments", Grey Papers.

9. Peel before the Select Committee on Military Organisation, P.P., 1860, vii, q. 3790; 24 January 1861, Granville to Lord Canning, quoted in Fitzmaurice, op. cit., i, p. 390; de Fonblanque, op. cit., p. 83; the Queen's statement: "In order to prevent doubts as to the powers and duties of the C-in-C with respect to the Government of Our Army and the Administration of Military Affairs", 11 October 1861, included in P.P., 1868–9, xxxvi, p. 591.

10. H. Gordon, op. cit., p. 51, Biddulph, op. cit., p. 10 et seq.; War Office organisation, 20 January 1857, Panmure to Queen Victoria, and 21 January 1857, Queen Victoria to Panmure, Douglas and Ramsay, op. cit., ii, pp. 340 and 343; Wheeler, op. cit., p. 174 et seq.

11. De Fonblanque, op. cit., p. 144; Godley before the Select Committee on Military Organisation, P.P., 1860, vii, q. 1829; 18 November 1859, Florence Nightingale to Sidney Herbert, quoted in Stanmore, op. cit., ii, p. 369.

12. Bacon quoted in Clode, op. cit., ii, p. 395; commissions etc., noted ibid., ii, p. 394; Graham's remark after the Select Committee on Military Organisation, quoted in Biddulph, op, cit., p. vi.

13. Royal Warrant on the Commissariat, 28 October 1858, included in P.P., 1857, xv, p. 187; 13 October 1855, Memo. by Trevelyan, PRO WO 43/103/159744.

Selected Bibliography

MANUSCRIPT SOURCES

BRITISH MUSEUM (*Additional Manuscripts*)
Aberdeen Papers
Gladstone Papers
Palmerston Letterbooks

PUBLIC RECORD OFFICE

Private Papers
Ellenborough Papers
Granville Papers
Russell Papers

Official Records
WO   3: Commander-in-Chief's out letters.
WO   4: Secretary at War's out letters
WO   6: Secretary of State for War's out letters
WO 28: Headquarters Records of the Crimea
WO 33: Miscellaneous Papers (1853–1930)
WO 43: A collection of papers, subdivided into VOS (very old series)
            and OS (old series)
WO 44: Ordnance Department, various
WO 45: In letters of the Board of Ordnance
WO 46: Out letters of the Board of Ordnance
WO 47: Proceedings of the Board of Ordnance
WO 58: Commissariat Department out letters.
WO 59: Minutes of the Commissariat Department
WO 60: Accounts of the Commissariat Department

OTHER ARCHIVES
Airey Papers, Hereford Public Record Office, Hereford.
Brown Papers, National Library of Scotland, Edinburgh.
Dalhousie Muniments, Scottish Record Office, Edinburgh.
Estcourt Papers, Gloucestershire Record Office, Gloucester.
Grey Papers, University of Durham.
Herbert Papers, Wilton House, Salisbury.

Kingscote Papers (including 'The Crimean Journal of Colonel R. F. N. Kingscote'), Gloucestershire Record Office, Gloucester.
Newcastle Papers, University of Nottingham.
Palmerston Papers, Broadlands Archives, Romsey, Hants.
Raglan Military Papers, National Army Museum, Chelsea.
Raglan Private Papers, Cefntilla Court, Usk, Monmouth.

AUTOBIOGRAPHIES, EDITED PAPERS AND MISCELLANEOUS UNPUBLISHED MATERIAL

All printed sources are published in London unless otherwise stated

Anglesey, Marquis of (Ed.): *One Leg: Life and Letters of the First Marquis of Anglesey* (1961)
Anon. *Contemporary Notes from the Crimea*, JSAHR, xlvi (1968)
Benson, A. and Esher, Viscount (Eds.): *The Letters of Queen Victoria*, Vols. I, II & III (1908)
Brett-James, A. (Ed.): *Wellington at War: a selection of his wartime letters* (1961)
Brown, G.: *Memoranda and Observations on the Crimean War 1854–5* (1879)
Calthorpe, S. J. G.: *Letters from Headquarters*, Vols. I and II (1856)
Costin, W. C. and Watson, J. S.: *The Law and the Working of the Constitution, Documents 1660–1914*, Vol. II (1952)
Douglas, G. and Ramsay, G. D. (Eds.): *The Panmure Papers*, Vols. I & II (1908)
Fitzherbert, C. (Ed.): *Henry Clifford V.C.: his letters and sketches from the Crimea* (1956)
Gordon, A. (Ed.): *General Orders issued to the Army in the East* (1856)
Raikes, H. (Ed.): *Private Correspondence of Thomas Raikes with the Duke of Wellington* (1861)
Strachey, L. and Fulford, R. (Eds.): *The Greville Memoirs*, Vol. IV (1908)
Symons, A.: Higher Army Administration 1836–1918 (dated 1939, but unpublished; in the Ministry of Defence Library, Whitehall)
Walshe, A. and Stocqueler, J. H. (Eds.): *Standing Orders* (1855)
War Office, The: *Commissariat Regulations and Instructions* (1853)
War Office, The: *Warrants and Regulations concerning Finance* (1841)
Ward, S. G. P. (Ed.): *The Hawley Papers*, JSAHR, Special Publication No. 10 (1970)
Wellington Duke of (Ed.): *Wellington with His Friends, Letters of the First Duke of Wellington* (1965)
Wrottesley, G.: *The Life and Correspondence of Sir John Burgoyne*, Vols. I and II (1873)

OFFICIAL PUBLICATIONS

PARLIAMENT

Hansard
Parliamentary Debates

Parliamentary Papers

1833: Report from the Select Committee on Army and Navy Appointments, vii, p. 1

1837: Report of the Commissioners appointed to inquire into the practicability and expediency of consolidating the different Departments connected with the Civil Administration of the Army, xxxiv, Pt. I, p. 1

1849: Interim Report from the Select Committee on Army and Ordnance Expenditure, ix, p. 1

1850: Interim Report from the Select Committee on Army and Ordnance Expenditure, x, p. 1

1851: Final Report from the Select Committee on Army and Ordnance Expenditure, vii, p. 753

1852: Reports of the Committee appointed to inquire into the Naval, Ordnance and Commissariat Establishments, xxx, p. 361.

1852: Report from the Commission of Inquiry into Ordnance and Commissariat Establishments abroad, lix, p. 395

1854: Report from the Select Committee on Small Arms, xviii, p. 1

1854: Report on the Organisation of the Permanent Civil Service, xxvii, p. 1

1854: Copies of all Correspondence between government departments and the contractors for hay during the last two months (dated 4/4/1854), xli, p. 73

1854–5: Report from the Select Committee on the Army before Sebastopol, ix, Pts, I, II & III

1854–5: Report from the Select Committee on the Royal Military College Sandhurst, xii, p. 1

1854–5: Copies of any Correspondence with the Secretary for War on the Subject of the Construction of a Railway or Tramroad from the Harbour of Balaclava to Sebastopol, xxxii, p. 574

1854–5: Papers relating to a Commission appointed to inquire into the irregularities which have taken place in the Transport of Stores & c. to the East, xxxii, p. 577

1854–5: Order in Council regulating the Establishment of the Civil Departments, xxxii, p. 677.

1854–5: Copies of Correspondence relating to the state of the Harbour of Balaclava, xxxiv, p. 107

1856: Reports from the Commission of Inquiry into the Supplies of the British Army in the Crimea, xx, p. 1

1856: Report of the Board of General Officers appointed to inquire into the Statements contained in the Reports of Sir John McNeill and Colonel Tulloch, xxi, p. 1

1856: Army, Commissariat and Ordnance Accounts 1854–5, xl, p. 31

1856: Copy of a letter from Commissary-General Filder covering Remarks in those parts of the Reports of Sir John McNeill and Colonel Tulloch, which relate to the duties of the Commissariat Department, xl, p. 337

1857: Return concerning the late Army of the East, (Sess. 1), ix, p. 1

1857: Return of casualties in the Crimea, (Sess. 1), ix, p. 7

1857: Return of those staying in the Crimea throughout the war, (Sess. 1), ix, p. 11

1857: Memorandum and explanation of Sir Charles Trevelyan in regard to a Section of the Report of the Board of General Officers appointed to inquire into certain statements of Sir J. McNeill and Colonel Tulloch, (Sess. 1), ix, p. 83

1857: Copy of the Order of instruction issued by the War Department during the past year for the Disbandment of the Land Transport Corps, (Sess. 1), ix, p. 163

1857: Report from the Select Committee on Transport Corps allegations in Petitions of Members of the Land Transport Corps complaining that the War Department had not fulfilled Conditions under which they were enlisted, (Sess. 2), ix, p. 293

1857–8: Report from the Select Committee on Petitions of Officers alleging that they had not received the rate of half pay to which entitled, x, p. 249

1857–8: Copy of the instructions given by the War Department to the Board appointed to investigate claims preferred by men who served in the late Land Transport Corps, xxxvii, p. 355

1857–8: Despatches of General Codrington to the Secretary of State for War concerning the Land Transport Corps, xxxvii, p. 357

1859: Report of the Committee appointed to inquire into the existing organisation of the Commissariat Department, xv, p. 187.

1859: Report of the Commission appointed to inquire into the State of the Store and Clothing Depots at Weedon, Woolwich and the Tower & c., (Sess. 2), ix, p. 285

1860: Report of the Select Committee on the Effects of alterations as to the War Office and Board of Ordnance 1855 & c., vii, p. 1

1862: Returns of Men voted for the Army in each year from 1816 to 1862 both inclusive, xxxii, p. 265

1863: Secretary at War abolition bill, iii, p. 191

1866: Copies of the Patents issued to successive Secretary of State for War, xii, p. 877

1868–9: Copy of any documents now in force upon the subject of the respective Duties and Authority of the Secretary of State for War and the C-in-C, xxxvi, p. 591

1888: Report of the Select Committees on Army Estimates, ix, p. 1

SECONDARY PUBLICATIONS

Anderson, O.: *A Liberal State at War* (1967)

Anderson, W. H.: *Outline of the British Army up to 1914* (1920)

Ashley, E.: *The Life of Henry John Temple, Viscount Palmerston*, Vols. I and II (1876)

Atkins, J. B.: *The Life of Sir William Howard Russell*, Vol. I (1935)

Bagehot, W.: *The English Constitution* (Fontana 1968)

Baker, H.: *The Territorial Force* (1954)

Beales, A. C. F.: *The History of Peace* (1931)

Bell, H. C. F.: *Lord Palmerston*, Vol. II (1936)

Biddulph, R.: *Lord Cardwell at the War Office* (1904)

Briggs, A.: *Victorian People* (Harmondsworth, Middlesex, 1967)

Bright, J. & Rogers, J. E. T. (Eds.): *Speeches of Richard Cobden* (1903)

Burn, W. L.: *The Age of Equipoise* (1964)

Cantlie, N.: *A History of the Army Medical Department*, Vols. I and II (Edinburgh & London, 1974)

Chesney, K.: *Crimean War Reader* (1960)

Clode, C. M.: *The Military Forces of the Crown*, Vols. I and II (1869)

Conacher, J. B.: *The Aberdeen Coalition 1852–1855* (Cambridge, 1968)

Connell, B.: *Regina versus Palmerston 1837–1865* (1962)

Craig, G. A.: *The Politics of the Prussian Army 1640–1945* (1968)

Curtiss, J. S.: *The Russian Army under Nicholas I, 1825–1855* (Durham, N.C., 1965)

De Fonblanque, E. B.: *Treatise on the Administration and Organisation of the British Army, with especial reference to finance and supply* (1858)

Emerson, G. R.: *Sebastopol, the Story of Its Fall* (1855)

Eyck, F.: *The Prince Consort: a political biography* (1959)

Fergusson, J.: *The Perils of Portsmouth* (1851)

Finer, S. E.: *The Life and Times of Sir Edwin Chadwick* (1952)

Finer, S. E.: *The Man on Horseback: the Role of the Military in Politics* (1967)

Fitzmaurice, E.: *The Life of Granville George Leveson Gower, Second Earl Granville K. G. 1815–1891*, Vol. I (1905)

Forbes, A.: *A History of the Army Ordnance Services*, Vols. I and II (1929)

Fortescue, J.: *History of the British Army*, mainly Vol. XIII (1930)

Fortescue, J.: *The History of the Royal Army Service Corps* (1930)

Gleig, G. R.: *History of the Life of Arthur, Duke of Wellington*, Vol. IV (1860)

Glover, R.: *Peninsular Preparation* (Cambridge, 1963)

Godwin-Austen, A. R.: *The Staff and the Staff College* (1927)

Gooch, B. D.: *The New Bonapartist Generals in the Crimean War* (The Hague, 1959)

Gordon, H.: *The War Office* (1935)

Griffiths, A.: *The English Army* (1878)

Griffiths, A.: *Wellington: his comrades and contemporaries* (1897)

Guedalla, P.: *The Duke* (1931)

Guggisberg, F. G.: *The Shop: The Story of the Royal Military Academy* (1902)

Hackett, J.: *The Profession of Arms* (1963)

Hamer, W. S.: *The British Army Civil-Military Relations 1885–1905* (Oxford, 1970)

Hardinge, Charles Viscount: *Viscount Hardinge* (1891)

Hay, G. J.: *The Constitutional Force* (1906)

Head, F.: *The Defenceless State of Great Britain* (1850)

Hibbert, C.: *The Destruction of Lord Raglan* (1961)

Howard, M. E. (Ed.): *Studies in War and Peace* (1970)

Howard, M. E. (Ed.): *The Theory and Practice of War* (1965)

Howard, M. E. (Ed.): *Wellingtonian Studies* (Aldershot, 1959)

Huntington, S. P.: *The Soldier and the State* (Cambridge, Mass., 1967)

Kinglake, A. W.: *The Invasion of the Crimea*, Vols. I–VIII (Edinburgh and London, 1863–87)

Le Marchant, D.: *Memoirs of the late Major-General Le Marchant* (1841)

Lewis, M.: *The Navy of Great Britain* (1949)

Longford, E.: *Wellington, the Years of the Sword* (1970)

Longford, E.: *Wellington, Pillar of State* (1972)

Luvaas, J.: *The Education of an Army: British Military Thought 1815–1940* (1965)

MacMunn, G.: *The Crimea in Perspective* (1935)

Martin, T.: *The Life of His Royal Highness The Prince Consort*, Vol. II (1876)

Martineau, J.: *Life of Henry Pelham, Fifth Duke of Newcastle 1811–1864* (1908)

Maxwell, H.: *The Life of Wellington*, Vol. II (1907)

Moore Smith, G. O.: *The Life of John Colborne, Field-Marshal Lord Seaton* (1903)

Morley, J.: *The Life of Richard Cobden* (1878)

Morley, J.: *The Life of William Ewart Gladstone*, Vol. I. (1905)

O'Malley, I. B.: *Florence Nightingale 1820–1856* (1931)

Omond, J. S.: *Parliament and the Army 1642–1904* (1933)

Paret, P.: *Yorck and the Era of Prussian Reform* (Princeton, N.J., 1966)

Pemberton, W. B.: *Battles of the Crimean War* (1962)

Pemberton, W. B.: *Lord Palmerston* (1954)

Petrie, C.: *The Victorians* (1960)

Petrie, C.: *Wellington: A Re-assessment* (1956)

Pool, B.: *Navy Board Contracts 1660–1832* (1966)

Reader, W. J.: *Professional Men* (1966)

Ridley, J.: *Lord Palmerston 1784–1865* (1970)

Roads, C. H.: *The British Soldier's Firearm 1850–1864* (1964)

Robinson, G.: *David Urquhart*, (Oxford, 1921)

Russell, W. H.: *The Great War with Russia* (1895)

Sheppard, E. (Ed.): *George, Duke of Cambridge*, Vol. I (1906)

Sidney, E.: *Lord Hill* (1845)

Stanmore, Lord: *Sidney Herbert, Lord Herbert of Lea*, Vols. I and II (1906)

St. Aubyn, G.: *The Royal George — The Life of the Duke of Cambridge* (1963)

Stocqueler, J. H.: *A Familiar History of the British Army* (1871)

Stocqueler, J. H.: *A Personal History of the Horse Guards* (1873)

Thackeray, T. J.: *The Military Organisation and Administration of France* (1856)

Thomson, D.: *England in the Nineteenth Century* (Harmondsworth, Middlesex, 1950)

Thomson, H. B.: *The Military Forces and Institutions of Great Britain and Ireland* (1855)

Thoumine, R. H.: *Scientific Soldier, A Life of General Le Marchant 1766–1812* (Oxford, 1968)

Trevelyan, G. M.: *The Life of John Bright* (1913)

Vagts, A.: *A History of Militarism* (1959)

Verner, W.: *The Military Life of George, Duke of Cambridge*, Vol. I (1905)

Ward, S. G. P.: *Wellington's Headquarters* (Oxford, 1957)

Ward, T. H. (Ed.): *The Reign of Queen Victoria*, Vol. I (1887)

Wellesley, M.: *Wellington in Civil Life: Through the Eyes of those who knew him*, (1939)

Wheeler, O.: *The War Office Past and Present to 1914* (1914)

White, A. C. T.: *The Story of Army Education 1643–1963* (1963)

Woodham-Smith, C.: *Florence Nightingale* (1964)

Woodward, E. L.: *The Age of Reform 1815–1870* (Oxford, 1962)

Young, G. M. (Ed.): *Portrait of an Age* (1936)

Young, G. M. (Ed.): *Early Victorian England*, Vol. I (1951)

Young, G. M. and Handcock, W. D. (Eds.): *English Historical Documents 1833–1874* (1956)

OTHER MISCELLANEOUS PAMPHLETS

Anon.: *Observations upon the Peace Establishments of the British Army* (1822)

Anon.: *Some Observations on the War in the Crimea* (1855)

Anon.: *Life of Field-Marshal Lord Raglan* (1855)

Anon.: *Remedy for the Evils that have caused the Destruction of a large portion of the British Army before Sevastopol* (1855)

Anon.: *The Royal Artillery* (1855)

Anon.: *Military Administration, a Sketch* (1870)

Anon.: *Military Administration 1855–1870* (1870)

Burgoyne, J. F.: *Army Reform* (1857)

Ci-devant Cavalry Officer, A: *Army Reform: a practical method of reducing the Army Estimates a million without diminution of its numerical force* (1833)

Constitutionalist: *Army Administration in Three Centuries* (1901)

Le Mesurier, H.: *A System for the British Commissariat on Foreign Service* (1796)

Maxwell, P. B.: *Whom Shall We Hang?* (1855)

Officer, An: *Observations on the Army* (1825)

Two Mounted Sentries: *The Horse Guards — a satire upon the Duke of Wellington* (1850)

Weale, J.: *An open letter to the Right Honourable Lord John Russell, First Lord of the Treasury, on the Defence of the Country* (1847)

LIST OF MAJOR OFFICE HOLDERS, 1830–1856

PRIME MINISTER

Duke of Wellington	January 1828–November 1830
Earl Grey	November 1830–July 1834
Viscount Melbourne	July 1834–December 1834
Sir Robert Peel	December 1834–April 1835
Viscount Melbourne	April 1835–September 1841
Sir Robert Peel	September 1841–July 1846
Lord John Russell	July 1846–February 1852
Earl of Derby	February 1852–December 1852
Earl of Aberdeen	December 1852–February 1855
Viscount Palmerston	took office February 1855

SECRETARY OF STATE FOR WAR AND COLONIES

Viscount Goderich	November 1830–March 1833
E. G. Stanley	March 1833–June 1834
T. Spring Rice	June 1834–December 1834
Earl of Aberdeen	December 1834–April 1835
Charles Grant*	April 1835–February 1839
Marquis of Normanby	February 1839–September 1839
Lord John Russell	September 1839–September 1841
Lord Stanley, formerly E. G. Stanley	September 1841–December 1845
W. E. Gladstone	December 1845–July 1846
Earl Grey	July 1846–February 1852
Sir John Pakington	February 1852–December 1852
Duke of Newcastle	December 1852 until post effectively abolished June 1854

* Became Lord Glenelg, May 1835

SECRETARY OF STATE FOR WAR

Duke of Newcastle	June 1854–February 1855
Lord Panmure	took office February 1855

SECRETARY OF STATE FOR THE COLONIES

Sir George Grey	June 1854–February 1855
Sidney Herbert	February 1855, then resigned
Lord John Russell	February 1855–July 1855
Sir William Molesworth	July 1855–October 1855
Henry Labouchere	took office October 1855

HOME SECRETARY

Viscount Melbourne	November 1830–July 1834
Viscount Duncannon	July 1834–December 1834
Henry Goulburn	December 1834–April 1835
Lord John Russell	April 1835–September 1839
Lord Normanby	September 1839–September 1841
Sir James Graham	September 1841–July 1846
Sir George Grey	July 1846–February 1852
Spencer Walpole	February 1852–December 1852
Viscount Palmerston	December 1852–February 1855
Sir George Grey	took office February 1855

SECRETARY AT WAR

Lord Gower	July 1830–November 1830
W. W. Wynn	November 1830–April 1831
Sir Henry Parnell	April 1831–February 1832
Sir J. Cam Hobhouse	February 1832–April 1833
Edward Ellice	April 1833–December 1834*
J. C. Herries	December 1834–April 1835*
Viscount Howick	April 1835–September 1839*
T. B. Macaulay	September 1839–September 1841*
Sir Henry Hardinge	September 1841–May 1844*
Sir Thomas Fremantle	May 1844–February 1845
Sidney Herbert	February 1845–July 1846*
Fox Maule, Lord Panmure	July 1846–February 1852*
R. V. Smith	6–28 February 1852
William Beresford	February 1852–December 1852
Sidney Herbert	December 1852–February 1855, when post effectively abolished*

COMMANDER-in-CHIEF OF THE ARMY

Duke of Wellington	January 1827–May 1827†
Duke of Wellington	August 1827–February 1828
Lord Hill	February 1828–August 1842
Duke of Wellington	August 1842–September 1852
Viscount Hardinge, formerly Sir Henry	September 1852–July 1856
Duke of Cambridge	took office July 1856

* Admitted to the Cabinet immediately or during tenure of office
† No C-in-C was appointed May–August 1827

MASTER-GENERAL OF THE ORDNANCE

Sir James Kempt	November 1830–December 1834
Sir George Murray	December 1834–May 1835
Sir R. Hussey Vivian	May 1835–September 1841
Sir George Murray	September 1841–July 1846
Marquis of Anglesey	July 1846–February 1852
Viscount Hardinge	February 1852–September 1852
Lord Raglan	September 1852–May 1855, when post abolished

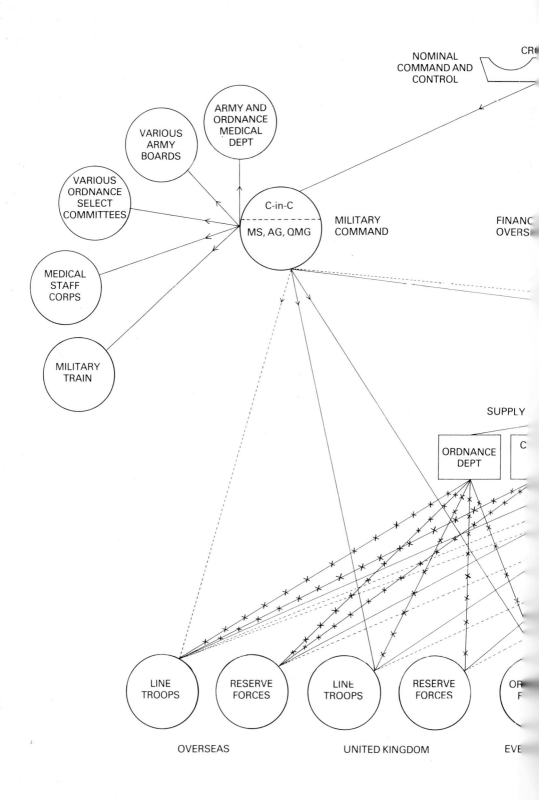

NOMINAL
COMMAND AND
CONTROL

CR

ARMY AND
ORDNANCE
MEDICAL
DEPT

VARIOUS
ARMY
BOARDS

VARIOUS
ORDNANCE
SELECT
COMMITTEES

C-in-C

MS, AG, QMG

MILITARY
COMMAND

FINANC
OVERS

MEDICAL
STAFF
CORPS

MILITARY
TRAIN

SUPPLY

ORDNANCE
DEPT

C

LINE
TROOPS

RESERVE
FORCES

LINE
TROOPS

RESERVE
FORCES

OR
F

OVERSEAS

UNITED KINGDOM

EVE